How to Sell a Book

What I've Learned Selling 100,000 Self-Published Nonfiction Books

David Kadavy

Copyright © 2024 by David Kadavy

All rights reserved.

No part of this book may be reproduced in any form or by any electronic or mechanical means, including information storage and retrieval systems, without the prior written permission of the author, except in the case of brief quotations used in reviews, articles, or any other purpose.

Contents

Note: no "kickbacks"	7
Introduction	9

1. DANCE WITH CHANCE — 13
- White-, black-, and gray-swan books — 14
- The portfolio approach and the never-ending lotto ticket — 16
- Write shorter books: Small books are small bets — 17

2. WRITE A BOOK PEOPLE WILL BUY — 21
- The four M's of a good book idea — 22
- Categories — 26
- Keywords — 28
- Idea/author fit — 31

3. BUILD THE AUDIENCE AS YOU BUILD THE BOOK — 35
- Community-first — 37
- An email list is a must — 39
- Explosive email courses — 40
- Lead magnets — 45
- Email newsletters — 46
- Social media — 49
- SEO — 52
- Having a podcast — 55

4. WRITE A TITLE AND CREATE A BOOK COVER THAT WILL SELL — 63
- "Turnkey titles" tell the whole story — 64
- Pass the "cocktail party test" — 65
- Subtitles — 67
- Book covers — 68
- Testing titles, subtitles, and book covers — 74
- Interior design — 77

5. WRITE AN IRRESISTIBLE SALES BLURB	79
Hook	80
Problem	81
Elevator pitch	82
Bullet points	83
Point of difference	85
Call-to-action	86
Your sales blurb is a writing tool	87
6. THE FIRST PAGES SELL YOUR BOOK	89
7. GET REVIEWS, BLURBS, AND FOREWORDS	94
How to get your first Amazon reviews	94
Handling negative reviews	97
Reader blurbs	99
Editorial reviews	102
Forewords	104
8. ADVERTISE YOUR BOOK	105
Ad-spend is education	107
Amazon Ads	108
Sponsored Products strategy	110
Lockscreen Ads strategy	115
Sponsored Brands ads	119
Evaluating Amazon Ads performance	119
BookBub Ads	122
Meta Ads	127
Other ad platforms	132
9. PICK THE PRICE THAT'S RIGHT	134
Ebook price "points"	134
Pricing across regions	137
Paper-book pricing	139
Direct-sales pricing	140
10. RUN PRICING PROMOTIONS	142
BookBub Featured Deals	142
BookBub Featured New Releases For Less	146
Amazon Kindle Deals	147

Kindle Deal restrictions and conflicts	149
KDP Select pricing promotions	153
11. INFLUENCE INFLUENCERS TO SELL YOUR BOOK	**154**
Meet influencers	154
Give books to influencers	156
Give books to strangers (who might be influencers)	159
Make micro-influencers out of those who take action	161
Pay influencers to promote your book	162
Be a guest on podcasts	166
12. GO "WIDE" (OR DON'T)	**175**
Wide ebook marketing	180
Aggregators make wide easy	183
Make your hard-copy books available everywhere, through IngramSpark	186
13. SELL DIRECTLY TO READERS	**192**
Start simple (or not at all)	193
"You can just put books in the mail"	195
Yes, you *can* beat Amazon	196
Why direct sales are the future	200
Premium editions and crowdfunding	201
Preview editions	204
Phased releases	207
14. INTERLUDE ON AUDIOBOOKS	**209**
15. DON'T LAUNCH THE "RIGHT" WAY	**213**
The slow-motion launch	214
Make the most of your launch moment	218
16. MAKE A BESTSELLER LIST (OR DON'T)	**221**
An Amazon bestseller is a "real" bestseller	222
Amazon's ranking algorithm, then and now	224
When and how to go for bestseller status	227
17. DO MEDIA STUNTS (AKA CREATE "PSEUDO-EVENTS")	**231**

18. WRITE MORE BOOKS	235
Two is two, three is six	236
Write in series	237
Write diversely	239
19. SELL FOREIGN RIGHTS	242
Translate yourself? (Nope.)	242
Finding foreign-rights deals	244
Is it a good deal?	245
English rights abroad	249
Hire a lawyer?	250
Foreign-rights agents	251
20. TRY IN-PERSON SALES	254
21. GO ON A BOOK TOUR (MAYBE)	258
22. 43 TACTICS TO SELL A BOOK	261
Appendix	267
Acknowledgments	271
Also by David Kadavy	273
About the Author	274

Note: no "kickbacks"

There are many apps, courses, and professional organizations that promise to help you strike gold in self-publishing. Some of them help, and some of them are scams. Many stay afloat through recommendations by self-publishing gurus. These gurus recommend the products, and get a commission when they refer a new customer, aka a "kickback."

Be assured I get no kickbacks for referring you to any products or services through this book. I haven't been paid to recommend any companies in this book, and there is no mechanism within this book, such as affiliate links, through which a company can tell I've referred someone. In other words, there's no way for me to earn a referral fee for products or services I mention in this book.

I do, however, earn referral fees from some of the companies I mention in this book, when I recommend them through other avenues, such as coupons I post on my website, or affiliate links in articles or emails. But not in this book. I'm trying to give the most honest and impartial information I can here. You paid for it, so that's what you deserve.

Nor do I consult or coach regularly on writing or self-publishing as a part of my business. A couple times a year someone will book a *call with me, but I haven't maintained long-term coaching or consulting contracts with anyone, as I'd much rather use my time and energy writing and selling my books.*

Introduction

I recently noticed I've sold more than 100,000 copies of my self-published, nonfiction books. After I was asked several times how I've done it, I decided to document what I've learned so far. Not only to share with you, but also to reflect and solidify in my memory what has and hasn't worked. 100,000 is far more books than I had expected to sell when I was an English-class dropout who didn't even enjoy writing. So now that I've established my career as an author, I hope writing this book will sharpen my own book-marketing skills.

Spoiler alert: What I know about selling a book involves a lot of work and sacrifice. There are many ways to sell a book, though no one way is a silver bullet. You'll rarely get quick and easy results, and much of your efforts will seemingly go to waste. As you've probably heard, the most important step to sell a book is to write a great book. I can't do that for you, but I can share my specific mental models on how to develop a marketable book. Aside from that, I'm hopeful that by sharing tactics I've learned, I can greatly reduce how much of your efforts go to waste.

As I've tried to make clear with the subtitle of this book, my experiences are primarily with writing and selling nonfiction books. There is an overwhelming amount of information about how to sell

Introduction

a self-published fiction book. As I've built my career as a self-published nonfiction author, I've had to wade through it, and try to discern what is relevant to nonfiction. I've at times felt very lost, because I couldn't find what I was looking for. So what I share in this book is wisdom hard-won through my own experimentation, my successes and failures. Fiction authors won't find in this book a repetition of the standard advice about cranking out a book a month in a rapid-release series full of cliffhangers, but maybe they'll find something fresh and useful. I myself am dipping my toes into fiction, and as I pursue it further I plan to use some of the same audience-growth strategies I talk about in this book.

In case you're curious or incredulous, I'll briefly "show the receipts" for my claim of having sold 100,000 copies of my self-published nonfiction books. I share screenshots to support each of the following, in the Appendix.

- Just on Amazon, I've sold more than 75,000 copies.
- My ACX dashboard shows nearly 15,000 audiobooks sold.
- PublishDrive, just one aggregator I've used, shows I've sold about 5,000 ebooks.
- IngramSpark, which distributes my hard-copy books, mostly outside of Amazon, reports a bit over 4,000 sales.
- Findaway Voices, which distributes my audiobooks outside of Audible/ACX, shows 2,000 more sales, just in 2023.

These numbers alone add up to more than 100,000, and don't include sales from other aggregators, sales directly from retailers other than Amazon, sales directly to my readers, or Findaway Voices sales outside of 2023. So my lifetime self-published book sales are comfortably over 100,000 copies.

Introduction

Nor does this 100,000 include the nearly 18,000 copies I've sold of my first, traditionally-published, book.

My self-published books are also translated or in-progress in more than a dozen languages. The cumulative first-print-runs of these deals are around another 30,000 copies. I don't know the sales numbers of all these foreign translations, but in total I may have sold nearly 150,000 copies, across all books.

Selling 100,000 books puts me far from the league of authors such as J. K. Rowling and Stephen King, or even Mark Manson and James Clear. But I'm proud I've sold my books to enough people to fill Madison Square Garden, and I'm excited to share with you what I've learned. If you have already self-published a book, I hope this helps you sell more copies. If you have not, I hope it helps make your first book a hit.

Paradoxically, by writing a book you're sure will sell some copies, you reduce your potential to sell many copies. That's because publishing is a dance with chance.

Chapter 1
Dance with chance

A foundational principle I work by and that I think is useful for most authors is to think of yourself not as someone following specific steps to achieve a clear goal, but as someone dancing with chance.

Professional golfers such as Tiger Woods are experts at dancing with chance. They accept they won't always take a perfect swing. Even if they could, they don't have total control over factors such as how the wind will change once the ball is in the air, or how it will bounce when it hits the ground. They know how to work with randomness to get the ball in the hole in as few strokes as possible.

In creative work, such as writing and publishing books, you don't have perfect control over how readers will react to your book, in part because it's affected by larger cultural trends we don't have perfect knowledge of and don't understand.

Additionally, most people, especially creative people, don't have perfect control over their own behavior. I know I don't. When you set out to write a book, chances are it will end up being a different book by the time you're done. That's if you can even get yourself to finish writing the book.

White-, black-, and gray-swan books

Randomness will take you places you didn't expect nor could have foreseen. Each book idea you pursue is a dance partner. Some dance partners will back-lead and improvise, others will follow your lead completely. It's up to you to choose an idea with the level of unpredictability you're comfortable with.

When I approach an idea for a new book, I'm not only asking myself whether I can stay curious about the topic long enough to write a book, but also whether or not I think the book will sell.

Whether or not I think the book will sell doesn't determine whether I'll write the book or not. That's because, in my mind, there are three types of books you can choose as dance partners: white swans, black swans, and gray swans.

These three types are inspired by the book, *The Black Swan*, in which Nassim Taleb talks about how explosive successes can't be predicted. The concept of the black swan is based upon the pre-modern European belief that black swans didn't exist, because Europeans hadn't seen them. You can see millions of white swans and never be totally sure black swans don't exist. But you need only see one black swan before you know they do.

Like black swans, books that sell millions of copies can't be predicted. Books that will surely sell some copies are very ordinary, like white swans. But you can mix characteristics of the two to create gray swans, books that are likely to sell some copies, but also have a chance to sell a lot.

How to Sell a Book

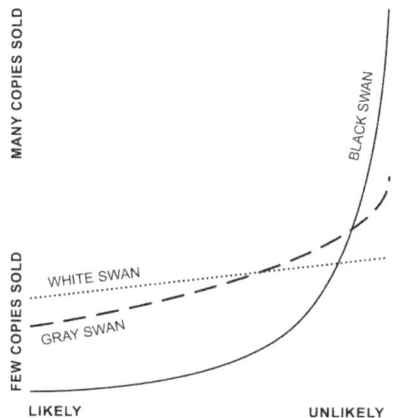

You can write a white-swan nonfiction book simply by writing a useful book on a topic that people search for books about. You'll sell some copies, but, like white swans, there are probably lots of books out there like it, so it won't stand out.

You can't turn a book into a black swan, but you can be sure a black-swan book's attributes will be unusual. If there's never been a book like it and it's hard to categorize, it has an infinitesimal chance to be the breakout book of the century. But because it's so unusual, the more likely outcome will be that it sells next to nothing.

You can virtually guarantee a book to sell some copies by making it a gray swan: Make it solve a clear problem and fit into a clear category, but make it unusual enough to stand out. A gray-swan book doesn't have as much potential as a black-swan book, but it has more than a white-swan book. A gray-swan book doesn't have as high a floor on its minimum sales as a white-swan book, but it has a higher floor than a black-swan book.

The portfolio approach and the never-ending lotto ticket

Writing books and getting them to sell is subject to chance. In other words, you have to get lucky. But, writing books is a tremendous amount of work, and even if you're somewhat successful at it as I have been, you still don't make a ton of money.

So I approach the business of self-publishing books with a constant sensitivity to how I'm allocating my resources, such as my time and money.

Venture capitalists and publishers themselves take a portfolio approach to dancing with chance. They make lots of small bets, and hope some of them are hits. Ninety-percent of traditionally-published books sell fewer than 2,000 copies in their first year. The other ten percent help keep publishers in business.

The portfolio approach is much harder to take when you're an individual, because writing and publishing a book can be so much work. It's hard to spread resources across many bets when you don't have many resources.

Many professional investors use a "barbell strategy." The barbell strategy is visualized as a very lopsided barbell, with a lot of weight on one side, little weight on the other side, and virtually nothing, only the bar, in between.

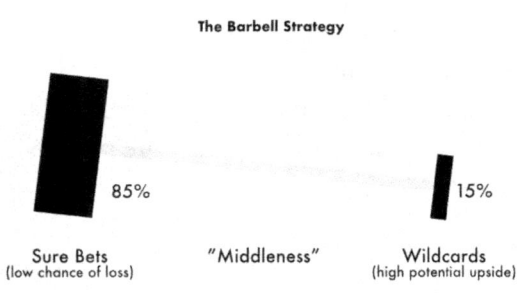

Inspired by Nicholas Nassim Taleb's *The Black Swan* | kadavy.net Feel free to re-use

Investors who use the barbell strategy make very safe investments in which they won't lose money with most their resources, and with the rest of their resources make smaller investments that have tremendous potential upside. If you make a 1,000x return on ten-thousand dollars, you'll make ten million dollars, but maybe you've risked all your money. If you had invested a thousand dollars, you'd have still made a million dollars, but without risking everything. As long as you can stay in the game, you essentially have a never-ending lotto ticket.

Early in my career, the safe side of my barbell was freelance work. As my more risky bets have paid off, I've built up to the point where almost all my income is from my books, and I no longer freelance. Therefore, books have become the safe side of my barbell.

But I allocate my resources carefully amongst white-, black- and gray-swan books.

Write shorter books: Small books are small bets

It's risky to put everything into a black-swan book idea, especially if it's your first book. This is one reason that, in addition to my full-length books, I've written a lot of "short reads." Some of my short reads are forty pages. My longest is about seventy-five. My shortest full-length book is 140 pages, and my longest is over 300.

By writing short reads, I sharpen my skills in coming up with book ideas and writing and marketing books. I get to experiment with black-swan book ideas, without losing years of my life on books that don't sell, forcing me to find a job and practically ending my career as an author.

Another benefit of writing short reads is many books just don't need to be that long. It's become a cliché humble-brag to claim a book you've read was "just a blog post with 250 pages of filler" – a claim now so ubiquitous I wouldn't be surprised to hear it about

Dance with chance

War and Peace. But it's no doubt true of many books today, especially in the Business and Self-Help genres, in which I write.

Books are intentionally made this long by traditional publishers, because that's the way the economics work out. There are overhead costs to printing a book, so it might as well be long, and many mainstream readers just feel like they're getting their money's worth if a book is longer.

In my experience, shorter books do, indeed, sell fewer copies at a cheaper price. But for me as an individual playing a portfolio strategy, writing shorter books is a win all over. I get the idea out there, my readers get a straightforward solution, I learn from another book's sales performance, and I make some money to feed myself until I finish my next big book. Plus, it keeps me in practice. I feel rusty if I haven't published a book in a while.

Shorter books are also great because people can actually finish them. People's time is more fragmented and attention spans are the shortest they've been. So even if people enjoy a book, they'll often not finish it.

Eric Jorgenson, the current CEO of Scribe Media, has self-published some shorter books. While *The Almanack of Naval Ravikant* and *The Anthology of Balaji* are each around 250 pages, Eric made sure to break them up with subheads, illustrations, pull-quotes, and larger typesetting. Eric says, "These all create momentum and make the book easy to finish. If you finish a book, you're more likely to recommend it."

My white swans

I put very little of my resources into white-swan books. My most white-swan book is *How to Write a Book*. People clearly want to write books, and while this book makes use of my style, it doesn't take a lot of risks. I'm amazed it's sold 12,000 copies.

I could also call *Digital Zettelkasten* a white-swan book. It clearly is written for a very specific topic. But I was really surprised how big the market was. It's sold nearly 16,000 copies, not including its two translations in foreign markets.

Both these books are "short reads," so they didn't take nearly as much work as my main books.

My black swans

Since I still don't have a lot of resources yet for big, risky bets, my attempts at black-swan books have all been short reads. My clearest bid toward a black swan has been the whacky, *In Defense of Papyrus*. I don't know what possessed me to write this book (which is a strong sign a book is a black-swan book). I just got obsessed with the Papyrus font and went with it. It actually was a ton of work per-word. It took me a year to write. Like most black-swan plays, it didn't turn into a black swan. It's my least-selling book at under 100 copies, though as I had hoped, it has led to some press coverage.

My gray swans

I've put the most resources into my gray swan books, and so far, they've all sold well. My first book was *Design for Hackers* – which was traditionally-published. Clearly there was already a market for web-design books, but this had a twist. Amazingly for a technology book, it's still selling thirteen years after its release. It's sold nearly 18,000 copies.

My next book was *The Heart to Start: Stop Procrastinating & Start Creating*. This book was my entry into the Self-Help/Creativity market of which *The War of Art* and *The Artist's Way* are seminal works. It's sold over 30,000 copies.

My latest book is *Mind Management, Not Time Management*. It spans both the very popular Time Management category, as well

Dance with chance

as that of Self-Help/Creativity. It's my best-seller, with more than 40,000 copies.

By allocating most of my resources to gray swans, I've been able to use book sales as the secure side of my barbell. I hope to make more black swan attempts with longer books, as I build my resources.

If you already have a secure income, you may be willing to risk writing black-swan books. If you want a higher chance to, like me, build a career as an author, you may want to write shorter white-swan books, and longer gray-swan books. But whether explicitly, as with white-swan books, or more subtly, as with black-swan books, you must start by writing a book people will buy.

Chapter 2
Write a book people will buy

Unless you're willing to put in the work to write a book and risk selling zero copies, you should assess whether or not your book idea has a market. Ideally, you would do this before writing the book, but if you're inexperienced and/or tend to have a bottom-up approach to projects, realistically you'll do this while writing the book. It's really common to have a feeling that you want to write a book, but have no idea what you want to write a book about. The best way to find out is to start writing the book.

But you have to think of your book as a product someone will buy because it does something for them. That could be something as practical as a detergent that gets out grease stains, or as impractical as the pet rock and whatever that did for people.

Knowing how to identify readers' desires, address them with your book, and communicate the value in your marketing can be so subtle, anyone who does it well is probably getting lucky. Otherwise, traditional publishers would only produce hits. But there are elements that can increase the chances you write a book people will buy.

The four M's of a good book idea

A book is much easier to sell if the idea for the book is good. A good book idea should be Marketable, Memetic, Memorable, and Made for the author.

Marketable

A book idea is Marketable if it promises something worth paying for. What's worth paying for might not be obvious. If your book is about how to live as an expat in a particular country, that has obvious utility. But a book can be Marketable in more subtle ways. It can confirm one's beliefs or affirm one's identity, which is much of the value of most political books. It can make you feel smart, which is part of the appeal of history books, pop-psychology books such as those by Malcolm Gladwell, and brain ticklers such as books by Nassim Taleb.

Two books can cover similar content, but be Marketable in very different ways. *Deep Work* and *The Shallows* were both responses to digital distraction. But the former was Marketable because it promised enhanced productivity, espoused focus, and made one feel pride in their work. The latter was Marketable because it was a "chicken little" book: Here are the reasons the sky is falling, just as you suspected.

Memetic

A book idea is Memetic if it has features that help it spread. Just as the shape of one virus will give it an affinity to the lining of the intestine, whereas another will affect the nasal passages, books will be shared and recommended based upon their qualities. Or, they won't spread at all. Nir Eyal's *Indistractable* was also a response to digital distraction. Instead of the paranoid posture of

The Shallows or the focus on personal productivity of *Deep Work*, it was somewhere in-between. *Indistractable* exudes a posture of resilience and personal ownership. It acknowledges that distraction is a challenge, but stresses that it's nothing new.

Nir's book is far more Memetic than if he had gone with his first idea. Early in his journey of talking about the content in *Indistractable*, he was considering the title *Un-Hooked*, which would have been an acknowledgement of his previous book's title, *Hooked: How to Build Habit-Forming Products*. This small fact contains a big lesson in creating Memetic book ideas: Good book ideas are status symbols for the reader. *Un-Hooked* wouldn't pass the "cocktail party test," which I'll talk about later. Telling others you're reading a book about how to get unhooked from your digital devices doesn't feel empowering, but telling them you're reading a book about being indistractable does.

Memorable

A book will have a hard time being Memetic if it isn't Memorable. The title and/or concept and/or content has to stick to the mind well enough to be passed on.

You can have the coolest concept in the world for your title, but if it's not easy to understand and remember, nobody can recommend it. If you say the book's title aloud, do you have to repeat it before someone can understand it? If you ask someone to repeat it back to you, do they butcher it? I haven't perfected this, myself. It's fascinating to hear what people come up with when they say my own book titles to me. "Hey David, I loved *The Art of Starting*!" (It's *The Heart to Start*.) "I was just reading *Time Management, Not Mind Management*." (The exact opposite of my title and the very concept of my book.)

Coming up with a Memorable title doesn't have to be guesswork. One of the books I re-read most often is Mark Forsyth's *The*

Write a book people will buy

Elements of Eloquence, which breaks down various structures in language that make short phrases Memorable, or even mis-remembered. Some that you may have learned in school include alliteration, the repetition of a consonant sound, as in *The Great Gatsby*, or assonance, the repetition of a vowel sound, such as in *East of Eden*. More obscure structures include chiasmus, which is a fancy way of saying the phrase crosses over or reverses itself, such as in the phrase, "winners never quit, quitters never win." The structure of that phrase is ABCCBA, with "win" and "quit" repeated in different forms. Because they're used both as nouns and verbs, the phrase also uses polyptoton.

These structures don't have to be repeated too formulaically to make a title Memorable. *The 4-Hour Work Week* is almost a chiasmus of assonance. If you say "the" with a long e, like in "week," those sounds provide bookends. In between are the short o's of "hour" and "work." While "four" has a long o that prevents the title from being a perfect chiasmus, there's still plenty of alliteration in the repetition of the r's in "four," "hour," and "work," and the w's at the beginning of "work" and "week." That's a lot of literary devices packed into just five words.

I liked the title *Mind Management, Not Time Management*, aside from the concept it expresses, because it contained two parallel phrases, each ending in "management." There's a lot of repetition of m's, n's, and t's. It still gets butchered, maybe because it's nine syllables, but there's something about the phrase that seems inherently embedded in the human mind. I've numerous times seen people on X say the phrase without knowing my book exists, and get high engagement while they were at it.

These literary devices help, but I have to admit they aren't necessary. One of the biggest mysteries to me in the Self-Help genre is how *The Obstacle is the Way* became a hit with such an awkward title. Saying it feels like trying to roll dice in your mouth.

Ryan Holiday's follow-up title, *The Ego is the Enemy* is much more poetic, with just the right amount of assonance.

You can also write a Memorable title by using a technique I call "idiom jacking." Basically, take a well-known expression, and change it into a title, in a way that's relevant to the book's offering. *The 4-Hour Work Week* "jacks" the idiom of the forty-hour work week. *Never Split the Difference* modifies the well-known idiom of "splitting the difference" in a negotiation.

A Memorable title isn't enough if it's not unique. You want to be able to search the title in Google and not have too many pages come up that already include it. *Eat, Pray, Love* includes very simple words. But those Memorable words hadn't been strung together like that before.

I'll talk more about titles later, and they aren't the only things that need to be Memorable. The thesis of your book should also be easy enough to grasp to be summed up in a short sentence, and provocative enough to be remembered when it is. It also helps to have lots of Memorable anecdotes or stories within your book that will get passed on. There were lots of books in the aughts that spread through memorable anecdotes, such as *Freakonomics* and *The Tipping Point*. *The 4-Hour Body* (2010) was full of Memorable promises, such as a 15-minute orgasm and the "slow-carb diet."

Made for the author

A book idea is Made for the author if the author is the only person who could write this book. A lot of would-be authors take this to mean if they aren't the most-renowned expert on one subject they can't write a book, and that's not the case. Dr. Robert Lustig didn't have to be the greatest doctor in the world to write *The Hacking of the American Mind*. But he gained a unique perspective on how the brain uses dopamine when he was researching his previous book, *Fat Chance*. He gained the unique perspective to write that book as chairman of the Obesity Task Force of the Pediatric Endocrine Society.

You can gain the unique perspective to write a particular book in the process of writing it. Tim Ferriss made himself the only person who could write *The 4-Hour Body* by conducting and tracking lots of weird experiments. Liz Gilbert funded the soul-searching travels she chronicles in *Eat, Pray, Love* by first getting a book deal to write about the travels she hadn't yet taken.

Choosing a book idea that's Made for the author is a part of what I call idea/author fit.

Categories

If you want a chance for your book to sell, it has to fit into one or more categories. These categories exist because people buy books that fit into these categories.

Familiarize yourself with the categories books fit into. See what books are shelved where at your local bookstore or library, take a peek at the standard BISAC "subject codes," or, my personal favorite, explore the categories on Amazon's Kindle Store. Amazon has the widest-ranging categories, including things like "Paranormal Demons & Devils Romance" and "Lapidary" (gem polishing).

Amazon is a great place to browse categories and assess the market of a book idea, because you can see directly how well each book sells, and thus get a good idea of the sales potential within a given category. On each book's Amazon page, you'll see its current sales rank. You can enter that sales rank into a sales rank calculator, and see approximately how many sales per month a book makes to achieve a given rank.

How to Sell a Book

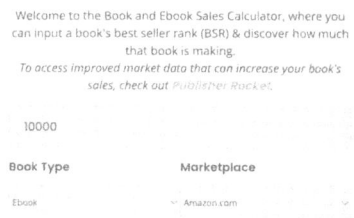

A book's overall Amazon rank, and ranking in up to three categories, is listed on its page, under "Product details."

This sales rank calculator on the Kindlepreneur website estimates a Kindle ebook ranked 10,000 sells 15 copies per day.

For example, at the moment I'm writing this, the Kindle edition of *Getting Things Done* ranks 23,439 overall in the Kindle store, which is about 360 books per month. In one of its main categories, "Stress Management," it ranks fourteen overall. The number one book in that category currently ranks 703 overall, which translates to about 4,000 sales per month.

Where there's potential, there's competition. Yes, it would be great to be at the top of Self-Help and sell 14,000 ebooks a month, but because there are so many books in that category, you'll have a ton of competition. But, if you write a book that fits in that category and some of its many subcategories, and does a decent job of delivering on its promise, you'll sell at least some books.

By contrast, the top book in the less-popular category of "Craft & Hobby Dough" is ranked 148,712, which translates to less than thirty sales per month. So you could write the greatest Dough book of all time and still make very little dough.

When publishing through Amazon's Kindle Direct Publishing (KDP), you can choose up to three subcategories, which will also include your book in all the parent categories. You'll want to choose the most specific subcategories possible that are relevant to your book. You used to be able to email KDP support and request your book to be manually added to up to ten subcategories, but they no longer honor those requests, and can even override your category selections, based upon your book's content and/or the behavior of shoppers.

Keywords

Realistically, not many people browse through Amazon's categories, looking for books. More likely, they search for keywords, and Amazon suggests books to them.

You can assess the market potential of your book by searching for keywords you can imagine people searching to find your book.

Just as it's common to feel like you want to write a book but not know what about, it's also common to not have a good idea what people will search for to find your book. If you enter a search phrase into Amazon, and it doesn't show up in auto-suggest, you have a problem. Nobody is searching for that search phrase, and thus it doesn't show up.

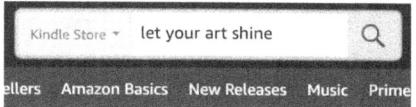

Searching for "Let Your Art Shine" on Amazon's Kindle Store. Notice no auto-suggest appears.

I'll talk more about titles in a bit, but the subtitle is a good place to express what your book is about in plain language that people search for. When I first published *The Heart to Start*, the subtitle was *Win the Inner War and Let Your Art Shine*. Terrible. Nobody searches for those things.

Now the subtitle is *Stop Procrastinating and Start Creating*. People at least search for the first part of that.

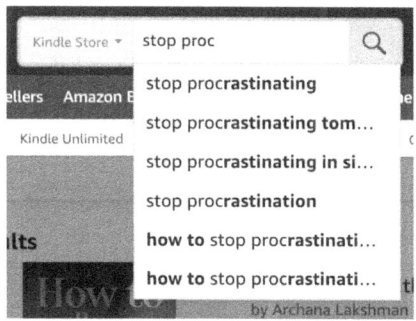

As with categories, you can estimate the potential of your book idea by searching keywords and seeing the ranking of books in the search results. But if you don't actually see the keywords you searched in the titles and subtitles of the books, it probably isn't searched for at a high rate. Though there are exceptions. When I was assessing the market potential of *Digital Zettelkasten*, there were no books with Zettelkasten in the title or subtitle.

Write a book people will buy

Mine was first, and caught the developing wave of interest in the topic.

Ideally there will be some books with those keywords in the titles and subtitles, but if you get pages and pages of results, you have a lot of competition. That doesn't mean you shouldn't try. "Time management" is an incredibly competitive keyphrase, but my book, *Mind Management, Not Time Management* ranks in the top ten at this moment. That's due to a combination of the keywords being right in the title, the frequency with which people click and buy the book after searching "time management," and whatever other secret sauce is in Amazon's algorithm.

Just because people aren't using your keywords doesn't mean they aren't searching for a book like yours. At the least it means they aren't using the words you expect. Finding the keywords people will use to search for your book is an iterative process. If you're writing a white-swan book, you may be able to figure it out just by brainstorming, running a bunch of searches, or asking ChatGPT for ideas.

As you get toward more gray- and black-swan ideas, you're more likely to need to discover the right keywords through the process of writing the book. I can't tell you how long I explored to realize "time management" was a keyword for my book, *Mind Management, Not Time Management*, and indeed that that was the title. It's kind of embarrassing because I had already written a blog post by that name, eight years prior to releasing the book.

Even if you don't have a keyphrase in your title or subtitle, you can include up to seven of them in the metadata you create when uploading your book to Amazon's KDP. Doing so will help your book rank for searches for those keyphrases, and may even influence whether your book is included in certain categories. One of the many features of the app Publisher Rocket is recommendations of keywords that help influence whether a book is included in given categories.

Idea/author fit

If you want to write a book that sells, it helps a lot if you're the only person who can write that book. Ideally, your book idea fits you, the author.

My first book was *Design for Hackers*, and that was a good fit for me because I had a degree in graphic design and had won awards as a designer, but had also worked for Silicon Valley startups as a designer and coder, so had a lot of familiarity with the audience and the problems they faced.

I was lucky to stumble into an idea that fit me. I created the conditions for that luck by writing about a variety of subjects on my blog until I hit a vein of explosive demand. My soon-to-be publisher, Wiley, recognized that and reached out.

It's really common to think you can write a book you have no business writing. I say it's really common, because that's what I tried to do next. After *Design for Hackers*, when I knew I wanted to write another book, but not about design, I had a lot of ideas for books that feel harebrained in retrospect, and that weren't a good fit for me as an author.

I hope I never said it, but somewhere in my mind, I felt I wanted to write a book like *Thinking, Fast and Slow*. That was ridiculous, because that book was written by an academic who had spent forty years pioneering the field of behavioral economics, running tons of studies and teaching students, and I have an undergraduate degree in graphic design.

But that was a starting point, and fortunately I didn't finish another book until I had explored and scrapped many ideas, many of which were just not good ideas, but all of which simply didn't fit me as an author. My second book ended up being *The Heart to Start*, which was a pretty good fit, because, rather than spending decades as an academic, I had spent decades struggling to put creative work into the world, and more than a decade making tremendous sacrifices to make that the main focus of my life.

The Heart to Start (HTS) was my first self-published book. I made a lot of mistakes, some of which I've been able to correct, such as the subtitle, but it sold over 30,000 copies in about six years.

My search for idea/author fit for my next book wasn't much easier, but I think it was just as good, if not better. My unique experience of developing a system for managing my creative energy made me the right person to write *Mind Management, Not Time Management* (MMT). Sometimes the right sources of idea/author fit are right under your nose, and you don't notice them. I somehow missed well into the process that I had written a successful blog post called "Mind Management, Not Time Management," which had led to collaborating with behavioral scientist Dan Ariely on a time-management app that had sold to Google and become integrated into Google Calendar. MMT sold over 40,000 copies in a little over three years.

HTS and MMT each had their own long idea/author searches, but both came from a somewhat-failed prior search. The series these books are in is called *Getting Art Done*, which was one of my ideas for my second book. But as I explored the idea, I realized it should be three books. The third book in that series is my main project right now.

Choosing the right idea for you as an author looks easy if you're a world-renowned expert with credentials, like Daniel Kahneman was when he wrote *Thinking, Fast and Slow*. But if your journey is off the beaten path like mine, it takes a combination of exploring what you have to offer, along with being realistic about how much authority you have in a topic, and also realizing unique points of view you don't notice you have because you are you. It's really an exciting and often uncomfortable process of self-actualization.

A good north star as you search for an idea that fits you is, Can you sum up who you are and what the book is about in a short sentence, and have it make sense? The basic format you want to fill out is, "[This book] is [about this] by [this person]."

"*Thinking, Fast and Slow* is a book about behavioral economics, by a pioneering researcher in the field," is the most basic way to match an idea to an author.

But you don't have to have official credentials to make a compelling idea/author statement.

"*Eat, Pray, Love* is a book about a soul-searching journey, by a recently-divorced woman who travels to Italy, India, and Indonesia." Liz Gilbert's black swan didn't have anything to do with her official credentials. She just had a compelling story people wanted to read.

The beauty of the internet age is that credentials in an idea/author statement can be what Daniel J. Boorstin called a "pseudo-event": The author has earned the right to write about the topic because they've written about the topic. "*The Subtle Art of Not Giving a F*ck* is a self-help guide by a guy who has a popular blog about self-help." That's been enough to sell more than ten million copies.

Doing also helps you learn what you want to teach in the book. The experiments of various academic fields often don't replicate, and studying things in a lab isn't the only way to learn. So learn by doing, then tell the story. In *Mind Management, Not Time Management* I tell the story of how I redesigned my life around my system for managing creative energy.

Even for white-swan books, you don't have to be an expert in the field. While I had experimented with various note-taking methods before discovering the Zettelkasten method, I wrote *Digital Zettelkasten* shortly after immersing myself in the method and applying it to my writing process. I purposely wrote the book about a specific way of applying the method (*Digital*), and an abstract way of thinking about it (as in the subtitle, *Principles, Methods, and Examples*) because, not being a highly-experienced

Write a book people will buy

expert, I wasn't trying to write the definitive guide on the topic. I was just describing the mental model that had helped me make use of the method. The idea/author statement for the book might be, "*Digital Zettelkasten* is an introduction to the principles, methods, and examples of an obscure note-taking method, by an author who uses it to write articles and books." It's sold more than 16,000 copies.

No matter how well you've researched your category, keywords, and idea/author fit, though, it's easier to sell a book if you have built an audience.

Chapter 3
Build the audience as you build the book

There's nothing you can have closer to guaranteed sales of your book than already having readers who are looking forward to it. There's no better way to get readers, and to make those readers look forward to your book, than building the audience as you build the book. By building the audience as you build the book, you get to see which of your ideas resonate or don't, while finding out who wants to hear what you have to say, and building your marketing skills.

The "I don't have an audience" Catch-22

Beginning authors often look at audience-building as a Catch-22 situation: You can't sell a book because you don't have an audience. You can't build an audience because you don't have an audience.

It's easy to beat yourself up when in this situation. How do you find the motivation to write *anything*, much less a whole book, if you don't already have someone who wants to read it?

It's trite, but true: You have to start somewhere. I started writing online regularly in 2004. Yes, I've been at it twenty years. When I started, I was living in Nebraska. No relative nor anyone

Build the audience as you build the book

I've grown up with or even went to college with has played a significant role in building my audience. When I started, people like me didn't do things like this. My audience started from zero.

The "must be nice" trap

It's also easy to get caught in the "must be nice" trap. That's where you look at one advantage someone else has that you don't, and conclude that's the reason they've made it and you haven't. Believe me, I have and sometimes still do fall into the "must be nice" trap.

For example, some might look at my twenty years writing online and say, "must be nice!" Yet I look at people starting now and think, "must be nice!" I started in the dawn of blogging, and the first time a blogger asked for money, it was very controversial. They're starting from scratch with all sorts of audience-building tools, business models, and a rich community of creators making a living online. I'm a middle-aged guy, set in my ways. I have to really make an effort to disrupt myself and keep up with changes in the landscape.

The "must be nice" trap is often lined with beliefs about timing. "It was easy then," because people read blogs. Or "It's easier now," because growth-focused networks like Medium and Substack are out there. I can tell you after twenty years writing online, there's always some hot new way to build an audience.

I've successfully built this audience, and have also done it from scratch under a pseudonym. As I talked about in my *Ten Passive Income Ideas* short-read, I used that pseudonym to write a blog that made me $150,000 and funded my writing under my real name. After building an audience twice, the best strategy I can recommend is just stick around and try lots of things for long enough for luck to strike a few times.

Community-first

To build an audience as you build a marketable book idea, start with a community-first approach. Find a community where people are regularly talking about the topic you'll cover in your book. It could be a Discord or Facebook group, a forum, a subreddit, or a hashtag or topic on a social network. Observe that community. Become a part of it if that suits you, but it's not absolutely necessary.

When your book comes out, this community will be the place people are talking about it. So it's important to understand this community for two reasons. One, every community has a different culture, and you need to shape your book idea and the way you'll sell it to suit that culture. For example, a lot of subreddits are hostile to any form of self-promotion. But if you look at the most-popular posts all-time on that subreddit, you'll get an idea what kind of content does well there, so you can adapt your message in a way that will get people talking about your book, without violating the community's norms. Two, understanding the community will help you build your audience as you build the book. If you become an active member of that community, and generously share your knowledge and help others, you'll get better at talking about your ideas in a way that resonates with that audience, while becoming a respected authority whose book launch members of that community will look forward to.

My first book, *Design for Hackers*, was successful thanks to the Hacker News community. I had been writing articles on my blog about various topics, and had gotten in sync enough with the community, it felt like I could write at will articles that would rank on the front page. As I was making a proposal to speak at a conference, I made writing a detailed article that ranked highly on Hacker News my main strategy for getting votes for my talk idea. My first article on design ranked at the top of Hacker News, and an editor

Build the audience as you build the book

at Wiley reached out. My second article prompted another publisher to approach me. My book deal announcement, the launch of my book, and my book tour were all strongly supported by that community.

My *Getting Art Done* series has been successful thanks to the audience I built writing on Medium, for the communities formed around the Creativity and Writing tags. By writing for those communities, I got a keen sense of what resonated and didn't for those readers. When I announced I was writing a book, many of those readers signed up for my email list, which has since become instrumental in promoting books in that series.

Digital Zettelkasten has been successful because Zettelkasten and other note-taking methods have vibrant communities, always talking about the topics. I immersed myself in the content those communities created as I learned about Zettelkasten, myself. I wrote the book that contained the information I wished I had when I started. While I'm not very active in those communities, other than an occasional discussion on X, the launch of *Digital Zettelkasten* was met with enthusiasm when I shared it in the Zettelkasten subreddit. (Importantly, I launched the Kindle edition at the lowest price Amazon allows, 99¢, which probably helped garner community support.)

If there's not a place where people talk about the topic of your book, that may be a sign your book idea isn't marketable. However, you might have an idea you feel will appeal heavily to a certain community, even if it's not directly related. But this is an advanced strategy with a high failure rate – a black-swan play. Crazy things can happen, though. The runaway success that was *Fifty Shades of Grey* started as *Twilight* fan-fiction, written in a forum.

If there's not a place where people talk about the topic of your book, you can also create that place. By creating free content around that topic, you can attract people from related communities to build your own. This would be a tremendous amount of work, but it would virtually guarantee a captive audience once your book came out.

An email list is a must

The best place to have your audience is on an email list. You can have a social media following of millions and a tiny algorithm change or shutdown of a site can take that away from you overnight. Yes, things have changed and will change about email, but it's the closest you can have to a direct line to your readers.

If you do not have an email list, put this book down and start one now. MailChimp is very popular, tons of creators use Kit (formerly ConvertKit), and I've been with ActiveCampaign for close to a decade because I like to get really sophisticated with automations, and it has more-advanced tiers I can grow into if my business model changes. But if you're just starting, it really doesn't matter, so long as it's a service that allows you to export your list of subscribers. Then you can always switch as you learn what you like and don't like about an Email Service Provider (ESP).

Why not just have a spreadsheet of emails you copy and paste into Gmail? Because these ESPs help keep you from breaking the law. And if you do things against the law, you may or may not have legal trouble, but it will hurt your "sender reputation." So emails from your email address will go straight to spam folders and not to inboxes, where you want them.

Don't let the perfect be the enemy of the good here. Just open an account with an ESP, and worry about the rest later. Many offer free plans under a certain number of subscribers. They'll ask for a mailing address that has to be at the bottom of your emails, and that can be a real buzzkill if you don't want to put your real address there. There are a ton of services to get an address that isn't your home, such as VirtualPostMail, the UPS Store down the street, or your post office. And yes, that's annoying and it's an extra expense, but if you're in business, you gotta do it. Or just put your own address on there, if you don't mind living dangerously.

Explosive email courses

Email courses are the best way to build your audience while building your book. They're great because, one, it makes sense for people to give you their email address if that's the way you're delivering content, and, two, because once you have their email address, you can easily tell them when your book is out.

I developed a really powerful "explosive email course" formula that has been successful for me, and many others who have tried the same formula. The important element of this formula is timing. At the time I developed it, many email marketers were doing simple "drip" sequences: you signed up for their email list and they immediately started sending their "five-day course" on their topic.

I debuted my formula in a free email course called *Summer of Design*, which brought my email list from 5,000 subscribers to over 30,000 in only three weeks. In many ways, it was like a traditional drip sequence, in that it sent out a series of emails. But, as I said, the important element is timing. I announced *Summer of Design* with a landing page that outlined a schedule for *when* I was going to send each email, complete with a countdown timer for when the course was going to start.

How to Sell a Book

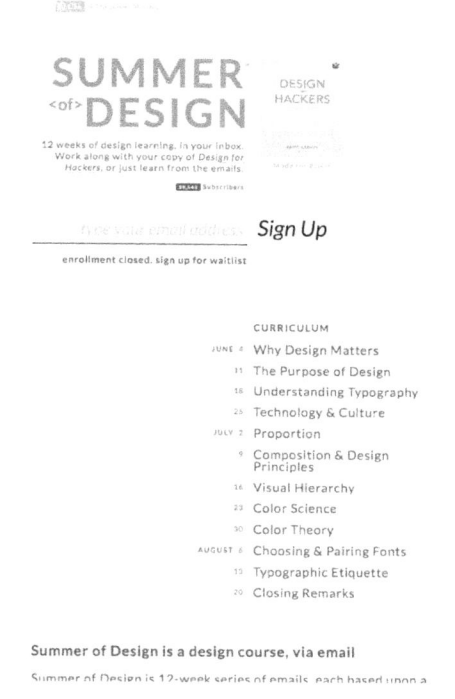

The simple landing page I used to launch *Summer of Design*, which grew my email list 6x.

Instead of independently getting each email "on-demand," subscribers were getting each email collectively, at the same time. This collective event created a sense of community. The deadline to sign up before the first lesson also gave subscribers time to invite their friends, and the urgency of that deadline further motivated sign-ups. Also important, instead of giving away the content whenever, I reinforced that the content was valuable stuff I had worked hard on, by giving it away only on my terms.

Many others have since used this explosive email-course formula, with great success. Noah Kagan uses it for *Summer of Marketing*. Robbie Abed, author of *Fire Me, I Beg You*, used it for *Summer of Quitting*. Your email course doesn't have to have

Build the audience as you build the book

anything to do with summer: Phil Thompson and Katie Lauffenburger of Wonder City Studios use it for their email tour of Chicago residential architecture. I've repeated this formula many times, such as with my email course, *100-Word Writing Habit*.

When I debuted *Summer of Design*, I promised twelve lessons, each based upon one of the twelve chapters of my book, *Design for Hackers*. So, I wrote the book before making the email course. Now, I do things the other way around: My *Getting Art Done* series started with an email course in which I promised a short chapter on creative productivity every day for thirty days. The course served as a first draft, which has been divided into three books, the third of which I'm currently writing. I expanded my *100-Word Writing Habit* email course into a book by the same name, and have now created an associated habit-tracking wristband and journal-prompt workbook.

Here's a diagram describing the explosive email course formula I developed more than a decade ago, and still use effectively.

Email course viral loop

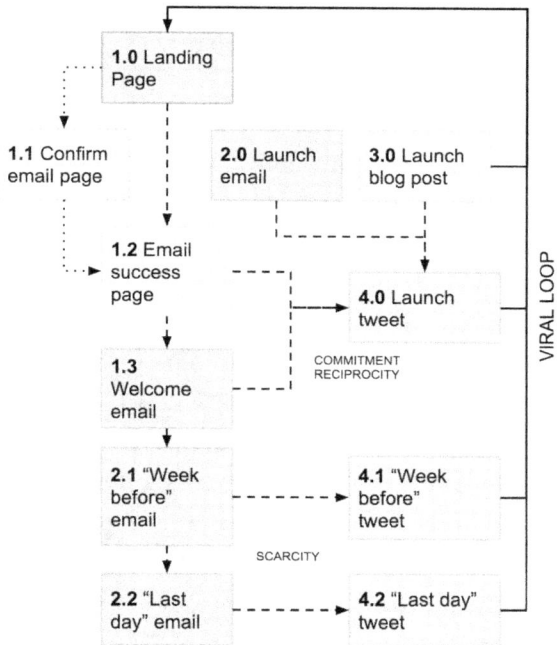

The Landing Page (1.0), is where readers sign up. Sign-ups are driven by a "viral loop," which consists of emails and social media posts that are timed and designed to make the best use of persuasive principles (as written by Robert Cialdini in his book *Influence*).

For example, in the Welcome email (1.3), the focus is on the principles of commitment and reciprocity. They've signed up for the course, and to help them commit to following through, you can encourage them to share on social media. For example, "Studies show that if you make a public declaration, you're more likely to follow through on a commitment. So share on social media!"

They can also be driven by a feeling of reciprocity. For example, "I've invested hundreds of hours in assembling this free course. The only payment I ask is that you share it with your friends and followers."

Build the audience as you build the book

Another persuasive reason for people to share your course is by inviting a commitment buddy. Even if everyone who signed up only got one more friend to sign up, you'd grow your email list quickly!

As the start of the course approaches, the focus shifts to the principle of scarcity. You send emails to students one "week before" (2.1) and on the "last day" (2.2) to sign up. By encouraging them to share on social media, perhaps once again by invoking commitment or reciprocity, a potential student who sees it's their last chance to sign up will be highly motivated to do so.

Once the first cohort of your email course is complete, you can run your course on autopilot by starting a new session every week. I won't get too deep into the technical details, but you can set up an automation in an ESP to start a new email sequence, say, every Wednesday, and find free countdown timers to put on your website, which reset at the same time each week. If a countdown timer is too technical, you can just show on the sign-up page, "Next session starts Sunday at 8 p.m." for example. Your email course will automatically build your audience and showcase your content while you do other things.

Not only do email courses help you build your audience, but building email courses also serves as fantastic motivational fuel to build your book. I've begun every email course by building a landing page, with a schedule listed of which emails I'll send by which dates. Once I announce the course, I'm motivated by the fact I haven't yet written the emails! I usually have written a few rough lines of each beforehand, but it's not until the date of the first lesson is coming closer I actually write the first email. As the course continues, I'm presented with one deadline after another, until the course is done. Others who have tried my email course formula have used the same tactic to motivate themselves, and reported it works for them.

Once your email course is done, you now have a very basic and short draft of your book, and hopefully some subscribers who have already enjoyed the content. In the case of my *Getting Art Done* email course, I had an entire first draft of a book!

Email courses are also products you can sell, to fund your writing. Some time after *Summer of Design* was finished, I started charging for access to it. Many people paid to receive the *Getting Art Done* series of emails – even people who had already been through the first iteration. An email course is in some ways better than a book: instead of having to open a book, your customer gets a little bit at a time, in a place they already check every day. In my experience, people will pay $5–15 for an email course that helps them. It's not a lot, but when you're first starting out, it's a thrill to get paid anything for your writing!

But don't put off starting your email list because you don't have an email course. Start your email list now.

Lead magnets

Less work than an email course but still an effective way to entice people to sign up for your email list is with a "lead magnet," or some freebie people get when signing up. I'm honestly surprised lead magnets work, but they do. Email courses seem like a better pitch to get someone to sign up for your email list, because they're sent via email. Lead magnets, which are often ebooks or one-page PDFs, you could just link to, so it always feels a little adversarial to say, "sign up for my email list and get this PDF."

Interestingly, some of the simplest lead magnets work best. I've experimented with giving away a forty-page ebook, and it doesn't seem to do any better than giving away a one-page PDF of "30 Journaling Prompts." I also give away "14 Tools to Quadruple Your Creative Productivity."

Since you're building your audience while building your book, make a lead magnet that helps you test content that might be in your book. You can see if one way of presenting the lead magnet might work better than another. For example, does "30 Journaling Prompts" lead to more sign-ups than "30 Writing Prompts"? Does "Quadruple Your Creative Productivity" work better than "Quadruple Your Writing"? This is information you could use to write a more effective title, chapter name, or subhead.

Lead magnets are a great resource to build your email list with advertising. In the chapter about advertising your book, I talk about how to build an automation that ensures you're only getting the best leads from this "cold" traffic.

Like with the email course, don't put off starting your email list because you don't have a lead magnet. Start your email list now.

Email newsletters

Email courses are short, and lead magnets are even shorter. They're both great for getting readers onto your email list, but they don't keep them there.

Even if a reader stays subscribed after receiving a lead magnet or taking an email course, if you send an email announcing your book a year after your latest email, they'll likely have forgotten you. They won't be accustomed to opening your emails and may erroneously report your email as spam, which will harm your sender reputation and make it less likely those who do remember you get your emails.

Keeping your relationship with your email subscribers "warm" is just one reason it's a great idea to have a regular newsletter. It can be quarterly, monthly, weekly, even daily.

The other reason to have a newsletter is to build the audience as you build your book. The way a comedian goes to open mics in the process of building an act, your newsletter is a chance to test out the ideas you're working on and considering including in your book. Sending a newsletter on a set schedule is a way to keep yourself accountable to a writing schedule, in the process of writing your book.

Some email newsletters are very long, in which the author sends out entire articles. Some email newsletters are very short, in which the author sends out a few bite-sized items. I recommend sending a short newsletter. I've noticed myself if one of my favorite writers sends a long article as a newsletter, I'll put off opening it, and likely won't open it at all. Email is just not the place for reading long articles. But if I know the email will be short, I'll open it right away.

I kept this in mind when I developed my weekly newsletter. I noticed Tim Ferriss had *Five-Bullet Friday*, which simply promised five interesting things each Friday. James Clear had *3-2-1 Thursdays*, which promised three ideas from him, two quotes from others, and one question to ponder. I designed *Love Mondays* to include one short essay from me of about 100–200 words, and two of what I call "ABCs": Aphorisms (Quotes), Books, Cool (tools, gadgets, and/or articles). It takes about two minutes to read the whole thing, so opening the email is low-commitment but high-payoff. My readers consistently report finding the emails insightful, and that it's one of the few emails they open right away. And my open rates are high.

Design your newsletter to share a collection of bite-sized things you are naturally creating or collecting, or as a way to motivate yourself to create or collect such things. I naturally read books, highlight quotes along the way, and seek out useful gadgets or tools. But I now seek out more books, quotes, and cool tools or gadgets because I share them in my newsletter. Most importantly, I pursue my ideas more intentionally because I have to write about them every week in my newsletter.

Just because you write about a particular subject, don't be afraid to share things that seem unrelated but can have a wide appeal. As someone who sells books, you'd better hope your readers

Build the audience as you build the book

would love to receive book recommendations, and everybody loves a cool tool or gadget or an interesting article or documentary. One of the most clicked-on items I've shared in my newsletter is a pair of my favorite headphones.

Your newsletter is a good chance to mention "by the way..." new projects you're working on. I often put those in as a "P.S." It's also great for supporting other authors or saying thank you to podcast hosts for having you as a guest. Share another author's work, and maybe they'll share yours. Share with your readers a link to a podcast that interviewed you, and other podcast hosts will get the hint that if they help you, you'll help them.

Read up on the current laws for email marketing, such as Europe's GDPR. You want to be clear up-front about what emails people will get. I tell new subscribers they'll get occasional project announcements in addition to the weekly newsletter, so I can send a dedicated email once in a while, when I launch a new book. After signing up, they can edit their preferences to either receive only the email newsletter, or the occasional announcements.

Don't feel like you have to have your email newsletter all figured out from the beginning. I developed *Love Mondays* over time, through a series of trials. I tried a book-recommendations list, like Ryan Holiday's, but just wasn't into making books the main focus. Then I tried something I called, only to myself, *Friday Night Highlights*, and sent out an email on a few Fridays, each with a highlight from my reading. I eventually settled on *Love Mondays*, and have sent it for more than 250 consecutive weeks.

My newsletter is a main focus for me, because it's that important to have a place to share and get feedback on my ideas as I build them into books, and to have an engaged audience I can tell about new books once they're out. I create a month's worth of emails at a time. I review my open and click stats carefully and document and improve upon my process to constantly increase the quality of emails and make producing and sending them easier. I now have more than 10,000 subscribers. (I didn't automatically sign up the 30,000 I once had for *Design for Hackers*, as I pivoted away from design.)

I'll keep saying this: Don't put off starting your email list because you don't have a great newsletter idea, nor an email course, nor a lead magnet. Start your email list now.

Social media

Social media is the shiniest object in audience growth. It's the most obvious thing to pay attention to, but, like many shiny things, it can be a distraction. Still, it can be useful if you're intentional about it.

You may have heard the analogy that building an audience on a social media platform is like building on rented land. This is an apt analogy, as a lot can change with little warning. The algorithm can change, the platform can go through troubled times or shut down, or your account can simply get banned for no reason. Your email list is indeed where your focus should be. It's the most direct line to readers that is also very unlikely to be suddenly taken away from you.

But just because a social media platform is built on rented land doesn't mean you shouldn't build. It just means you should be careful about your motivations as you build. You're building your audience as you build your book, and nowhere should that be your goal more than on social media. What you share on social media should primarily be about testing out your ideas and seeing whether they resonate. Building an audience is secondary.

Generally, what's compelling as cocktail-party conversation will be compelling as an X post or video reel, and will be compelling when communicated within a book. There are subtle differences amongst these various mediums, but many of them can be mitigated by adapting the message to the medium. That's what's useful and fun about sharing your ideas on various social-media

Build the audience as you build the book

platforms. By adapting your message to various mediums, you improve your writing and communication skills, while getting feedback on what resonates or doesn't, thus honing your message.

Many authors wonder, What's the *best* social media channel? There isn't one for everyone. The best social media channel is the one you like using. Period. You might think it's the one where you can best grow an audience, but if it doesn't interest you, what's the point? For example, I recently dabbled in TikTok by posting every day for a couple months. I grew my account to 30,000 followers, and some of my videos were getting millions of views! But, I have been on X (Twitter) seventeen years as I write this. My follower count has remained the same for as long as I can remember. I can grow on TikTok, but can't seem to grow on X. But, I just *like* X better. I find using X energizing. It's where the smartest, most-interesting people spend a lot of their time and converse. I came to find using TikTok exhausting. Yes, my work was getting more exposure there, but it got to where I didn't even want to look at the comments because so many were mean-spirited or juvenile.

I love X as a place to build an audience as I build my book, because it's where I can share the most basic version of an idea and get feedback. That then serves as a starting point for building on that idea, sometimes until it becomes part of a book. The process of condensing an idea into an X post is part of the value. My best X posts, determined not only by audience reaction, but also simply whether I like the idea, go into a spreadsheet, where I sort through them and narrow them down to ideas for my weekly newsletter. I expand the best ideas into newsletters, then the ideas shared in the newsletters often get adapted into my books.

This is an iterative process, so what I'm writing in a book I'll often share as an X post, to improve the way I express the idea. When I was writing *Mind Management, Not Time Management*, I often created posts based upon short passages from my draft. The process of adapting the ideas to X (then Twitter) helped me make those passages snappier. Many of the "most popular highlights" in the Kindle version of *Mind Management* became worthy of being highlighted because they were directly lifted from tweets I had written based upon less-eloquent passages in my draft. These very same passages may have started as even-less-eloquent tweets. In this way, an idea can get passed back and forth several times between X and my longer-form writing.

This isn't to say I don't enjoy creating on TikTok at all, or that TikTok can't serve the same purpose. It definitely can, and indeed I've found it valuable to adapt my ideas to yet another medium. But I just enjoy X more, so X is the best social network for me to spend time as I build an audience while building books. While my X follower-count hasn't grown in recent memory, I still believe it helps me sell books, as I converse with many readers new and old there. X is where I've announced many of my email courses, which has added subscribers to my email list, which is my most powerful marketing channel.

Some people don't like to spend time on any social network at all, which also can be fine. You don't need social media to sell books, as there are plenty of readers who spend a lot of time browsing Amazon and reading books, and none at all on social media. So as long as you're publishing books regularly, you can still sell books. My only concern with not using social media at all is whether the author is getting useful feedback on their writing. By useful feedback, I don't mean some critique group with other writers. I mean feedback from real readers. A writer who doesn't use social media to me seems like a stand-up comedian who produces an hour-long set without ever stepping on-stage. It could be done, in theory. But it's not the best way.

If you don't know what social media platform you like, try a lot of them. But don't give up easily, make a concerted effort. In my experience, it really helps to publish every day for a couple months, not only to get a feel for the culture of the platform, but also

Build the audience as you build the book

because the algorithms that help content spread on social media reward consistency. These platforms aren't just competing to get people's attention so they can sell ads, they're also competing to motivate creators to create content. One way they do that is by rewarding consistency. So by creating consistently, you're giving them what they need to function, and your content will receive a boost for that.

Think broadly when you think "social media." Aside from the big platforms at this moment like Facebook, X, and Instagram, there are all sorts of places where your potential audience might congregate. It might be a Facebook group, the comments on a popular blog, a subreddit, or a Telegram group. Groups like these generally won't let you promote your own work, and that's for the best. Being overtly sales-ey doesn't work in the big places either, it's just nobody's stopping you. What's important is you can express your ideas in a way that resonates with others. If you can do that outside your book, chances are you can do it inside your book too. And you'll have an audience of people looking forward to your book.

Think of social media as a place to test out ideas. You might need to try various platforms to find one that suits your communication style and that you actually like. Use social media to build your book, and you'll build an audience in the process.

SEO

If social media is the shiny object, the first authors pay attention to, Search Engine Optimization (SEO) is the diamond in the rough few bother to dust off and cut and polish to achieve its potential. Writing content on your website about topics people search for isn't as exciting and doesn't have as immediate potential payoff as spending hours on social media, but it can attract a highly-relevant audience. Relative to social media, SEO often has less competition.

Writing articles to attract search traffic is also a great way to build your audience as you build your book.

SEO is an entire industry that uses advanced and often-shady tactics, and changes rapidly, but you don't need to keep up with it all to benefit from SEO. The basics are very simple: Write quality content on topics people are searching for, making sure you're including the right keywords in your pages' titles, headers, body text, and in the alt attributes of images. And get links.

The best thing about SEO is, rather than trying to get the attention of people who are merely bored and wasting time on social media, you're getting the attention of people who are actively searching for information on a topic, and are actually looking for articles to read about it. That tells me they're more likely to be a reader – someone who actually buys and reads books.

The major downside of SEO is the feedback cycle is incredibly long. You can spend dozens of hours researching and writing an article, and it may be months before you see results, if any. That makes it difficult to tell whether you're doing a good job, and to use that feedback to improve.

My SEO strategy for building my audience and selling books has generally been to write quality articles about whatever interests me, use basic SEO best-practices in my writing, and review the data periodically to see if there's any low-hanging fruit. You can guess what topics you have a chance to rank highly for and attract traffic from on search engines, but you don't really know until you try. You get that data by writing articles, and with that data, you write more articles.

For example, years after writing an article about one of my favorite distraction-free writing devices, the AlphaSmart – basically a keyboard with a small black-and-white LCD screen – I noticed in Google Search Console the article was ranking for "distraction-free writing devices." It was ranking very poorly, as the article wasn't at all optimized for that keyphrase, but I could see in the data that

Build the audience as you build the book

there was a good amount of volume for that keyphrase, and that volume was growing.

So, I wrote a dedicated article on distraction-free writing devices, optimized for that keyphrase, and linked to it from my article on the AlphaSmart. That article is now the most popular on my website. As with all my articles, within the page is a call-to-action to sign up for my email list to receive a lead magnet.

I could be much more strategic with what I choose to write about for the sake of SEO, but this opportunity presented itself organically from my interests, and serves as a relevant source of new email subscribers. I really love to play around with distraction-free writing devices, and by the time I wrote the article, I had already written about the topic in *Mind Management, Not Time Management*. People who are searching for distraction-free writing devices are exactly the kinds of people who would be interested in my book.

If I were more disciplined, I would probably have articles on a bunch of cleverly-chosen topics around creativity, productivity, and time management, to constantly bring in new relevant readers. But I've done fine simply writing the highest-quality articles I can about topics that interest me, keeping SEO in mind. Some of my other popular articles are about a meditation challenge I did and summaries of books I've read. I believe there's some overlap between those who enjoy these articles and those who would enjoy my books.

With the rise of AI large language models, such as ChatGPT, SEO is changing rapidly. Many in the industry are seeing their search traffic plummet. I believe this is because people who work in SEO naturally are very strategic about what they write about, and they optimize to their detriment. ChatGPT can do a better job of conveying the information in their articles, and their articles may even be written by ChatGPT. My search traffic, however, is moving in the opposite direction. I've always written about a variety of topics on my blog, which has never been the "right" way to do SEO, but I think we're entering an era where writing content in a human voice, about your own experiences and interests, gives you the edge. That's far more difficult for a large language model to emulate.

Besides the content in your articles, another important element of SEO is getting links, especially from popular websites that are also relevant to your topic. SEO experts do elaborate link-building campaigns to do this, but I don't. I don't keep up on trends in SEO, but with how much the internet has changed over the years, I'd guess links from other websites are far less powerful than they used to be. But you should share links to your articles on your social media pages, such as X. Even better if people on these networks like your articles enough to share them, too.

You can get deep into SEO if you want to, but I'm telling you I do okay without overthinking it. The main focus is always still building my audience as I build my books.

Having a podcast

At various points in time it has been, and maybe will in the future once again be, trendy to start a podcast. A podcast can be a way of building your audience as you build your book.

But, as with social media, you should be careful about your motivations in running a podcast. A podcast can be an incredible amount of work, and it's definitely hard to grow. In fact, marketing genius Noah Kagan once told me of his podcast, "It's the hardest thing I've ever tried to grow."

Don't start a podcast with dollar signs in your eyes. Start it with relationships in mind. An interview-based podcast is a fantastic way to build relationships. Aside from going to a prestigious college, landing a job at a startup full of smart people, or writing a successful book, I can't think of any better way to build your network than hosting an interview podcast.

Build the audience as you build the book

I ran a podcast for eight years and more than three-hundred episodes. Even though I quit, I wouldn't trade the experience for the world. I didn't go to a prestigious college, so, aside from landing jobs in Silicon Valley at startups full of smart people and writing a successful book, there's nothing that's done more to build my network. Running my podcast also helped me build my books while I've built my audience, which also means I've learned a ton from my guests.

Thanks to my podcast, I've talked to Seth Godin for an hour, twice. I've talked to a childhood hero, Steve Case, founder of America Online. I've talked to David Allen, author of *Getting Things Done*, twice. I've talked to Elise Bauer, who runs my favorite recipe website, *Simply Recipes*. I've gotten to pick the brain of creativity neuroscientist John Kounios for more than two hours. I've gotten to share with my audience interesting friends, such as Laura Roeder, Phil Thompson, and Saya Hillman. I've gotten to know better friends who live far away, such as Nick Gray and Tynan.

The value of these conversations goes well beyond the conversations. I spent an average of about ten hours preparing for each, which means I thought deeply about the work of each guest, which forced me to ask myself what I wanted to learn. Then, while editing each episode, I listened to every conversation several times. I gained a massive amount of experience in paying attention to what made a conversation interesting or dull, and therefore in guiding future conversations to be educational for myself and interesting for listeners.

I was fortunate to already have an audience when I started my podcast, so I was able to attract some great guests early on. But I was really surprised who was willing to be a guest, and, if you try, you'll be surprised, too. If you're running the "must be nice" script in your mind, you're probably thinking of me as someone who has interviewed Seth Godin, David Allen, and Jason Fried. But before

I had started my podcast, I hadn't done any of that. I still had to start from scratch, and work hard and risk rejection to get great guests. If you're going to run an interview podcast, my best tip for attracting great guests is to be genuine, and generous.

Be genuine by inviting guests you truly find fascinating, and not just because they have audiences. One of my best episodes was with Rob Hunter. He's a software developer, and doesn't have an audience at all. He's just a friend with an interesting story to tell, about us spending a year wandering from cafe to cafe in San Francisco, working on projects on our laptops, and how we both eventually "made it" in our own ways. Or there was Paul Bennett, a friend-of-a-friend who I just *had* to interview because he and his wife had sailed around the world while running a business, twice.

Be generous by making the invitation to your podcast all about *them*. Don't think of it as you asking the favor of them being on your podcast, though it very well may be a favor. Think of it as you offering to help them in some way. You love their work, and want to share it with others. So if there's a big guest you're hoping to one day land, pay attention and reach out when they're, say, launching a new book. I got Steve Case as a guest when he was launching his book, *The Third Wave*, and therefore looking for podcasts to be on. (Thanks Robbie Abed, for the idea.) I was able to get Mark Manson on my podcast when he was launching his soon-to-be mega-hit, *Subtle Art of Not Giving a F*ck*. (Thanks Alex Pyatesky, for suggesting him.) I reached out again when he was launching his following book, *Everything is F*cked*, and he agreed to a second interview.

Now that I have enough of a platform podcast hosts invite me as a guest, I can tell you, I don't care about the size of the podcast's audience as much as I do that the host is genuine and generous. It's always an honor to be interviewed by someone who enjoys my work and wants to share it with others. It sucks to be interviewed by someone who doesn't actually care about my work and only sees

Build the audience as you build the book

me as a way to build their audience, or, worse yet, as raw material for producing just-another-interview within which they can sell ad spots.

I see being on podcasts as another way to build my audience as I build a book, and I think many other authors do, too. Hosts who are familiar with my work always ask me questions I've never thought of before, but that organically connect with what I've already created. So being interviewed is a great source for new ideas. This book is in fact a product of being asked by podcast hosts how I've sold 100,000 books. Interviews are also a chance for me to talk about ideas I'm currently working on, just to see how they sound when I speak them aloud to another person. Interviews are a part of my writing process!

Having guests with a platform is indeed a source of growth for your podcast, but by no means make that a main motivation for inviting a guest, and don't expect your guests to share. Personally, I never even asked guests to share episodes, though they did many times. At the very least, alert each guest once their episode is out.

A little on how not to treat guests: I've received a rash of emails lately in recent years from people running an "online summit," which is a bit like a podcast. They must have received a template from a course they bought because the con is always the same: They send you an email, inviting you to be interviewed for their online summit, and talk about the audience they're going to share it to. They then try to get you on a "short call," where they tell you that to be a guest in the summit, you have to promote it to your email list. They do this on a call because that's where people are less likely to refuse, because nobody receiving this terrible idea via email would agree to it. When you dig deeper you realize they have no audience whatsoever, and the "audience" they've promised to share to is your audience. Okay, your audience and that of any other sucker who has agreed to be a guest in the summit.

The whole thing is so phony and desperate. Maybe this works

somewhat for the host and guests, but I can't imagine it working any better than getting a bunch of irrelevant readers from the other guests desperate enough to agree to share to their list. And it seems very disrespectful to readers who have entrusted you with their email addresses to participate in one of these schemes.

The model could work, in theory, if you yourself have an audience you've earned to bring to the table, you don't obligate your guests to share, and you run a genuine and valuable summit. But the part that bothers me is the contrived sharing agreement, and the way these hosts go about pressuring guests into sharing. These people are looking for a shortcut to building an audience, and there are no shortcuts. I do some tricks with my inbox to make sure I rarely see these emails anymore, and whenever I receive them, I block the sender into oblivion. They are dead to me, and everyone selling them email templates can go to hell.

That said, I *always* share podcast episodes in which a genuine and generous host has interviewed me. I even keep a checklist of places I can share, making sure I don't miss one. This is a fundamental of building an audience as you build your book: Use whatever channels you have such as social media or your newsletter to reciprocate when someone makes a genuine effort to appreciate your work. If they're just in it for access to your audience, don't give them what they want. That's a shitty way to treat your readers and will just feed the vultures. If these attitudes seem contradictory, just think about the difference between dating, and prostitution. Reciprocate genuinely when it feels right, not just to grow your business.

My books are full of quotes and stories from my podcast conversations. Inviting a subject-matter expert to be interviewed privately for a book you'll finish someday, with nothing in it for them other than the off chance you'll find a quote to use in your book, is asking a lot. Creating a podcast on which you publish your conversation and promote their work in the process is asking much

Build the audience as you build the book

less. And by creating the podcast you create source material for your book.

If your podcast gets enough listeners, it can be a source of revenue, but this shouldn't be a goal. When my podcast was active, it was in the top five-percent of all podcasts, with a few thousand downloads per episode, and well over a million downloads in the first several years. But I never made more than a few thousand dollars per year from podcast advertising. When I did have advertisers, a good portion of my energy went to selling my ad spots, writing and recording the spots, addressing last-minute requests of sponsors, and trying to collect payment.

Many of these problems can be addressed if your podcast is huge, such as by having strict policies, and/or joining an agency or podcast network. But even when I had an agency selling advertising spots for me, it felt like I was spending too much energy dealing with advertisers, for too little money. So I couldn't spend enough energy on what really mattered: creating quality content.

Taking advertising for your podcast shifts incentives away from building your audience while you build your book. If every new interview means more ad slots, you start feeling pressure to interview people not because you want to, but because you'll make more money, or simply to deliver ad slots you've already sold. Then there's the question of whether the advertisers who want to advertise on your podcast are ethical companies you want to associate with. After running ads for several years, I stopped taking advertisers because I wanted my focus to be on the learning and content I generated from making the podcast.

A couple years before quitting my podcast, I quit interviewing guests. I had already been publishing essays every other episode, in which I would read an article I had written. I quit interviewing guests because I had learned what I had wanted to learn from guests. I kept reading articles because I was still learning from doing that.

How to Sell a Book

There's a tension between the goals of interviewing guests and exploring your own ideas. In fact, I think it's very hard or nearly impossible to do both well at the same time. Think about your favorite interviewer, and they might be a great interviewer, but chances are they haven't shared with you a lot of life-changing ideas. Or if they have done both, they've been in different eras of their career, or they've merely been a messenger of life-changing ideas they've collected from their guests. They're rarely sharing life-changing ideas during a period when they're conducting great interviews, and vice-versa. I got to a point where I felt I had to decide: I could work ninety percent harder to be a ten percent better interviewer, or I could reallocate the energy I was spending interviewing toward exploring my own ideas. I realized even if I had to work ninety percent harder to be five percent more insightful, I'd rather strive to become a five percent more insightful writer than a ten percent better interviewer.

But even though for a period I was making more progress toward building my audience while building my book by reading articles on my podcast, I eventually quit the podcast altogether. Why? Mostly because my return-on-investment for sharing ideas on my podcast waned. For the first several years I read articles on my podcast, it was incredibly valuable. I learned a lot about audio production and vocal performance, which from day one I had known would help me produce my own audiobooks. Reading my writing aloud also greatly improved my prose writing. If a sentence is awkward to speak it will be awkward to read. It's not that I don't still have a lot to learn about audio production, vocal performance, and writing compelling and clear prose, but I found myself in another dilemma: I could use time and energy to read my articles aloud, learning at a much slower rate than I did before, or I could reallocate those resources toward something that would help me learn as fast or faster, while building my audience more effectively. I chose the latter, and now the time and energy I was using

Build the audience as you build the book

to produce my podcast I now use to improve and grow my newsletter.

I also quit the podcast due to a lack of feedback, versus other mediums. People are busy doing other things while they listen to your podcast, such as driving or doing chores. So you get little or no idea how your messages are resonating. Contrast that with video reels on TikTok, where you get many different forms of engagement and a graph of when all viewers were or weren't engaged, with X posts, where you at least get likes, reposts, bookmarks, and replies, or with an email newsletter, where you get opens, clicks, and occasional replies. Unless you have a huge podcast audience, you're screaming into the void, and getting a huge podcast audience is incredibly hard. It's not impossible, but if you want to write and sell books, there are better uses of your energy.

So, start a podcast if you're willing to put in the time and energy. Learn as much as you can and make as many friends as you can. Then when you start learning at a slower rate, quit. You can always keep the episodes you've published up as a record of your learning. I pay $5 a month with Libsyn to keep episodes of *Love Your Work* published, and people still listen to them. I also regularly re-listen to my own interviews and essays, and always notice something I hadn't before.

* * *

If you build your audience as you build your book, you'll have readers eager to buy your book on launch day. But more will buy if you write a title and create a cover that will sell.

Chapter 4
Write a title and create a book cover that will sell

Your title is the most important one-to-eight words you write for your book. Choosing a title for your book can make or break its performance. A good book with a bad title won't sell, and a poorly-written book with a great title will. At least, at first.

As with the idea for the book itself, there are trade-offs in naming a book. A book title can be straightforward, which will ensure it sells to those looking for a book on that subject, or a book title can be abstract, which could start a new cultural phenomenon, but will more likely cause it to be ignored.

Deep Work is an example of an abstract title, a bet on adding a new term to the lexicon, which worked. "Deep work" is now a term people use, including blocking off time on their calendars for them to do "deep work."

How to Win Friends and Influence People is a straightforward title, which may make many readers cringe were it released today. But there had already been books about etiquette and social influence, and it was the first to explicitly state what it was for.

There are tons of nonfiction books with straightforward titles on a variety of subjects. Which book shows up on Amazon when someone searches for the subject of a book determines which book

Write a title and create a book cover that will sell

will sell a lot of copies. Having the keyword right in the book title is the easiest factor you can control that helps you get top search ranking. But it results in titles that are best for white-swan book ideas, such as *The Orvis Fly-Tying Guide*.

"Turnkey titles" tell the whole story

The straightforward titles of white-swan book ideas mix with the abstract ideas conveyed in gray- and black-swan book ideas in what I call turnkey titles. Turnkey titles are book titles that sum up the main takeaway of the book, right in the title.

What do you suppose *The Obstacle is the Way* is about? Once you know it's a stoic-mindset book, it's pretty clearly about that the obstacle is, well, the way. If I asked you to guess what *The Checklist Manifesto* was about you'd probably guess, that checklists are important.

Something very cool about turnkey titles is that you can often get value from the book without even reading the book. The title alone is thought provoking or inspiring enough to light a fire inside you. The first time you heard the title, *Start With Why*, it probably got you thinking about the "why" behind many things you do. Even though I've never read *The One Thing*, I often think about it when running my own business. It reminds me to intensely focus on the "one thing" that matters in my business.

While you can get value just hearing a turnkey title, these books seem to sell very well. Part of that is probably because the titles arouse curiosity. Part of that is probably because the titles are memorable, and so are top-of-mind when people are deciding what to read next. Another part is probably that, whether you read the book or not, merely buying the book is a way to instill in your mind the message conveyed by the title.

Pass the "cocktail party test"

Conveying a simple statement with your book title won't automatically make it a good title. It has to be a compelling statement, not only to those who hear the title, but also to those who say the title.

What I mean by that is a good book title has to pass what I call the cocktail party test. Imagine you're at a cocktail party, and you're telling a stranger you'd like to impress about the book you're reading. How does it feel to be the person saying this book title to someone else?

If the answer is embarrassed or weak, it's generally a bad title. But, there's some subtle psychology to this: What is embarrassing to say in one circle is not in another. What sounds weak in one circle sounds strong in another.

In some circles, saying you're reading Donald Trump's *Never Give Up* will make others think, "Now here's a strong, determined person. I like them!" In other circles, you'll get kicked out of the party just because of who wrote the book. Author aside, the title will cause some to shout, "Never back down, never what!?" and burst into laughter (it's a meme, look it up).

In the same party where you'll get kicked out for reading *Never Give Up*, saying you're reading *Daring Greatly* will make you seem sensitive and emotionally intelligent. On the surface, these are very similar titles, both of which convey determination in the face of adversity. What's the difference? Put aside the fact that there's very little overlap in the social networks of those who read books by Donald Trump and those who read books by Brené Brown. I think the main difference is that *Never Give Up* conveys determination in the face of external forces, whereas *Daring Greatly* conveys determination despite internal struggles. You "give up" when circumstances you believe to be beyond your control force you to. You "dare" when you're scared to do something. In the Trump

Write a title and create a book cover that will sell

crowd, you never admit fear. In the Brown crowd, being "vulnerable" is a badge of honor.

Who will or won't be into a certain book and title isn't always clear. It generally feels good to say you're reading a book called, *So Good They Can't Ignore You*, but in small circles, it may be seen as overly-ambitious and -earnest. *Deep Work* passed the cocktail party test when it came out in 2016. It feels good to believe the work you're doing is "deep." But an anti-productivity movement has spread throughout culture such that some of the same people who liked *Deep Work* might now be more interested in *How to Do Nothing*.

Titles that pass the cocktail party test tap into the desires of the people who might recommend the book, and those desires are mostly about how they want to perceive themselves, and be perceived by others. A desire to be perceived a certain way might inspire a purchase, but won't necessarily inspire action. I don't think it's a mistake that I once purchased the book, *Thanks for the Feedback*, but never read it. I'd like to think of myself as someone who craves feedback, and as an author who has his books reviewed by readers publicly, receiving feedback, both glowingly positive and brutally negative, is a fact of life. But as is true of many people, if I have a choice between seeking out feedback and doing just about any other thing, I'll choose the latter. So I didn't read the book.

For an extreme case of a book that seems on the surface like it might pass the cocktail party test, but is so boastful it only works as a joke, look no further than the book, *How to Live with a Huge Penis*. Only a few of the 4,000+ Amazon reviewers were disappointed the book didn't contain information to help them with their little problem. To the rest, it's clearly a gag gift. If you go deep on this you could imagine it being recommended at a cocktail party more often than *How to Live with a Tiny Penis*, which surprisingly can't be found. That book title would not pass the cocktail party test, but I could imagine it selling decently as a white-swan book idea to those searching for help with a bigger problem.

Subtitles

The title of a white-swan book is a good place to simply state the keywords you expect people to search for to find the book – provided it still sounds natural. But when you write a slightly more-abstract book, your title will be more abstract, and won't necessarily show up in searches. The subtitle is a good place to clarify an abstract title, while also including keywords that will help people find the book.

Keep in mind that in basic SEO terms, the words you use in your subtitle are just as powerful at helping your book show up in searches as the words you use in your title. I don't want to get into too much detail about SEO nor HTML here, but at least on Amazon, the title and subtitle both show up in the same "tags" in the HTML code which search engines such as Google use to figure out what the book's sales page is about.

I purposefully stuffed as many relevant keywords as possible into the subtitle of *How to Write a Book*. I was curious whether it would work, and, frankly, I thought it would be funny. The subtitle is, *An 11-Step Process to Build Habits, Stop Procrastinating, Fuel Self-Motivation, Quiet Your Inner Critic, Bust Through Writer's Block, & Let Your Creative Juices Flow* (*Short Read*). By conducting dozens of test searches on Amazon, I determined that people search for "build habits," "stop procrastinating," and "writer's block". All those keyphrases are relevant to the content I shared in the book, so I just strung them all together into a statement that comprises my subtitle, which barely fits in the field available to fill out on Amazon KDP.

Looking at all those keyphrases now, I realize they're each competitive enough it would be challenging to write entire books

Write a title and create a book cover that will sell

about those keyphrases and show up in the first page of searches. As such, with those keyphrases in the subtitle of one book, it doesn't show up on the first page of results for any of them. But, the book has sold well beyond my expectations, about 12,000 copies.

Book covers

When a person decides whether or not to buy a book, one of the first things they see is the cover. The cover of a book triggers a snap judgment in their mind and heart that tells them if this is the kind of book they'll like. They'll form this judgment of a book by its cover based upon the covers of past books they've read in the genre. Any saying about not judging a book by its cover exists precisely because people do.

Since I once had a career as a graphic designer, I design almost all my own book covers. I don't agonize over my covers. I try to simply communicate what the book is about, with clear typography, and a style that is congruent with other covers within the genre and that will stand out amongst other covers. Then again, I have years of training in design and have developed my own style, so while I don't agonize over my covers, there's still a lot of past thought that goes into them.

If you're eager to get some books out there, and are okay with lower sales until you get better at selling books, I don't think there's a problem with designing your own covers, so long as you have at least minimal design skills. Search and you'll find tools you can use to design your covers. You just want to be able to export a JPEG.

If you're willing to spend some money and/or don't want to risk a sub-par design, by all means, hire a cover designer. Reedsy.com is one good place to find book professionals of all types, including cover designers. Charlie Hoehn, editor of three *New York Times* bestselling books, author of the self-published *Play it Away*, and founder of Author Alliance warns that, "The fastest way to kill book sales is skimping on your cover design. Just like a compelling YouTube thumbnail determines if someone clicks on a video, your cover instantly determines whether readers will want to read your book, or ignore it because it screams 'amateur hour.' Invest at least $2,000 to hire a top-tier book cover designer from INeedABookCover.com. Trust your designer, go bold, and let your cover be an investment that pays off for the rest of your life."

Whether you're designing your cover yourself or art-directing a professional designer, do some research. Look at books in similar categories as your book idea, and notice the colors and style. Are the covers highly-illustrative, or dominated by typography and solid blocks of color? Are the images light or dark? Smooth or rough? Are the colors bright or muted?

The same approach for white- to black-swan book ideas apply to covers. Want to be assured of some sales? Make your cover as much like similar books as possible. Want a tiny chance to set a new trend? Make it as different as you can. Want the best of both worlds? Make it both fit in and stand out.

I have a template I use for most my short reads. I just use the Minion font, and play with the sizing and spacing, and pepper in a few rule lines. As a designer I'll be the first to admit they aren't fantastic covers. But they clearly display the title and subtitle of the book. These are mostly informational books, and the straightforward graphic style communicates that you'll get straightforward information.

Write a title and create a book cover that will sell

The covers for my short reads often follow the same simple template.

For my two big self-published books, I've developed a graphic theme. *The Heart to Start* is an abstract geometric representation of a sun rising, which also symbolizes the dawn of one's creative journey. *Mind Management, Not Time Management* represents green rolling hills, which mirror the energy fluctuations talked about in the book, and also represent the green mountains around Medellín, Colombia, where much of the book takes place.

These geometric shapes match up when the books are put together. Since the physical books are different sizes, the shapes are at a different scale on the ebook version, since they show up as the same size on online stores such as Amazon.

How to Sell a Book

Getting Art Done
2 book series

Since the hard-copy versions of HTS and MMT are different sizes, the ebook covers are slightly different, so the patterns match.

The third book in the *Getting Art Done* series will carry on this theme, so that they all match up.

It's interesting to me that traditional publishers often make drastically different covers for each of various books in a nonfiction series, and sometimes even have different covers for ebook, paperback, and hardcover editions. Then they have different covers for different markets, such as the U.S. versus UK.

The book covers in Nassim Taleb's *Incerto* series aren't especially alike.

Maybe this does impact sales, but I doubt by much. I get the feeling there's some political struggle within the publishing company that convinces whoever's working on the book to have

Write a title and create a book cover that will sell

extra work for each edition, or maybe it helps keep the in-house designers busy.

You can always change your cover if you don't like it. With Kindle editions, some authors even change their covers every couple weeks to see what converts best.

I've only made one major cover change in my self-publishing career, and didn't see a big impact on sales.

I changed the cover of *The Heart to Start* years after publication, but can't say it had a noticeable impact on sales.

Maybe I could sell a few more books if I hired a professional book-cover designer to design my covers, but I'd rather spend my time, energy, and money writing more books, which will *definitely* lead to selling more books.

See your covers in context

I don't overthink the content of covers, but one thing I do pay attention to is how the covers will look in a sales context. The old way to test this would be to mock up a book, put it on the shelf at your local bookstore, to see if it stands out. And you could still do that and it could be useful.

I prefer to go to the Amazon sales page of a similar book, take a screenshot of books under "Customers also bought," and mock up my cover on top of one of the books, to see how it looks. Does it

How to Sell a Book

both stand out and fit in? That's what I'm going for, with gray-swan books.

A mockup from the design process for the cover of *The Heart to Start*, in context in Amazon's "Also-Boughts"

Another place many ebook sales probably take place is right on the Kindle home screen. Many readers prefer a black-and-white e-ink screen, so I like to see how my covers will look when converted to black and white and placed in context. What stands out in color won't always stand out in black and white.

Testing titles, subtitles, and book covers

I strongly recommend testing in some manner your titles and subtitles, especially for gray- and black-swan book ideas. This can be as simple as talking to a friend and watching their reaction when you say the title. If you have a friend who will actually tell you the title sucks if they think it does, even better.

Pay attention to how you feel saying the title to friends and strangers. Does the title make you feel strong or weak or judged when you say it? Does it roll off the tongue? Do you have to repeat it because they don't understand you the first time? Do they have at least a vague idea what the book is about based upon the title? A white-swan book title should be crystal clear. A black-swan title should be vague at first glance. A gray-swan title should be somewhat vague, and arouse curiosity.

To back up your title, subtitle, and cover ideas with hard data, run some ads to test performance. But be careful where and how you test. Some people throw up some Meta ads and see how they perform, but I'm skeptical of that.

I personally like to test my titles, subtitles, and book covers on the BookBub ad platform. BookBub is an email list readers subscribe to, to get alerts on ebook discounts. So at the very least, you know you're advertising to people who buy books. They cover many different genres, so you can target on the platform by genre, and by author.

BookBub Ads are supposed to be for advertising a book that's already out, but I often run ads using titles, subtitles, and covers that are destined to never exist. To comply with BookBub's policies, I link my ads to a landing page on my website that includes a "Follow me on BookBub" button (collecting email subscribers through their ads is unfortunately against BookBub's policies).

The landing page is very basic, and the ads I run are usually very basic, designed to isolate the performance of whatever variable I'm testing. For example, if I'm testing a title, I use the most generic cover imaginable.

If I already have a title and am testing covers, I include an image of a book with that cover. If I already have a title and a cover, I test out subtitles as a headline.

Write a title and create a book cover that will sell

FROM 'TOO MANY IDEAS' TO 'DONE'

By running an ad targeting readers of one author, you can get a drastically different click-through rate than by targeting readers of another author. So this is something to pay attention to as you get a feel for where your book belongs, and who will be interested in buying it.

I've found as a self-published author, my books somehow perform best with readers of other self-published authors in my genre. Advertising to audiences of these authors is often cheaper than the big-name traditionally-published authors.

When testing, you want data that's strictly driven by the factor you're testing, such as title, subtitle, or cover. So, you're going to have a lower click-through-rate (CTR) than if you were advertising, say, a pricing promotion. When I advertise a pricing promotion, I can get CTRs above 3%, but when I'm just testing titles and subtitles with very basic ad designs, I'm lucky to get above 0.5%.

Don't draw too many conclusions or even test via ads unless you're willing to become somewhat statistically literate and collect enough data. At such low CTRs, it's statistically likely to have two ideas that seem to perform very differently to the naked eye, but are actually performing the same. For example, if out of 1,000 impressions each, two different ideas get 7 and 9 clicks respectively, you may think the second is better, but statistically, that's not a big enough difference. Get another 1,000 impressions, and your results may very well reverse. However, if you get ten times the impressions and clicks for each one, in other words 10,000 impressions and 70 and 90 clicks respectively, now there's a very good chance the second idea is better.

Look up how to run a Chi-Square test. I usually look for a Bayesian calculator, which I've been told by an expert is imperfect in concept because Bayesian reasoning doesn't actually work the way they purport to work. But I'm looking for a "90% chance to win" or higher of one option over another. If you have a good idea, you should see it beating other options convincingly over and over.

All this complication around drawing statistical conclusions is actually a good argument for using Meta Ads. Meta has tons of data and the brightest minds in statistics and machine learning ensuring they only run the ad creatives that are effective. But, their manual targeting is limited, so it's not as easy to see how your ideas perform across readers of various authors, or even ensure you're advertising to book-readers. Though logically, their algorithms probably detect your ad is about a book and serve it to readers.

Testing with ads can get expensive quickly, and doesn't lead directly to sales. So if you're not willing to invest a lot of money, skip it.

Interior design

I'll talk really briefly about interior design, or the typography within your ebooks and paper books. As a designer with coding skills, I design almost all my interior layouts and ebooks. I feel it gives my full-length books a sense of traditionally-published quality. I could hire an even better designer, but that would be expensive.

But I'm not sure to what degree a nice interior design helps a book's sales. I designed the interiors of both the ebook and paperback editions of *Digital Zettelkasten* using a really handy and easy-

Write a title and create a book cover that will sell

to-use program for Mac called Vellum. Vellum is not nearly as sophisticated as the programs I've used to design my major books' paper-book interiors: Adobe InDesign and Affinity Publisher. Nor is Vellum as capable as what I've used to design and code ebooks: an open-source program called Sigil. To my trained eye, Vellum puts me in a frustrating straitjacket in terms of what it allows me to do. But, it makes good-enough design really easy, and both paper and ebook editions come from the same source text, which makes fixing errata easier.

Digital Zettelkasten has sold 16,000 copies, and I doubt it would have sold more if I had spent hours longer making the best interior design I could. My educated guess is that a gray-swan book idea like *Mind Management* benefits more from a nicer interior design than a white-swan idea like *Digital Zettelkasten*. I won't pretend to know whether interior design can make or break a black-swan book. The same way Craigslist took down newspaper classified ads with a bare-bones design, an unprofessional design could be an asset to a book, if the content is subversive or has a grassroots spirit.

Once you've captured the attention of a prospective reader with your title, subtitle, and cover, it's time to build desire, and sell the book, with your sales blurb.

Chapter 5
Write an irresistible sales blurb

After reading the title and subtitle, and viewing the cover, a prospective reader will read the sales blurb. On an online store, such as Amazon, this is the description that shows up near the buy button. This is your chance to get them excited about your book, and ask them directly to take the next step.

Many traditional publishers' blurbs read a lot like the book itself, with long paragraphs and big words. I haven't collected a lot of data on this, but I believe it to be a mistake.

Copywriting, or converting a sale, is very different from the writing you do in most of your book. As Marshall McLuhan said, "the medium is the message," and the medium of a sales-page blurb is very different from the medium of a book. When someone is reading your book, you have some level of commitment from them. You can present more complex ideas, in more complex language, with more complex sentence and paragraph structures. They might be curled up on their couch with a hot tea next to them. They're not going to run away. This isn't the case when they're reading your sales blurb. They're more likely on their computer or mobile device, with mountains of distractions just a finger flick away.

The difference between the text in your book and the text on your sales blurb is like the difference between a movie in a theater

Write an irresistible sales blurb

and a short-form reel on a social media platform. In a movie theater, you've committed a good portion of attention to watching the movie. You've left your house, turned off your mobile, and grabbed your popcorn. So the images on the screen often move very slowly, even in portions of a blockbuster action movie. If you're swiping through social-media video reels, you're a lot less patient. A video needs to really grab you.

So your sales blurb needs to really grab the reader. It also needs to keep them interested, up until the point it asks them to take action. This is copywriting, not prose writing.

The format most of my sales blurbs follow is this:

- Hook (grab the reader)
- Problem (show you understand)
- Elevator Pitch (quickly make a promise)
- Bullet Points (basic format is teaser + mechanism)
- Point of Difference (why it's different)
- Call-to-Action (make the sale)

I'll go through each of these, in-depth, breaking down the sales blurb for my best-selling book, *Mind Management, Not Time Management*.

Hook

Your hook should be a short statement, about ten words or fewer, that arouses curiosity and gets the reader thinking about the problem your book will solve.

The hook for my description for MMT is:

You have the TIME. Do you have the ENERGY?

This is a statement I came across very often when

researching people's relationships with time management. I'd often hear them say, "I have the *time*. I just don't have the *energy*."

I don't think the hook I've chosen is fantastic at arousing curiosity. I think the hook I have for *The Heart to Start*'s sales blurb does a better job:

> **It's a terrible feeling.**

That's pure curiosity. What's so terrible? The next line, after the break, is, "To know you have a gift for the world." And that line does a good job of keeping the reader reading. Because what can be terrible about knowing you have a gift for the world? But I'll stop there.

This time/energy hook doesn't arouse a ton of curiosity, but it does perform the function of getting the reader thinking about the shortcomings of time management. And my book is clearly offering an alternative.

Both this "terrible feeling" hook and the time/energy hook I've tested through ads, against many other potential hooks. Better hooks are possible, but I'm confident they're better than most the other ideas I've had.

Problem

After pulling the reader in with the hook, you want to get them thinking about the problem your book is meant to solve. The next few paragraphs of my MMT blurb are like so:

> You've done everything you can to save time. Every productivity tip, every "life hack," every time management technique.
>
> But the more time you save, the less time you have. The more overwhelmed, stressed, exhausted you feel.

Write an irresistible sales blurb

"Time management" is squeezing blood from a stone.

Most of this is, again, taken from my research on what people say when they talk about time management. The final statement about squeezing blood from a stone performed decently as a tweet.

Elevator pitch

Now that you've got them thinking about the problem they want to solve, and they're nodding in agreement, reading the words of someone who clearly understands that problem, you're going to make a short promise to solve that problem.

For MMT, my elevator pitch is:

> Introducing a new approach to productivity. Instead of struggling to get more out of your time, start effortlessly getting more out of your mind.

That second sentence is really the meat of the pitch. The first sentence is an age-old copywriting trope. It releases the tension and slight negativity of thinking about the problem, and segues into the solution. It's like that moment in a commercial for some ab-exercise product, when the frustrated woman doing crunches in black-and-white suddenly turns to color with the new product: "*Introducing....*"

The paragraph that follows is also part of the elevator pitch:

> In *Mind Management, Not Time Management,* best-selling author David Kadavy shares the fruits of his decade-long deep dive into how to truly be productive in a constantly changing world.

I'm basically saying: book title, who wrote it and why they matter, and why this book matters in "this world."

I don't have a lot to work with, traditionally-speaking, to stress why I'm the person to write this book. I say I'm a best-selling author, so that's *something*, then I mention that I spent a decade diving deep on the topic. I don't have a PhD to tout, and I'm not a coach to Fortune 500 executives or anything like that. I did use the principles in the book to advise a startup on a time-management app that sold to Google and became a part of Google Calendar, which is highly-relevant, but I never found a crisp way to write it in copy. The elevator pitch should probably have something about that, but it doesn't.

The final part about the "constantly changing world" is trying to make the reader think about why this book matters right now. This could be punched up based upon what's going on at any given time, such as "in a world where AI tools are causing us to question our humanity." But a constantly changing world is enough. The world is always changing, and we always think it's changing more than ever.

Bullet points

At this point, we've pulled the reader in with the hook, shown them we understand their problem, and teased a solution. Now it's time to introduce them to the ways we're going to provide that solution, while at the same time building curiosity so they'll want to know more.

But remember, they're on a computer or mobile device, so their attention is still fickle. Thus, bullet points are a good way to provide a lot of enticing information in a short period of time. Bullet-points also break up the text block to make it look less intimidating when they're skimming. If a reader has skipped over the hook and everything else above, each bullet-point is a potential entry point into

Write an irresistible sales blurb

your blurb, to capture their attention and entice them to read the whole thing.

The general format I like to follow for bullet-points is: **hook**/mysterious mechanism. For example, the first bullet-point in my blurb for *Mind Management, Not Time Management* is:

> **Quit your daily routine.** Use the hidden patterns all around you as launchpads to skyrocket your productivity.

I already knew "Quit your daily routine" would make a good hook, because I had already written a blog post and podcast episode with that statement in the title. That blog post got more views than most, and the podcast episode got more downloads.

The "mysterious mechanism" that follows is full of copywriting tropes. I promise to reveal to the reader "hidden patterns." We've all been helped by having something hidden pointed out to us, so that's intriguing. Then there's the hyperbolic metaphor of "launchpads to skyrocket your productivity," which paints a picture in the mind of the reader.

Some of you probably think this is cheesy, and I have to admit I cringe a little when I write stuff like this. But the fact is we read and are influenced by copy like this all day, without thinking it's cheesy. It's only when we pay close enough attention by writing it or learning about it that it seems a little ridiculous.

In any case, I've made a promise, and teased the mechanism through which I'll deliver that promise. The blurb doesn't give me enough space to explain exactly how the mechanism works. That's what the book is for, and I want them to buy or at least read the sample of the book.

Some other bullet-points in my blurb:

- **Do in only five minutes what used to take all day.**

Let your "passive genius" do your best thinking when you're not even thinking.

- **"Writer's block" is a myth.** Learn a timeless lesson from the 19th century's most underrated scientist.

Hopefully you can see how I'm grabbing the attention of the reader with the hook that begins the bullet-point, and following it up with a mechanism, introduced in a mysterious enough manner to arouse the reader's curiosity.

I usually include three to five bullet-points in my sales blurb, depending upon the length of the book.

Point of difference

Now that I've given the reader a sampling of what they'll learn in the book, and aroused their curiosity for how they'll learn it, it's time to take this blurb home.

It would be jarring to go right to the call-to-action now, so I like to tie up everything I've said by this point by presenting the book's point of difference. That is, why is this book different from other books in the category? While reading your blurb, the reader's mind will naturally try to compare your book to others they may have read or considered. So this is your chance to drive home why your book is one-of-a-kind.

For *Mind Management, Not Time Management*, I present the point of difference as such:

> *Mind Management, Not Time Management* isn't your typical productivity book. It's a gripping page-turner chronicling Kadavy's global search for the keys to unlock the future of productivity.

Admittedly, I don't provide a great deal of point of difference here, other than saying that this "isn't your typical productivity book." What I *wanted* to say here was that the book isn't a mindless regurgitation of story, study, takeaway; story, study, takeaway. But I wanted to keep a positive tone and talking shit about other books is not a good way to do that. So, my promise here ended up a little generic.

Call-to-action

Finally, we present the call-to-action (CTA). This is the most cringe-inducing part of copywriting for those not used to it. I remember, while working at my first startup, the Director of Marketing ordered me to put "click here" on a button. I tried not to roll my eyes as I reluctantly agreed to do it. It seemed so stupid. It's a button. Who doesn't know you're supposed to click?

But when we ran a test, the results were undeniable. And I've seen this repeated many times in my career, on websites, in email subject lines, and on sales pages. If you want someone to take a particular action, you need to straight-up *tell* them what action you want them to take. Statistically speaking, they will do it. Yes, there are varying degrees of CTAs, from the very blunt, such as "Buy it now," or the more gentle, such as "Learn more." Surprisingly, the sales blurbs of many books by traditional publishers ignore this key copywriting tool completely.

I like to preface the CTA in my blurbs with a final summary promise. What will everything I'm promising help the reader *do*? For *Mind Management, Not Time Management*, I start my call-to-action with:

> You'll learn faster, make better decisions, and turn your best ideas into reality.

And my actual CTA follows, with:

Buy it and start reading today.

Do I know that this particular CTA converts better than any other for this particular blurb? No. But through many repetitions of writing copy on ads and landing pages, this felt like the right one. I want the reader to buy it, which will lead to the action the reader can picture themself doing, start reading it, and when do I want them to do that? Today.

I've also used less-forceful CTAs, such as for *The Heart to Start*. I lead the CTA with:

Take your first step and click the buy button.

Which is on-theme, because the book is about finding the courage to start things. This also includes a more gentle request, which is not to "buy" but merely "click the buy button." I then follow that up with:

Download *The Heart to Start*, and unlock your inner creative genius today!

Instead of "buy," I say "download" (this is for the ebook version). I then follow it up with the benefit they'll receive, that they'll unlock their creative genius.

For those who are shy about sales, writing a CTA can feel really uncomfortable. But try it, *today!*

Your sales blurb is a writing tool

Don't put off writing your sales blurb till after you've written your

Write an irresistible sales blurb

whole book, because writing your sales blurb is a great writing tool for the book itself.

As you write elements of your sales blurb, such as your elevator pitch and especially the bullet-points, you gain a sense of whether your book will sell well. If your elevator pitch feels flat, it's probably because you aren't yet clear on who your book is for, and what it is and isn't about. And if you're not clear on those things, the book will suffer. So, you can go back and forth, writing your elevator pitch, making it crisper, then re-writing or editing your book to make it meet the promises made in your elevator pitch.

Your blurb's bullet-points have the most influence on the meat of your book. If you have boring bullet-points, chances are your book is boring, too. Like with the elevator pitch, you can go back and forth, writing compelling bullet-points, then changing the content of your book to match.

Your title, subtitle, cover, and sales blurb may be enough to convince many readers to buy. For the rest, you have to sell the book in its first pages.

Chapter 6
The first pages sell your book

Your final chance to get someone to buy your book, maybe your *best* chance, is with your book's opening – its first several pages. I personally like to download the sample of an ebook and read it before buying. For me, it's a bit of a game. I download many samples, start reading, and see if I can resist buying each book. When I find myself struggling to even reach the end of a sample, I ask myself, *What could the author have done better?* When I find myself rushing to buy the book just a few pages in, I ask myself, *What made me want to buy?*

Writing the first pages of your book is a bit like writing your blurb, in that you're not just writing, but *copywriting*. However, you have a little more time to hold the reader's attention since they're actually reading your book, and nobody wants to read an entire book that reads like a sales blurb.

Unfortunately, you don't get to choose at what point the sample of your book ends. For Amazon's Kindle, it seems as if there are actual humans choosing when to end the sample. Kindle samples usually end at a point where what will follow has been sufficiently built up, and there's a good amount of unanswered questions in your mind that make you want to keep reading. But the beginning of your book has to be well-written for your sample to be

The first pages sell your book

compelling enough to keep the reader reading until the end of the sample.

I think there are two wrong ways to begin your book. One is with a dry presentation of facts about what will follow. Here's a made-up example:

> People around the world love carrots. In this book, I will tell you why carrots are orange, why people love them, and why they're delicious. In chapter one, I will explain why carrots are orange...

This could be good if you, as the author, are the only person in the world who knows about carrots, and your reader just really wants to know about carrots. But it's dry, not fun to read, and stiff as a carrot.

I read a lot of biographies of artists to write my books on creative productivity, and nothing can strike horror in my soul worse than picking up the one biography available for an artist, and reading a first sentence that goes: "Smacky McPeterson was born on July 7, 1901, in Mobile, Alabama." While it seems logical to begin a biography with the subject's birth, surely there are countless other moments from Smacky's life that would be infinitely better with which to begin the book.

The other wrong way to begin your book is with a personal story that doesn't immediately tie to what the book is about and the needs of the reader. Don't get me wrong, a personal story can be good. My books are full of them. But it's important when telling the story to signal to the reader that you aren't droning on about yourself with no purpose: You understand their concerns and are here to help.

For example, here's a story from the first page of *The Heart to Start*, but re-written the *wrong way*:

How to Sell a Book

At my high school graduation party, one of the older kids from the neighborhood was there. We got to talking about the snow-removal business he had started. But I was really confused at how he had started it. He had rebuilt the engine of an old truck, and installed a snow plow, and was making money clearing parking lots every winter at places around town, such as the grocery store or even the K-Mart.

Funny, even as I write that, I feel like it's not *that bad*. Mostly because it's a book about starting things, and here I am confused about how this older kid started his snow-removal business. And a snow-removal business is kind of a weird thing to write about, which makes it interesting. Or maybe it's only interesting to me because I lived it.

In any case, the story as it's told here doesn't tie back to the concerns of the reader and signal to the reader that I'm "here."

Instead, I open the book by directly addressing that the book isn't even necessary:

> I'll start off by introducing the elephant in the room: You don't need this book to get started. If you can put this book down and start creating your art, then that's exactly what you should do.

Maybe some readers do put down the book or close the sample and go make something. That's great if they do. But many readers are probably intrigued that I'm being honest about whether or not they need the book, and take the first step in admitting to themselves that despite the fact that the book is logically unnecessary, they still need help.

In any case, this opening at least establishes that I'm talking about what the book is about, rather than launching into a personal story with no context. The above paragraph goes on for a few

The first pages sell your book

sentences, then the story gets told in the following paragraph. But that second paragraph starts off with some context, too:

> For me, it's never been that simple. I've been an independent creator for ten years now, making a living from writing, podcasting, and teaching what I learn along the way.

This establishes some authority for the subject. Like I've said, I don't have a PhD and didn't go to a well-known school, so all I have is what I've done. So I talk about what I've done. Now that I have established context, I tell the story:

> I still remember the first time I met a real "starter." He was an older neighborhood kid who was running a snow removal business. As he sipped on a Coca Cola at my high school graduation party, I couldn't stop drilling him with questions. *How did you rebuild the engine on that truck? How did you install the snow plow? How did you find your customers?* He kept shrugging his shoulders and giving me the same frustrating answer: "I just *did* it."

Some key differences from the way I told the story above include the following: I start off by establishing the point of the story. It's the first time I met a "starter," someone who has no trouble starting. I then illustrate my curiosity at how he was able to do what he did. I close by illustrating my frustration at not being able to learn from him.

It's about the same number of words as the previous version of the story, but the actual version does a better job of sticking with the purpose of the book and the concerns of the reader. There's an argument to be made that in some other kind of book, such as a memoir, the first version of the story is better. But for the book in which the second version is told, the second is undeniably a better fit. It establishes a theme that I harp on for the next several pages: That there is a gap between people who tell us to "just do it," and those for whom just doing it doesn't come naturally.

Work really hard on the opening and first several pages of your book. This will be easier if you write or at least revise heavily the first part only after you've written everything else. Yes, write the beginning of your book at the end of the project.

Your table of contents (TOC) also is a sales tool. Especially when considering nonfiction books, prospective readers will look at your TOC to see what to expect. Like with your title, you can either make a straightforward promise of what information will be found in a given chapter or under a given subhead, or you can present something more abstract. I like to review my TOC as I'm well into editing the book, to make sure my chapter names and subheads strike a balance between informative and provocative. Sometimes I'll use phrases that have performed well on social media or title and subtitle tests, but for whatever reason weren't right for those purposes. Intentionally writing a strong TOC can sell a book, but can also improve structure and flow, which can also sell a book.

*** * * ***

Even if readers like what they see in the first pages of your book, some will still not be convinced to buy. They need some encouragement from reviews, reader blurbs, and a foreword.

Chapter 7
Get reviews, blurbs, and forewords

Every author wants their book's Amazon page to be full of positive reviews. In part, because they know they as a reader pay close attention to reviews before buying a book.

If you want positive reviews, then, the logical thing is to do whatever you can to get positive reviews, including asking friends to review your book, even writing a review for them to copy-and-paste, or paying some service that promises a bunch of positive reviews. But don't do any of that. Your reviews will be obviously fake, and you won't be able to sleep at night.

There is a simple two-step process to getting lots of positive reviews: One, write a great book. Two, ask.

How to get your first Amazon reviews

The asking is the part I can teach you in this book. Wherever there is someone who has read your book, ask for an honest review. One of the best places to do this is within the book itself. The Kindle prompts readers to rate and review your book once finished, but at the end of *The Heart to Start*, I make an additional personal request for the reader to "click on a star rating," which is linked to the rating/review page for the book.

I ask for the reader to click on a star rating because it's a much lower-commitment thing to ask for than to write a review. Writing a review is *work*. But everyone has time to click on a star rating. Once they click on a star rating, Amazon's interface is set up to try to motivate them to write a review. They have professional interface designers crunching data and running tests to figure out the best way to do this. So, I ask readers to click on a star rating, and let Amazon take care of the rest. Even if they don't write a review, their star rating will at least register.

Thanks in part to my personal request for the reader to click on a star rating at the end of *The Heart to Start*, the book has a *ton* of reviews. More than my other books, by far. I think it gets so many reviews in part because it's my shortest full-length book, so readers actually get to the end, where I make the request. I've also seen books with a page right in the middle or after the first chapter that asks for reviews. It makes sense, because few people finish even the books they like.

I currently do nothing to try to get reviews for my books. I have enough readers that I feel confident that I will get some reviews. It would probably help if I did more, but I'd just rather do something else with my time and energy.

I did find one way to get *The Heart to Start* lots of reviews in the beginning, but it requires some finesse. Many businesses will offer incentives to motivate customers to review their products and services. I once went to a hair salon, for example, that displayed a sticker in their store, promising a discount on a haircut in exchange for a five-star review. As far as I know, the FCC has made this illegal in the United States, but businesses still do it. And it leads to phony reviews.

Offering a bonus in exchange for a positive review is illegal and

Get reviews, blurbs, and forewords

unethical. But writing a review of a book is work, so it still helps to find some way to motivate readers to share their *true* opinions of your book. You can do this by offering a bonus for filling out a survey for your book. Build the survey using Google Forms or comparable tool, and send it to your email list, explaining that you will be holding a drawing of survey respondents for an Amazon gift card. Stress that whether their opinion is positive or negative has no influence on their chances to win. I think I offered a $20 card, in 2017. (By the time your book is out, you should have an email list.) It doesn't take much, as people love free money.

Once you've received responses, and drawn your winner and sent them a gift card, you can reach out to other respondents individually. Your message can be something like this:

Subject: Click on a star rating?
Hi [name],
Thank you so much for taking the time to fill out my survey for my book, [book name]! While I've already drawn a winner for the gift card, your opinion helps me improve my writing.
Can I ask you a favor? You've already been very helpful by filling out the survey, so it's up to you. Can you please click on a star rating for the book on Amazon? All you have to do is go to this link and click on the stars:
[Share the link directly to the page to rate your book on Amazon. Test it in a private browser window not logged into Amazon first, to make sure it's the correct link!]
If it helps, in your survey, you gave my book a rating of [number], out of five.
While you're on that page, it would be extra helpful if you also wrote a review. Or, you could just copy and paste what you wrote in the survey:
[What they wrote in your survey]
No pressure. You've already been very helpful filling out the

survey, but if you have a minute to do this it would help more people like you find this book.

Sincerely,

[your name]

I won't go in-depth to every word of this email, but hopefully you can see that you're asking the smallest possible favor (click on a star rating), acknowledging that they've already been a big help and you appreciate it, and reminding them there's no pressure to do this, so it's up to them. You may have also gleaned that your survey questions should consist of a 1–5 rating and an open-ended question about whether they liked the book, so you can share those items in the email.

At this point you've already motivated them with the gift card to share with you their honest opinion of the book. There's nothing in it for them to post that opinion as a review, other than being your fan and a nice person. But what they wrote is right there in the email, so it's incredibly easy for them to post a review.

I Am Not a Lawyer and this is not legal advice, but I sense this is both a legal and ethical way to motivate readers to provide the first reviews of your book, and it only costs $20 for the gift card giveaway.

Handling negative reviews

This isn't exactly marketing related, but it looms so large for authors I'll talk about it anyway. Yes, you will get negative reviews. Yes, it sucks.

Some negative reviews are irrelevant, stupid, or factually incorrect. You might get a one-star review, for example, because Amazon printed your book poorly, which has nothing to do with the quality of your writing, and isn't your fault!

Get reviews, blurbs, and forewords

You can try to report to Amazon the irrelevant reviews, but don't expect much. Just get on with your life and keep writing.

But keep in mind that the most relevant, intelligent, and factually correct negative reviews can still feel like a personal attack. That's a natural reaction, especially at first. But they're a chance to learn what isn't working for a certain type of person about your writing. Even reviews that are deliberately nasty can have some kernel of truth you can learn from.

I've learned from writing several books to anticipate, before I finish writing the book, the kinds of negative reviews I'll get. And in fact, you want to get some negative reviews, because if all your reviews are positive, you didn't take any risks in your writing, and that's boring to read.

My reviews for *The Heart to Start* are overwhelmingly positive, but that book makes much less profit than others. I have more negative reviews for *Mind Management, Not Time Management*, but the book sells very well. However, the types of negative reviews I have for MMT are the ones I expected. I expected some complaints about "too many personal stories." But I learn what I teach in my books through personal experience, and most reviewers love the personal stories. *Digital Zettelkasten* has the most negative reviews, and they're puzzling to me because many of them strike me as factually incorrect. But that's been the easiest book to make a profit off, without advertising.

Decide who you're writing for and how you will or won't write, and be brave enough to stick to that plan. Then your book will be better and you won't be surprised by most your negative reviews. On occasion, you'll get a negative review the contents of which suggest you didn't accomplish what you set out to accomplish. Those are simply learning experiences.

Don't comment on your negative reviews or get in arguments with your reviewers. It will accomplish nothing. Negative reviews are a fact of life as an author, and can be useful. Learn to live with them.

Reader blurbs

The moment any traditionally-published book comes out, it already has blurbs printed on it, mostly from other well-known authors in the same genre as the book. Some think this makes no difference, but I can see how it would: These blurbs signal to the reader they're in the right place. The authors they respect, respect this author.

I feel a little sick writing about blurbs, because they're the most obvious fraud in publishing. I assume readers know these authors didn't read the book. I assume readers know these authors often didn't even write the blurb! I assume readers consciously know these blurbs are fraudulent, and will probably tell you the blurbs do nothing to influence their book-buying decisions. But the human mind is a master magician, and even though readers know magic isn't real and these blurbs are fake, deep down I know everyone loves magic and these blurbs work to some degree. At the very least, reader blurbs signal to the reader the publisher went through the extra work to deceive them. As Daniel J. Boorstin, who coined the term "pseudo-events," once said, "the public [enjoys] being deceived."

If you know the players in traditional publishing in your genre, it's obvious where these blurbs come from. If you buy a Publisher's Marketplace membership, browse the publishing deals, and see which agents represent which authors and which publishers habitually work with which agents, you will notice a pattern when you read these blurbs: *Hmmm, that guy has the same agent as this author! That lady's book was published by the same publisher! This guy is a client of the author's PR firm!*

In some sense it's innocent. Everyone working within a genre is naturally going to cross-pollinate. People with similar interests are

Get reviews, blurbs, and forewords

going to be friends, and who hasn't done a favor for a friend? But please. Joseph McSelfhelpauthor who's a professor by day is not spending his evenings pouring over mid-wit self-help books.

I think it also makes me sick to write about blurbs because I suspect some of my blurbs are fake. I've sent books to people who have sent blurbs suspiciously fast. I've had others ask me to write their blurb, and I've complied. I could refuse, but I also know everyone is very busy, and it actually makes sense for you to, if not *write* a blurb for someone else, at least tell them what you'd like to highlight in their blurb. You, the author, are reaching out to this busy, well-known person to write a blurb because they have some point-of-view that's congruent with the point-of-view you share in the book. If you're writing a book about apples, and the foremost expert on oranges writes a blurb, it makes sense, because they're both fruits.

If the world's foremost expert on oranges writes a blurb for your book about apples, don't be surprised if she goes on about oranges in her blurb, let's hope in a way that ties back to the importance of apples. If a busy, well-known person is writing a blurb for your book, that blurb is as much about them as it is about your book. You've given them a promotional opportunity, and, besides, them writing about oranges will help jog the memories of any readers who aren't sure they recognize their name. *Oh, right! It's the orange lady.*

If you don't want to participate in the fraud that is reader blurbs, you don't feel you know any well-known people to write blurbs, and you are afraid to reach out to well-known people you don't know, this is one area where the magic does *not* happen outside your comfort zone. Some blurbs would probably help, but it won't be the end of the world if you don't have any.

One area I do think blurbs help is if you want to get a deal with BookBub, a giant promotional email list. When I've had BookBub deals, BookBub's staff has often pulled blurbs from my Amazon page to include in their description of my book. They usually pull the blurb from the reader with "*New York Times* best-selling author" in his bio line. BookBub is dealing with millions of mainstream readers, and unfortunately, the mainstream is still enamored with and influenced by traditional authority triggers.

As a self-published author, don't feel like you need blurbs from the first day your book is out. Traditional publishers send out Advanced Reader Copies (ARCs) like six months in advance, to drum up blurbs they can print on the dust jacket. As a self-published author, you can add blurbs whenever you want, from readers who have actually read the book. I only send out ARCs a maximum of several weeks before launch. I've had some blurbs on my books when they've launched, but I've added many more after launch.

Maybe you don't know any well-known people to ask for a blurb, and as a self-published author, you don't have an agent or publisher to call in a favor for you. You can do without a blurb, but it doesn't hurt to start getting to know people you could picture blurbing a future book. Part of that networking should come from the process of building your audience as you build your book. For example, I ran a podcast for more than 300 episodes, and now have ongoing relationships with many of my guests.

My best blurb, from Seth Godin, on the cover of *The Heart to Start*, was a product of my podcast. I had Seth on my podcast, which in itself was the result of gently asking a couple times over the course of a year. On the podcast, Seth opened my mind to self-publishing. Once my first self-published book was out, I naturally wanted to send it to him. One day I woke up to a big spike in sales, and realized Seth had mentioned my book on his blog. I emailed him to ask if I could use what he wrote as a blurb for the book. His response: "I said it."

Get reviews, blurbs, and forewords

Editorial reviews

There are some legitimate opportunities for self-published authors to get editorial reviews from respected publications. *Publisher's Weekly* and *Kirkus* are the most well-known in the publishing world.

Publisher's Weekly has a website called *BookLife*, geared towards helping indie authors. You can list your book, submit it for review, and with some luck, your book can get reviewed for free. I submitted *The Heart to Start* and someone at *BookLife* gave the book a positive review, which was published in a print edition of *Publisher's Weekly*! This caused a slight spike in sales outside Amazon, and I know at least one librarian bought the book for her library after reading the review.

I submitted *Mind Management, Not Time Management* the same way, but it did not get picked up for a review. I later paid some money to enter it in the "BookLife Prize" contest. The book made it to some degree of semifinals for the contest, and someone wrote a lukewarm review for the book.

I used a quote from my BookLife Prize review on my book's sales page for a bit, but a couple years after *Mind Management* had been released, I paid for a review from *Kirkus*, something around $350. I got a very positive review, and my book was marked "recommended." I can't connect this to a lift in sales, but I now proudly use an excerpt from the review on the book's sales page.

I think paying for a review from *Kirkus*

> **The Heart to Start: Win the Inner War and Let Your Art Shine**
> David Kadavy. Kadavy, $10.84 trade paper (138p) ISBN 978-0-692-99569-3
> In this encouraging guide, Kadavy (*Design for Hackers*), shows how to jumpstart one's creativity. Kadavy uses material from his podcast, *Love Your Work*; entertaining metaphors; and vignettes from his life and those of a myriad of others such as a behavioral scientist, a board game creator, a singer-songwriter, and a chef to highlight the obstacles that prevent people from starting their creative projects. Original terms, such as "the Fortress Fallacy" (imagining one's project in its most ambitious possible form before even starting) and "Inflating the Investment" (overestimating how much time and energy projects will take) clearly illustrate the thinking that leads to procrastination. The practical advice and techniques that Kadavy provides for circumventing distorted thinking and ego-driven insecurities, such as "motivational judo," in which "you use the force of your own ego to kickstart your project," make it sound relatively easy to start creating, but Kadavy is careful to keep expectations realistic. Reassuring reminders not to be defeated by discomfort, perfectionism, and the fear of others' judgments, and to follow one's curiosity and passion, round out this lively, motivating entry into the self-help genre. (*BookLife*)

The review of *The Heart to Start*, in *Publisher's Weekly*

or *Publisher's Weekly* is far from the first way you should spend money to promote your book. But if your book is selling well, receiving positive reviews from readers, and making a profit, paying for an editorial review can be a good way to add some legitimacy to your sales page, and help you get other promotions such as a BookBub Featured Deal, which I'll talk about later.

Paying for an editorial review sounds like bullshit, but it by no means guarantees you'll get a positive review. Search on the web or in online communities of authors, and you'll find plenty who are unhappy they paid for reviews and had their books torn apart. My recommendation is only pay for an editorial review if you either are willing to risk the money going to waste, or if your book is already doing well. And even then, you might get unlucky and have a reviewer who hates your book, thus wasting your money.

Avoiding scam reviews

Now that I've talked about a couple legitimate sources of paid editorial reviews, it's a good time to talk about scams. I don't have an exhaustive amount of knowledge about scams, because I generally avoid almost all paid contests or other paid author services, other than advertising.

Everyone wants to be a successful author, and a great way to make money is by selling the dream. So there are lots of services out there, doing just that. They'll promise you they're the one thing standing between you and your big break. They're almost certainly not.

I'll just say, be very careful. If you're in doubt, see if you can find something on the web about service providers, written by the Alliance of Independent Authors. They have a "watchdog" service that evaluates service providers and warns authors of scams.

Forewords

I suppose having a foreword written by a well-known author in your genre or other well-known person related to your book's subject matter can increase your sales. I wouldn't know, because I've never had a foreword. I've asked a couple well-known people to write forewords for my books, but they have always declined. I don't have the patience or fortitude to keep asking for someone's approval and endure constant rejection, which is part of why I like self-publishing. So I've always just published the book anyway, without a foreword.

Go ahead, ask someone if they'll write your foreword. If you do so, you should make a case for why this is the right book for them to write a foreword to, and why it will be a good marketing opportunity for them. But if you can't get someone to write your foreword, it's not going to make or break your book.

A foreword *might* get someone who would otherwise ignore your book to take notice, but one more effective way to get your book noticed is through advertising.

Chapter 8
Advertise your book

Advertising your book isn't a substitute for an audience, but it can work symbiotically with your audience. If you have an audience of people buying your books, your advertising will often be more effective. If your advertising is effective, you'll grow your audience.

Two surprisingly-common yet contradictory viewpoints amongst novice authors are: One, you shouldn't have to spend any money to sell books, and, two, if you've spent money to sell books, your sales are somehow not real.

Those might not seem contradictory on the surface, but when these viewpoints are held within the same mind, they only serve to protect the person believing them. If someone believes sales are somehow not real if they're generated by advertising, I challenge them to profitably advertise a book: Spend $1,000 on ads, and make $1,001. To that challenge, they'll often reply that they can't afford to spend $1,000 on ads, which is nonsensical because we're talking about *profitably* running ads – so they'd get their money back, and then some. But to advertise their book profitably, they would have to have written a book that sells. So they've successfully reinforced their belief they shouldn't have to spend money to sell books,

Advertise your book

without challenging their belief that book sales generated by advertising are somehow not real.

When I lamented to Seth Godin on episode 177 of my podcast how much money I and other self-published authors were spending on ads, he said, "Publishing has always been really expensive, it's just the authors didn't know that. Now that you're self-publishing, don't be surprised it's going to be really expensive." Godin has been in the book business for decades, and brought to life more than a hundred books. He knows what he's talking about.

How much you have to advertise a book depends upon whether it's a white-, gray-, or black-swan book. If you've written a white-swan book and have the proper keywords in your title, subtitle, and backend keywords, you're more likely to sell some books organically. Advertising on keywords associated with your book will help, but you're less likely to find profitable keywords outside of your subject area. If you've written a book on making soap, for example, it's unlikely you'll make a profit bidding on keywords around car repair.

If you've written a black-swan book, you'll need some way to get readers early on. Besides promoting to your audience, advertising is a good way to do that. But advertising profitably will be difficult early on, because nobody is looking for a book on your subject and it's not clear what it's about from the book's title. You have to figure out what people who happen to be interested in your book are searching for, then hope they enjoy your book enough to share with their friends (it will have to pass the cocktail party test, of course).

Once again, gray-swan books are a happy medium. You can more-easily find profitable keywords, since your subject is clear, but because your book provides a twist, it can be appealing to a wider breadth of readers.

Ad-spend is education

Too many authors give up on ads too easily. They'll spend five dollars on ads, make no sales, then quit and conclude ads don't work. It's incredible that the same people who have spent $50,000 or more getting a college degree won't invest $500 to run some ads and learn in the process.

The goal of spending money on ads is to sell books and make a profit, but spending money on ads is also an education. Think of the first chunk of money you spend without making a profit as tuition. Spending money on ads is a great way to test directly your hypotheses about what will or won't sell books. So if you spend $50 buying 50 clicks on a keyword, with no sales, you haven't wasted $50: You've learned people searching that keyword are not good prospects for buying your book, at least given your current cover, title, description, and reviews.

Because you learn by spending money on ads, Bryan Cohen, author of *Self-Publishing with Amazon Ads*, has a very specific recommendation. "Run 100 clicks worth of Amazon Ads at a 39 cent bid ($39 in total) and check to see if your royalties are higher than your ad spend. If so, then you can keep running more ads to see more profitability. This can work even better if it's the first book in a series."

Another problem that causes authors to give up on ads is the ads simply won't run, especially on Amazon. As I'll get into, Amazon generally doesn't want to run ads on your book if they aren't confident they'll make more money running your ad than another ad. If you've just published your book and have no reviews, they know it will be very difficult to sell your book, so you better have made a sky-high bid before they'll run your ad. Even if your ad does run, you probably won't make any sales, since you have no reviews. So, unless you're willing to invest a large sum in your "edu-

Advertise your book

cation," don't run ads until you have made some sales organically and have some reviews. Then, as you learn and run ads profitably, you'll get more organic sales, which will in turn make it easier to run ads profitably, which will lead to more organic sales.

Keep in mind that no matter how much you spend on ads, it can't make people buy a book they don't want to read. You have to have a marketable book idea, achieve idea/author fit, and make a good sales pitch with your title, subtitle, cover, and sales blurb. If a book sells without ads, it will be easier to make a profit selling it with ads. If readers aren't compelled by your book, all the exposure in the world can't get them to buy it. The *New York Times* reported that despite her more than 97 million followers on Instagram, pop star Billie Eilish's book sold "only" 64,000 copies in the first six months, which was probably disappointing to the publisher that paid more than a $1 million advance. Justin Timberlake received a similar advance for his book, and despite his 53 million Instagram followers, "only" sold 100,000 copies in the first three years. Politician Ilhan Omar was only able to convert 3 million Twitter followers and 1.3 million Instagram followers to 26,000 sales in the first eighteen months after her book's release.

Amazon Ads

Amazon ads are the surest way to profitably advertise most books. Amazon still commands most of the U.S. market, and the incentives are aligned: You pay Amazon to advertise your book, and they make extra money if they successfully sell your book. So, they want to fill their ad slots with the ads that will actually make sales. Other advertising platforms don't directly earn extra when you make a sale, so in some sense they don't care how effective your ad is.

There are various types of Amazon ads, but the most important are Sponsored Products and Lockscreen Ads. Sponsored Products ads are displayed on search-result pages, and on the sales pages of other books.

Lockscreen Ads are displayed on Amazon's Kindle devices. They used to only appear before they were unlocked, but they now also display on a banner on the home screen.

Generally speaking, white-swan books are best advertised with Sponsored Products ads, black-swan books are best advertised with Lockscreen Ads, and gray-swan books work well with both ad types. This is because Sponsored Products ads can be targeted more specifically. You can target Sponsored Products ads to users

Advertise your book

who are searching for specific keywords or who are viewing the sales pages of specific books. You can only target Lockscreen Ads to readers who have shown an interest in specific but broad categories of books, such as "Business and Money > Business Life" or "Other > Nonfiction". So, if you've written a how-to book on a very specific subject, you have much more control with Sponsored Products ads over whether your ad is shown to people who are actually interested in that subject. With Lockscreen Ads, you have a chance to present a compelling idea about a broader category.

Amazon's ad features are always changing, but now I'll provide a high-level overview of important things to know about promoting with either type of ad, without getting into nuances of working with Amazon's ad platform, which change more rapidly than I could update this book.

Sponsored Products strategy

With Sponsored Products ads, you can target readers very specifically, based upon what they're searching for. For example, you can display your ad to readers searching for "frisbee golf," while not displaying it to readers searching for just "golf." But on what keywords will displaying your ad lead to sales? If you have a white-swan book, it may be pretty straightforward. For gray- and black-swan books, it probably won't be.

A three-campaign structure can help you discover what keywords lead to sales, so you can target specific keywords and control your costs. I'll preface this by saying this can be complicated and even intimidating, so don't get frustrated if it doesn't make sense the first or fifth time you read it. I'll also explain why you might not need it at all.

The three campaigns in this strategy each serve specific functions:

1. Discovery: An "automatic" campaign, which casts a wide net, so you can find keywords that lead to sales.
2. Research: A campaign that uses keywords that have led to sales, to discover even more keywords that lead to sales, but in a more-strategic and cost-efficient manner.
3. Performance: A campaign that uses proven keywords to make sales in the most-profitable way possible.

Here's how a keyword might travel through these various campaigns:

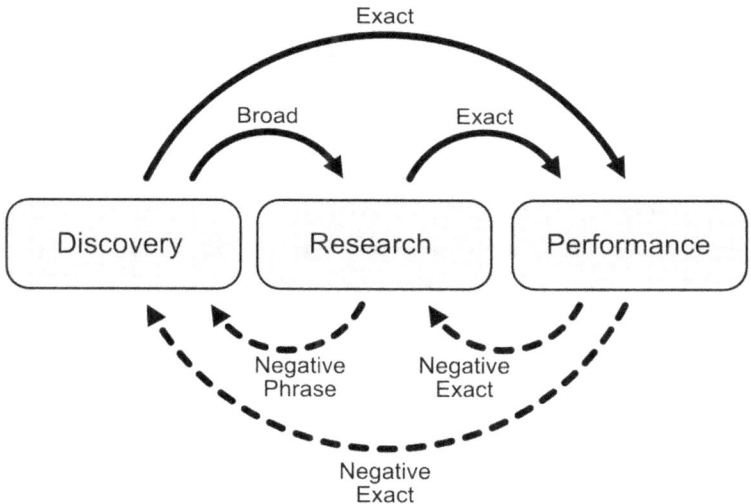

Redrawn with inspiration from an illustration on the now-defunct Prestozon blog.

1. **Keyword leads to a sale in the Discovery campaign.** The automatic campaign, through which Amazon uses its mountains of data to display your ad to

relevant readers, displays your ad when a reader searches for a keyword. The reader buys your book through this ad. Let's say the keyword they searched was "golf."

2. **Keyword is added to both Research and Performance campaigns.** Now, both the Research and Performance campaigns will specifically target the keyword "golf," but in different ways. Golf has been added to the Performance campaign as an *exact match* keyword. So it will only be displayed if the reader searches for "golf." It's also been added to the Research campaign as a *broad* and *phrase* keyword. As a broad keyword, the ad may be displayed when someone searches for variations of the word, such as "golfer," or "golfing." As a phrase keyword, the ad may be displayed when someone searches for phrases that include the keyword, such as "golf book," "golf practice," or, yes, even "frisbee golf."

3. **Keyword is also omitted from Discovery and Research campaigns.** Since the exact keyword, "golf," has already led to a sale and is in the Performance campaign, we no longer need our ad to run for that keyword within the Discovery nor Research campaigns. So, it's added to (or one might say omitted from) the Discovery and Research campaigns as a *negative exact* keyword. This means the ad will not be displayed for these campaigns when someone searches for "golf." It's also added as a *negative phrase* keyword to the Discovery campaign, which means the ad won't be displayed for that campaign when someone searches for phrases containing the keyword, say, "frisbee golf." The Research campaign is instead bidding on phrase searches.

4. **Bid for keyword is optimized within Performance campaign.** Since we're bidding specifically on the keyword "golf" in the Performance campaign, we can get our ad to display for cheaper than if we had bid on "golf" as a broad or phrase keyword. (We still are bidding on it as a broad and phrase keyword, but in the Research campaign, aside from the *negative exact* match of "golf.") We can run a test by bidding $1 per-click for a couple weeks, then dropping our bid to 50¢ for a couple weeks. If we make more profit in one scenario versus another, we can keep our bid there, or try further experiments, such as bidding 75¢ or 25¢.

Notice that since we've omitted the *exact match* keyword from our Discovery and Research campaigns, we won't compete with our own bid, which would increase our costs. Furthermore, since we only use broad and phrase keywords in our Research campaign and omit them from our Discovery campaign, we reduce our Research costs.

As you can see, this is a very deliberate and logical way of, through a process of elimination, finding exactly what keywords lead to sales, and bidding the minimum amount on those keywords to make the most possible profit per sale. But running campaigns with this model is expensive, complicated, and time-consuming. By design, you're spending money that won't lead to sales, so you can better spend money that will.

Logically, for example, if you were promoting a book about golf, you would omit "frisbee golf" from the beginning. But if you were following this model strictly, you would need to collect a lot of data to first be fully confident searches for frisbee golf don't lead to sales of your golf book. It wouldn't be totally unreasonable to pay for thirty clicks before you felt confident you could eliminate the

Advertise your book

keyword. Repeat this for dozens or hundreds of keywords, many of which it's less obvious won't work, and you are spending a lot of money figuring out which keywords do or don't work!

Additionally, regularly reviewing which keywords have led to sales in the Discovery campaign, and applying and omitting the proper keywords within all campaigns, is a tedious process. On top of that, how are you to keep track of all the bids you're testing within the Performance campaign?

There are automation tools available to run campaigns like this. I used to use one of them, called Prestozon, but it was purchased by Helium 10. The technology from the former got integrated into the latter, but at a much higher cost. This model worked great for me when I used it, and helped me scale up my ad spend and book sales, but I haven't used it for the last several years, if for no other reason than that I've been busy working on new books.

Whether you use this three-campaign model or not, it's worth at least understanding conceptually how it works, because it illustrates how to find and optimize profitable keywords.

Keywords aren't the only thing you can bid on for Sponsored Products ads, by the way. You can also target products, in other words, advertise on the sales pages of other books. Instead of keywords, a product is represented by ASIN, which is a string of letters and numbers that can be found on the book's Amazon sales page, and within its Amazon URL. For example: B08DQGLPSN. As keywords consist of exact match, broad, and phrase types, products can be targeted *exact* or *expanded*, the latter of which will target variations of the same book, and even related books.

When you build a campaign and choose one of your books to advertise, you can use a generic "creative," or write some copy to go along with your ad. I've experimented in the past with writing custom copy for my Sponsored Products ads, and didn't see much difference, so I run the generic creative. There are already enough other variables to worry about, such as the keywords, bids, and budget. That doesn't mean you can't find success writing your own copy for these ads.

Automatic Sponsored Products campaigns

Since I don't currently use the three-campaign strategy for Sponsored Products campaigns, I rely somewhat on keywords I've already harvested from this method in the past. For the rest of my campaigns, I use Automatic targeting (the type of campaign used for "Discovery" in the three-campaign strategy).

Amazon has a ton of data on who buys what, and complex algorithms to predict when an ad is likely to result in a sale, and since they make money when you make money, the incentives are aligned. In my experience, unless you're willing to invest a lot of time and money in learning about, tweaking, and maintaining ad campaigns, it's difficult to beat Amazon's Automatic targeting.

The main variables to play with are your default bid per-click, and your daily budget. Usually if I play around with these, I can run a profitable campaign. There are advanced variables, such as "campaign bidding strategy," which determines whether or not Amazon can deviate from your default bid based upon the chances of generating a sale, and "adjust bids by placement," which determines whether they can increase your bid to give your ad a better placement. I don't mess with these, because they make it more complicated to know whether I'm choosing a profitable strategy.

Lockscreen Ads strategy

In recent years, I haven't run many Lockscreen Ads, but they have at times been very profitable for me. It's much easier to get Sponsored Products ads to run at all (though not always, which I'll talk about). So Lockscreen Ads take a little more patience.

Unlike Sponsored Products ads, on which I've done fine with a

Advertise your book

generic creative, in Lockscreen Ads, your ad copy is king. Remember, these ads show up on someone's Kindle before they unlock it, so whatever copy you write is front-and-center, right below your book cover.

Some of my top-performing Lockscreen Ad creatives have been:

> David Kadavy's exciting new book is changing productivity forever. Read now.

> Take the *Heart to Start* challenge: Read the first sentence of this book, and try not to keep reading.

> "Things are not difficult to make; what is difficult is putting ourselves in the state of mind to make them." —Constantin Brancusi

I talked earlier about using BookBub Ads to test titles and subtitles. Writing copy for Amazon's Lockscreen Ads can also be a good opportunity to test and refine messaging, or use messaging that has already performed well in other contexts. The Constantin Brancusi quote performed well as a tweet, and is one of the "Popular Highlights" for the Kindle version of *Mind Management, Not Time Management*. When I was developing my formula for sales blurbs, I relied heavily on Lockscreen Ads to test copy.

Authors often get frustrated with and give up on Lockscreen Ads for a couple reasons: One, they can't get them to run, and, two, when they do run they don't appear to be profitable. Getting Lockscreen Ads to run is indeed a bit of a mystery. The variables you choose when starting a Lockscreen campaign include a bid per-click, a budget, and a schedule for when the campaign will begin and end. Placing a high bid per-click, say 40¢, will make it likely your ad will run, but then it's hard to make a profit because you're spending so much.

Even then, it can sometimes take weeks before your ad starts running. If you choose a very high budget, like $10,000, and a short schedule, like two weeks, that will often get a Lockscreen Ad to run. Once it's started running, meaning you're seeing impressions and clicks in your reports, you can extend the schedule, sometimes for six months. In my experience, the Lockscreen Ads never meet the crazy-high budget, but keep an eye on them just in case. If they were profitable, I would be happy. As a wise man named Chris Yeh once said, "I have an unlimited budget for advertising that clearly works."

But even with a high budget and short schedule, Lockscreen Ads with low bids tend not to run. Authors who swear by Lockscreen Ads usually advocate for running dozens and dozens of ads with low bids, like 5¢. Occasionally, for no apparent reason, one of the ads will start delivering a huge amount of impressions and lots of cheap clicks, which often results in lots of sales. I've experimented with this and have never had a successful Lockscreen Ad run for less than 14¢ per-click. However, I'm advertising in categories such as Business, whereas many of these authors are advertising in obscure fiction categories. When I was running lots of Lockscreen Ads, I had a spreadsheet that would randomly compile campaigns with various bids, categories, and creatives. An assistant would then copy and paste the information to generate lots of campaigns.

To make Lockscreen Ads even more mysterious and frustrating, their sales reporting is generally wrong. You might see a Lockscreen Ad generating lots of impressions and clicks, but that, according to the reports in your Amazon Advertising console, has resulted in no sales. However, in your KDP reports, you'll tend to see a spike in sales corresponding to your spike in Lockscreen Ad impressions

Advertise your book

and clicks. It's easy to make the connection if you have few sales and aren't running other promotions, but otherwise, it's hard to know if your Lockscreen Ads are working. According to Brian D. Meeks, from whose book, *Mastering Amazon Ads*, and Facebook Group I gained my initial knowledge of Lockscreen Ads, just focus on getting cheap clicks. I've run some tests, however, and my vague conclusion is that Lockscreen Ads reporting is directionally accurate. That is, if I have two ads delivering a high volume of clicks, and one is reporting an Average Cost of Sale (ACoS) of 400%, meaning supposedly for each dollar of book sales I'm spending four, and another is reporting an ACoS of 50%, I believe the second one is performing better.

While Lockscreen Ad reporting is far from perfect, based upon my data collection, an increase or decrease in clicks on Lockscreen Ads generally correlates with an increase or decrease in sales reported in the KDP Dashboard and the Amazon Ads Dashboard.

One probable reason reporting for Lockscreen Ads is poor is that they are presented when a reader is about to read a book other than yours – when they're picking up their Kindle. Sponsored Products ads are presented when a reader is shopping on Amazon's website or app, so are naturally more likely to directly lead to sales. But don't let that cause you to overlook Lockscreen Ads.

Sponsored Brands ads

The other type of ads currently available on Amazon, besides Sponsored Products and Lockscreen Ads, are Sponsored Brands ads. These enable you to advertise yourself as an author, alongside multiple books. I've only dabbled in these and didn't find them successful. They might be good if you have a complete series to advertise. I will try them again once I've completed my *Getting Art Done* series.

Evaluating Amazon Ads performance

The reporting on Sponsored Products ads is not as unreliable as on Lockscreen Ads, but it's still not perfectly accurate. Think about your own book-buying behavior and it clearly would be difficult to determine whether a particular ad has led to a sale. I might download a Kindle sample and not get around to reading it and buying for months or even years. Repeatedly seeing a book advertised may increase my awareness of that book, and that may help cause me to finally buy it after a friend has recommended it. Even if sales were perfectly attributed to the ads that led to them, there's often such a delay between an ad being seen and the book actually being bought, you won't always get data on which you can base day-to-day decisions.

Because sales reporting on Amazon Ads isn't perfect, you can't decide whether your ads are working solely based upon what you see in your ad reports. You have to look at your sales, and consider to what extent those sales could be generated by efforts other than Amazon Ads, thus Bryan Cohen's advice above to look at your

Advertise your book

royalties in comparison to your ad spend. If you turn off all your ads and a couple weeks or months later have no sales, then start making sales again soon after turning the ads back on, that's a good indicator your ads are generating sales – no matter what it says in your ad reports.

Earlier in your author career, when fewer of your sales are happening organically, it's a little easier to see how well your ads are working, especially if Amazon Ads are the focus of your marketing efforts. When I was getting comfortable with Amazon Ads, I kept a spreadsheet in which I tracked weekly basic stats on Amazon Ads, compared with my earnings as reported in the KDP dashboard. I generally found that spending more on ads led to more sales, even if my ads didn't appear to be profitable in the Amazon Ads dashboard.

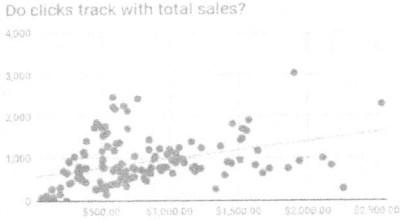

Over years of tracking, I generally found that when I generated clicks through Amazon Ads in a given week, I made more sales that week. But some weeks were outliers, due to organic spikes or other promotions.

Through evaluating data and refining campaigns, I got better at running ads profitably. Notice in the beginning I spent a lot on "tuition," running ads without making a profit.

Focus your ad efforts on one country

Unless you have a thriving author business you're scaling with support staff, you need to focus your efforts. Amazon has separate ad platforms for several countries and they're always adding more. Focus your ad efforts on the country where you'll make the most sales. For example, if your books are in English, that will probably be the United States.

It's tempting to try to run ads in Canada, the UK, and Australia, too, but that's likely to be a lot of extra work for little extra money. I personally used to run some Automatic Sponsored Products campaigns in the UK, but now don't even do that. It arguably wouldn't hurt, but I run my business independently, with no assistant nor other support staff, so there are better uses of my energy.

BookBub Ads

The biggest giant next to Amazon for self-published authors is BookBub. As I mentioned earlier when talking about running ads to test titles, subtitles, and covers, BookBub is an email list people subscribe to, which sends out discount and free ebook deals every day. In some fiction categories they have over two-million subscribers, and in Advice and How-To they have nearly a million. I'll talk about these pricing promotions later, but BookBub also runs an ad platform that displays ads in their emails and on their website. They have a lot of data on what readers are interested in, so their ads are an effective tool to sell your book or at the very least learn a lot about who is and isn't interested in your book.

As you've seen from the sample ads I've shared previously, BookBub Ads are classic rectangular image ads. You can design your own creative, or generate a basic ad right in the BookBub Ads platform.

A generic ad creative made within BookBub's ad platform.

After spending thousands on BookBub Ads and trying different designs, I've settled on a simple format I use for all ads other than those on which I'm trying to test something such as a title or subtitle: I display the book cover and the price, and if I'm targeting readers for a retailer other than Amazon, I showcase the retailer's logo.

An ad I made for BookBub's platform, featuring price and store logo

Since BookBub is advertising to readers who have signed up to receive deals, your ads will perform much better if your book is discounted. Obviously your book will be discounted if you have a BookBub Featured Deal, but you can run your own promotion even if you haven't been chosen for a BookBub Featured Deal. You'll have a much higher click-through rate, get cheaper clicks, and a higher rate of those clicks will convert to sales if your book is discounted and you advertise such. All of the above will also improve on the last day of your promotion if you make it clear in your ad it's the last day.

Advertise your book

An ad with last-day messaging

Keep in mind that when you apply for a Featured Deal, BookBub wants the price you're offering to be the best price for your book within the "recent" past. So a poorly-planned self-run pricing promotion can make you ineligible for a Featured Deal in the immediate future.

BookBub Ads can be targeted by country, category of interest, preferred retailer, and authors of interest, so you can learn a lot about selling your book while running BookBub Ads. It seems to me BookBub decides who is interested in a particular author based upon who has clicked on that author's deal or ads. Since I've run several BookBub Featured Deals, a Featured New Release, and many BookBub Ads, I have a pretty substantial audience of nearly 20,000 readers. I or anyone else can target this audience when setting up a campaign.

David Kadavy
19,423 Readers
2.35% CTR

My BookBub audience, which anyone can target for BookBub Ads, now contains nearly 20,000 readers. As you can see, I average about 2.35% CTR advertising to my own audience.

How to Sell a Book

Not every author will have a BookBub audience you can run ads to. You can see how many readers an author has when choosing them in the campaign setup. This is one of the factors that will affect the indicator which predicts whether you have the ideal audience size to run a successful campaign.

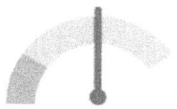

Audience: Defined

Max Daily Reach: **Fewer than 10k**
impressions

If the audience you're targeting for a BookBub ad is on the low end of this meter, that doesn't necessarily mean it won't run.

In my experience, an ad will indeed become expensive and not perform very well if the audience size is too big. But if the indicator says the audience is too small, your ad can still perform well, even if it doesn't run at a high volume.

Targeting the audiences of various authors all at once is a quick way to reach more readers. But, while you're able to see a breakdown in your campaign stats of the click-through-rates of followers of various authors, I still avoid mixing authors within a campaign, because you can never tell how those numbers get muddied, such as by one customer being included in multiple authors' audiences. Ideally, each campaign will be targeted at one author's readers, in one country, for one retailer, with the currency and retailer displayed on the ad. But, generating creatives and campaigns for all these is labor intensive. It isn't too bad if you really plan out the production and scheduling of your creatives and campaigns, and it's worth it to actually see the differences in performance amongst

Advertise your book

these various factors. If you're going to spend money on ads, you might as well learn.

When you set up a BookBub Ads campaign, you can choose its duration, budget, and whether the budget will be spread throughout the campaign or spent as quickly as possible. These factors are self-explanatory, but the factors that behave more counterintuitively are whether you bid on a CPM basis (cost per thousand impressions) or CPC (Cost Per Click). I personally haven't had much success bidding on clicks, and have more success choosing a high CPM, often above the suggested bid displayed during campaign creation.

After some trial-and-error, I've settled into running my BookBub Ads campaigns with a very high CPM bid.

Unfortunately, while BookBub makes it easy to see which of your ads get a higher click-through rate, after that, it's hard to know for sure if your ad led to a sale. On Amazon, you can sign up for an Amazon Associates account, generate a tag, include it in the URL on your ad, and track its performance, but running ads with your affiliate links violates Amazon's terms, so that account could get banned. To me, it's not worth the risk of something worse happening, such as my KDP account getting banned, too. That's one of my main sources of revenue!

Meta Ads

Though Meta currently runs the second-biggest ad platform to Google they of course aren't focused on books. But ads across Meta's platforms, specifically Facebook and Instagram, can be a good way to sell books.

Meta Ads cover too many placements and types of creatives, all which change too often, to be worth talking about in this book, and Meta Ads have had a limited contribution to the 100,000 sales I've made. My Meta ad spend has mostly been comprised of ads I've run to supplement pricing promotions with BookBub, which I'll talk about in a bit. It's simply easier to get people to click on your ad when you're advertising a sale, and as described regarding BookBub Ads, it's hard to be sure your ads are actually leading to sales on retailers. So using Meta Ads to advertise pricing promotions is better-suited for when you're trying to generate as many sales as possible, rather than optimize your profits.

It's much easier to gauge the effectiveness of your Meta Ads if you're selling direct through your website, such as a Shopify store, or a store directly on Instagram or Facebook, which can be set up through Shopify. Then you have the luxury of a tracking pixel the ads platform can use to attribute a sale to a particular ad – though this method is not perfect.

The best strategies for Meta Ads change frequently, and I'm not heavily-experienced with them anyway. That said, the current prevailing strategy amongst experts is to not do any targeting, and instead let Meta's back-end machine-learning algorithms determine who to display your ads to. Apparently they use millions of data points from the text of the ad and the creative, whether image or video, as well as a massive amount of data from more than a decade of delivering ads. So they can probably do a better job of targeting than any human who doesn't want to dedicate their life to optimizing their ads.

Advertise your book

This is a departure from what used to be the prevailing strategy, which involved testing various audiences based upon a catalog of interests Meta had identified from their user data, such as "Writing (communications)" or "Pottery (crafts)". Ad managers became connoisseurs of these interest categories, or pages of brands liked by users. The big pages had the most competition, so it was all about finding the more obscure and unexpected pages that just happened to be liked by people who would also respond to your ads. Meta has increasingly been removing interest categories as targeting options, so this is becoming an outdated way to target, and may disappear completely someday, in lieu of their automatic targeting options.

One of Meta's new and advanced targeting techniques is what they call Advantage+. You can run an ad with a simple image of your book and link to a landing page, and Meta will automatically find users ready to buy. But these campaigns tend to perform very well early on, then burn out quickly, as your ad has already been shown numerous times to everyone Meta thought was ready and willing to buy your book. You can quickly go from making a profit to throwing your money in a pit.

A campaign structure I've found effective recently is what's called the 3:2:2 dynamic creative system. It involves running "Dynamic Creative" ads within a single campaign and ad set with no targeting (unless your book is specifically targeted, say, to men or women). 3:2:2 refers to three creatives, two headlines, and two body copies. "Creative" in this case refers to images or videos – the same type for each Dynamic Creative ad.

How to Sell a Book

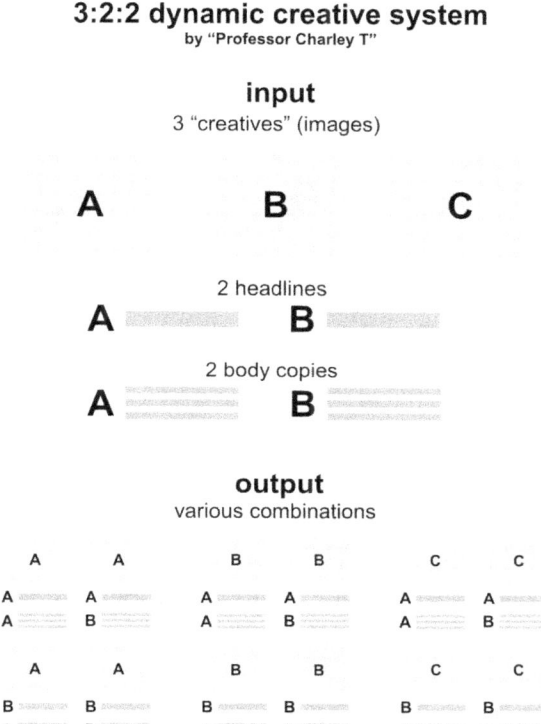

Dynamic Creative ads run various combinations of creatives, headlines, and body copies. Once the ad has run for several days, you make another 3:2:2 Dynamic Creative ad which includes the winning creative, headline, and body copy from the previous ad. In other words, against the winning creative, headline, and body copy, the ad will be testing two additional creatives and one additional headline and body copy.

This forces you to come up with lots of different ideas for how to advertise your book, and Meta's ad platform supposedly takes care of the rest. A frustrating element of this system is that most of the new ideas you come up with will get no exposure at all.

Advertise your book

DC 001 - kadavy typewriter, kadavy journaling, t...	22,924	49,338	4,282
Image "kadavy-journaling-30-journal-free-downl...	22,788	48,644	4,227
Image "free-download-kadavy-typing.png_105 (...	121	136	9
Image "overhead-typewriter.png_105 (773d446...	441	557	46

Meta's Dynamic Creative campaigns automatically run higher-performing elements, including images, headlines, and body text.

Sometimes a combination of Dynamic Creative elements will appear to be really effective because it has a high engagement rate, or even converts to a sale after very few impressions, but Meta's ad platform will not run the ad. A popular and logical viewpoint in these cases is, There's no mistake. Meta has tons of data and knows best. If your ad isn't running it's because it's not effective, at least in the sense that it doesn't contribute to a positive experience for Meta users, so they don't want to display it.

A Meta advertising method that has traditionally been popular is that of "retargeting," or running ads to people who have already shopped for your book or even added it to their shopping cart. This is only practical if you have control over the shopping experience, such as if you're selling directly through a Shopify store. But even retargeting is currently questioned by Meta Ads experts. Apparently Meta will retarget for you, so long as you have a campaign running. If Meta is so great at advertising to people it already knows are interested in your book, it makes sense that running a special retargeting campaign is unnecessary.

Advertising on Meta, I personally have learned a lot about book-buying psychology. In particular, I have been surprised to see that what I can advertise profitably on other channels I can't so easily advertise profitably on Meta, and vice versa. For example, my short read, *100-Word Writing Habit* hasn't sold great. Last I checked, fewer than 1,000 copies. But it performs better on Meta Ads than any of my other books. My theory is that it works better as an impulse buy: People like the idea of building a 100-word writing habit, and merely seeing the book motivates them to want to buy the book, as a souvenir of the idea and reminder they want to build a writing habit. Because *100-Word Writing Habit* has performed well on Meta Ads, I'm developing other products to complement the book, hopefully to increase the Average Order Value when readers order it from my Shopify store. For example, I've created a habit-tracking wristband, and have recently launched a workbook full of journal-prompts to help start a 100-word writing habit.

Using Meta Ads to build your email list

Meta Ads are also useful for building your email list. You can build Forms for collecting email addresses and run Lead Ads to drive traffic to those forms. Since the forms work directly within Meta's apps, there's very little friction for users to fill them out.

I've had success by promising a list of 30 journal prompts upon sign-up to my email list. That lead magnet has performed as well if not better than giving away an entire short read, *How to Write a Book*, although each appeals to users of different demographics.

If you grow your email list through paid traffic, it's very important to monitor the engagement of the people who sign up in this way, and prune out of your list those who aren't engaged. This is "cold" traffic, and aside from attracting people who simply give you fake or throwaway email addresses, it will also attract people who just like free stuff, or simply aren't going to engage with your future content for some other reason.

I don't find my email courses to be as effective as simple lead magnets when advertising to paid traffic, but they are very effective at warming up leads. My current-warm up sequence looks about like this:

- Lead signs up, send an email with lead magnet
- A couple days later, remind them of the lead magnet, and invite them to my *100-Word Writing Habit* email course
- A few days later, check to see if they've engaged with any emails (clicked in or opened)
- If they haven't engaged with any emails, wait a week and check again. Send anyone who hasn't engaged into a "reactivation" sequence, which will remove them if they don't engage.
- If they have engaged with emails, check to see if they've signed up for the email course
- If they have signed up for the email course, let them complete that course before talking about anything else
- If they haven't signed up for the email course, send an email telling them what to expect from the weekly *Love Mondays* newsletter they'll be receiving

This sequence is far from perfect, but it ensures my sender reputation and open rates don't get dragged down by people who don't want my emails, while allowing those who do want my emails to become happy long-time subscribers I can notify when I launch my next book.

Other ad platforms

There are other ad platforms besides Amazon, BookBub, and Meta, but those are the ones I've concentrated on. I've dabbled in Google AdWords, for advertising my Shopify store. I haven't seen anything convincing from it, but wouldn't rule out using them in the future. I've also gotten quality email sign-ups advertising a lead magnet on X (Twitter), but heartily recommend against it: At this time, there

How to Sell a Book

are many users who block every account they see ads from, and being blocked by many accounts works against your organic reach, as documented in the open-source algorithm for X.

No matter how enticing your book and your advertising, you'll make more sales, and more profit, if the price is right.

Chapter 9
Pick the price that's right

Having the right price for your book can be the difference between someone choosing to read your book, or a comparable one. Choosing a "price point" that's appropriate for your book helps meet reader expectations, which helps convert the sale. So it's worth it to think carefully about the prices of your books.

Ebook price "points"

A term that gets thrown around in marketing is "price point." Why don't people just say "price?" Including "point" implies strategic thinking. It implies that the price you've chosen, to the penny, is the perfect price to drive sales and/or maximize profitability. I also think including "point" implies that the price you've chosen will act as a sort of trigger that springs readers into action, causing them to buy your book.

There's more than 100 years of marketing research behind why you'll see books priced not at $1, but instead $0.99; not at $5, but instead $4.99; and not at $10, but instead $9.99. As much as we know the latter price is pretty much just as much as the former, somehow it makes it seem less expensive. We're just used to it.

How to Sell a Book

Amazon has massive amounts of data on what price points lead to sales, and they force the hands of self-published authors to sell their Kindle ebooks at those price points. Nowhere do they do this more explicitly than with their royalty rates. If you publish a Kindle ebook in the U.S. and agree to a 70% royalty rate, you have to price your book between $2.99 and $9.99. If you agree to the 35% royalty rate, you have to price your book between $0.99 and $2.98, or above $9.99.

There are some other differences between the 70% and 35% royalty plans, such as whether you have to pay for digital delivery charges (which can make a big difference if your ebook has a lot of large images). These terms are subject to change, so make sure to read up on them directly from Amazon if you're not sure which plan works for you.

With that in mind, generally if your book is priced at $2.98, you'll earn approximately $1.04 per sale. If you raised your price one cent to $2.99, you'd earn nearly double that. If your book is priced at $10, you'll earn approximately $3.50, and if you lowered your price one cent to $9.99, you'd earn double that once again, about $7.

The price of your book will affect whether readers will buy your book, thus affecting the number of total copies you sell, and the profit you earn. The lowest Amazon will allow you to price your book is $0.99 (to make a book free, you have to publish it free on another platform and ask Amazon to price-match, aka "permafree"). Generally, the cheaper your book is, the more copies you'll sell. But at a $0.99 price point, you'll be making about $0.34 per book. If you sold an impressive 1,000 books, you'd make $340. If you sold that amount at $9.99, you'd make close to $7,000.

So the right price for your book will depend upon whether it's more important for you to sell lots of copies, make the most profit possible, or simply attract readers who value your work. You'll sell more copies at $0.99, but will buyers value what you've written as

Pick the price that's right

much as if they had paid $9.99? And if you price your book at $4.99, you'll likely make more sales and more overall profit than if you had priced it at $9.99. Then again, if you price your book at $9.99, you can afford to spend more money on ads. If your book is meant to attract high-priced consulting contracts, you may attract more-qualified leads buying ads to sell your book at $9.99 than by practically giving it away at $0.99.

The happy-medium price point between offering your book for cheap and making a good profit per-sale is $2.99. This is the lowest price at which Amazon will give you a 70% royalty rate. Your reader gets your book for pretty cheap, and you get the best royalty rate possible.

The most-popular ebook price points end in ninety-nine: $0.99, $1.99, $2.99, $3.99, $4.99, and $9.99. You won't as often see prices between $4.99 and $9.99. A price like $5.99 isn't as strong as $4.99, because five is a psychologically significant level. When something is $4.99, your mind says, "Oh, it's less than $5!" When it's $5.99, it says, "Darn, it's more than $5." You might see $7.99, because that's just over $7, and at that point you're thinking about how much less it is than $10. But if it's less than $10, it might as well be $9.99. You'll also occasionally see a price point that ends in forty-nine. $3.49 and $4.49 are especially popular price points of this variety.

Pay attention to the prices of various books in your genre. If all the books of a similar length in your genre are $0.99, you'll have a very hard time selling yours for $9.99. If your genre is full of traditionally-published ebooks priced at $14.99, yours might look like a bargain at $9.99.

Speaking of traditionally-published books, apparently they don't have the same royalty structure with Amazon, because traditionally-published Kindle ebooks are usually priced above $9.99, especially in Nonfiction categories. For example, $14.99 is a popular price for traditionally-published Kindle ebooks. It makes no sense for a self-published author to sell a Kindle ebook for $14.99 (besides the royalty being unfavorable at this price point, I've tried). At that point, you're making less than $5.25 per book. Remember, if you sold it at $9.99, you'd make around $7 per book, and you'd sell more copies because it would be nearly 50% cheaper.

In 2014, author Hugh Howey shared data from a report by a now-defunct blog by "The Data Guy." The Data Guy compiled a report of sales data from the top 500 books (excluding the outlier top-ten books), and found $4.99 to be the most-profitable price point. Combining sales price and number of copies sold, $4.99 made the most money of all price points. When you consider it's in the 70% royalty-rate plan, it would also make most self-published authors the most profit. While this data is now ten years old, Amazon's royalty rates and associated pricing plans haven't changed significantly since then. (With all the inflation over the past decade, Amazon forces indie authors to sell ebooks at the same low prices, which is frightening.)

That doesn't necessarily mean $4.99 is the only price point you should consider for your ebooks, even if your goal is to maximize profits. If you have a loyal following of dedicated readers, many of them will be happy to support you by buying your book at $9.99, when it first launches. Additionally, pricing your book higher can build tension so that when you finally discount your book, such as through a pricing promotion, you'll have a higher sales velocity. That can catapult your book into high rankings on Amazon, driving further sales, which is useful if you're trying to generate enough sales to hit a bestseller list.

Pricing across regions

The price points I've talked about above are in U.S. Dollars, for the U.S. market. Each market has its own ideal price points. They follow the general rule of ending your price in a nine, which isn't

Pick the price that's right

the price you'd set if you'd simply calculated according to the exchange rate. Additionally, price points uncommon in one currency may be more common in another. For example, $4.99 in USD is currently worth $7.46 in Australian Dollars. So it makes sense to have a price such as $6.99 AUD or $7.49 AUD. Price points U.S. consumers are used to seeing such as $4.99 or $9.99 would be too cheap or expensive relative to the U.S. price point.

Amazon still forces the hands of self-published authors in pricing outside the U.S. On Amazon's Australia store, you might see an unusual price point of $21.99 for a traditionally-published Kindle ebook. But the highest price at which authors publishing through KDP can earn a 70% royalty is $11.99. There are other markets in which self-published authors can only earn 35%, unless they include their book in KDP Select/Kindle Unlimited – a serious decision I'll talk about later. Currently, those markets are Brazil, India, Japan, and Mexico.

Ideally, you would research price points in your genre in all markets. In reality, that's a waste of time. Here's a breakdown of my lifetime earnings across all Amazon markets (CreateSpace closed in 2018).

As you can see, 83% of my earnings are from the U.S. I haven't even earned 10% of what I have in the U.S. in my next-biggest market, the UK. I could grow my earnings in those other markets, but having the perfect price probably won't be what does it. And I'd rather try to grow the pile that's 83% of my earnings than one that's 6%. So I focus on the U.S., and trust that other markets will grow along with it.

The situation could potentially be different for you, such as if you write in German. But if you write in English, chances are the U.S. will be your biggest market. Self-publishing pioneer Joanna Penn, for example, is based in the UK and has said she makes the most money in the U.S. market.

To save time and energy, I use the help of my aggregator, which publishes my ebook outside of Kindle, to determine foreign pricing. PublishDrive has a "pretty pricing" feature. I enter in my USD price, then click the "pretty pricing" button to convert it into price points commensurate with exchange rates for the various markets. Then, I cross-reference those prices with the available markets in my KDP pricing dashboard, making sure I'm in the 70% royalty plan, where possible. If PublishDrive recommended a $10.99 CAD price for Canada, for example, I would adjust both Publish-Drive and KDP to be $9.99 – the maximum price at which you can currently earn a 70% royalty for Canadian Kindle ebooks.

In the above case I don't *have* to change the PublishDrive price, too, but it's a good habit to keep your prices the same across all retailers. If my price was, say, £0.99 on retailers on PublishDrive, and £1.99 on KDP, Amazon would likely price-match down to £0.99, which would knock me down to the 35% royalty rate. Instead of earning nearly £1.40 per sale, I would earn about £0.34 per sale.

Paper-book pricing

Deciding on a good price for hard-copy books, such as paperback and hardcover, is not as straightforward as pricing ebooks, because there are more costs to consider when determining your profit. For example, I sell the paperback of *Mind Management* through KDP for $19.95. It

United States	$198,785.75
United Kingdom	$14,393.27
Germany	$7,438.17
Canada	$5,679.91
Australia	$3,125.33
Spain	$2,082.70
France	$1,998.42
CreateSpace US	$1,869.49
India	$1,796.39
Italy	$1,589.60
Netherlands	$883.01
Brazil	$632.64
Japan	$527.53
Mexico	$499.15
Poland	$109.31

Breakdown of my earnings by country in various Amazon markets.

costs $4.14 to print, and I earn a 60% royalty rate on the list price, so I earn $7.83 per book. So, the printing cost makes the math a little more complicated, changes based upon the length of your book, and is subject to change if costs of raw materials fluctuate. But, Amazon breaks down the math for you as you set prices in KDP, and there's a calculator available to plan pricing as you plan the length of your book.

You'll still generally see the same pricing patterns on paper books, with prices ending in nine. I, personally, like to end pricing on paper books with a five, so for example $19.95. It just feels a little more sophisticated to not try to squeeze those extra four cents out of someone, and physical books are sophisticated products. But, Amazon may adjust the pricing of your book to whatever they deem more profitable. Amazon currently sells my $19.95 paperback for $17.96, but I still earn the $7.83 per book I was promised when I set up my $19.95 price.

Direct-sales pricing

Currently on books I sell directly on my Shopify store, I fly in the face of more than a century of marketing wisdom and price my books by whole numbers. So ebooks are $7, $10, or $15. Paper books are $15, $20, or $28. Selling direct feels to me like a more intimate exchange. If your friend asks you to Venmo $8.78, you might send $9 or even $10. If you're selling books in a yard sale, you aren't going to price them at $4.99. You'll price them at $5.

On Amazon it makes sense to optimize your pricing, because your books are competing within the same store with millions of other books. A less-than-optimal price could potentially be the difference between your book being recommended by the algorithm, or not. But people who are buying directly from me might have followed me for a decade, so it feels strange to play some weird game with pricing.

I'm not married, though, to the idea of pricing on whole numbers. I have been experimenting with running ads to drive sales on my store, so if I'm trying to convert cold traffic, it makes sense to present pricing that's familiar to customers. But then it wouldn't feel right to ask cold customers to pay $9.99, and loyal followers $10, so I'd probably opt to just charge $9.99, if it made my ads more profitable.

Your everyday pricing can affect your sales a little, but running pricing promotions will affect your sales a lot.

Chapter 10
Run pricing promotions

Some readers are simply not going to buy your book unless they get a deal. Maybe they have a personal policy of only buying books on sale, maybe they aren't curious enough about your book to buy it at full price, maybe they mean to buy your book but will never get around to it otherwise, or maybe they simply can't afford full-priced books.

It's hard to believe that by running a pricing promotion you can virtually alter the space-time continuum and cause someone to read your book instead of another – but this is indeed the case. By running a pricing promotion, you get your book into the hands of more readers. This leads to more sales at higher prices, after online-bookstore algorithms boost your book, and those who bought at a discount recommend it to their friends.

BookBub Featured Deals

As I mentioned earlier, in some fiction categories BookBub has over two-million email subscribers, and in Advice and How-To they have nearly a million. Your book can be one of the books BookBub sends out to all these subscribers. Sounds great, right? There are three catches: One, you have to pay to have your book included;

two, you have to discount your book; and three, they're extremely selective. Being willing to pay them doesn't guarantee they'll want to include your book.

In a BookBub Featured Deal, as it's called, your book is one of the few books featured, within a category, that BookBub sends via email to interested readers and displays on their website. Nonfiction books are most commonly discounted to $1.99 or $2.99. Some authors give their books away for free, which is more common in fiction categories. Some books are discounted only to $3.99, which seems to be reserved for traditionally-published books.

My book, as featured in its very first Featured Deal, on BookBub's website

I've run several of these deals, and have sold anywhere from 600 to 2,700 books during the periods in which my book has been discounted. How many books I've sold has depended both on how new the book has been, and how much I've spent on ads to support my deal. The deal itself can cost a lot, and depends upon which category your book is chosen for, in which countries your deal is running, and what price your book is discounted to.

At the moment I'm writing this, an International deal to the Advice and How-To category for a book discounted to $1.99 would cost $1,339. If the book is discounted to $0.99, the deal would cost less, $781. This deal would be emailed to at least 870,000

Run pricing promotions

subscribers in the U.S., Canada, the UK, and Australia. BookBub estimates the deal would sell between 200 and 4,500 copies.

How much money you make with a BookBub Featured Deal will depend upon your goals. If your goal is to make a bestseller list, you will likely lose money. If you're going for a bestseller list, you'll want to supplement your deal with lots of additional ads on Book-Bub's ad platform, and other ad platforms. In my first BookBub Featured Deal, my initial loss was about $4,000. I sold over 2,500, which wasn't enough to get my book on the *Wall Street Journal* bestseller list. But, I did get my book into the hands of thousands of readers. No doubt many of those readers recommended the book to others, who purchased it at full price. I broke down the exact numbers from this first BookBub Featured Deal in a post on my blog, called, "Why I Lost $4,000 on my BookBub Featured Deal (& Why I'd Do it Again)."

You may like the idea of getting thousands of new readers for your book, and be willing to pay thousands of dollars for the privilege, but BookBub is very selective of which books they send to their subscribers. I didn't get my first BookBub Featured Deal until *The Heart to Start* had been rejected fourteen times. Since BookBub asks you to wait four weeks after a rejection before applying again, that was well over a year of applying, awaiting a reply, receiving a rejection, and waiting for another chance to apply. It wasn't until my fifteenth attempt that BookBub finally accepted the book for a Featured Deal.

What causes BookBub to accept a book for a Featured Deal? Primarily, your book has to have lots of signals it's a good book. It should have a well-designed cover, lots of strong reviews, and hopefully an editorial review or two, and/or blurbs from well-known authors. What makes a cover good, and how many reviews or blurbs do you need? That is a mystery known only by BookBub's editors, and even they probably couldn't articulate their criteria.

Even a good book with all of the above isn't guaranteed a

How to Sell a Book

BookBub Featured Deal. BookBub's editors have access to a ton of data about reader preferences, so may take into consideration factors such as the season, or what other books for which they have deals scheduled. Even after I've done several Featured Deals, my books still get rejected often. What's rejected now may be accepted next month, so keep trying.

If you're determined to get a BookBub Featured Deal, keep a document in which you log each attempt, and all of the information you need to fill out in the form, including at what price you offered to promote. That way you can streamline your application process by copying and pasting. Each time you get a rejection email, set yourself a reminder to try again in four weeks. Meanwhile, familiarize yourself with the platform, subscribing to receive deals for books in your category. That way, you can get a feel for the editors' preferences. Apply with various popular price points. If you have an editorial review or great blurb, paste it into the comments section of your application. Maybe try running some BookBub ads, to see how your book appeals to readers. The repeated rejection may be tough, but just consistently and dispassionately keep applying, on auto-pilot.

Once you get a Featured Deal, remember, you're responsible for making sure your pricing is correct on the day your email goes out. Don't try to time this perfectly. Just discount your book well in advance, especially if your book is distributed through aggregators, such as PublishDrive or Draft2Digital. I once scheduled a deal through an aggregator, and for unknown reasons my book wasn't discounted on time through Apple Books. So my deal didn't go out to BookBub's Apple Books readers, and I missed out on hundreds of sales. I was going for the *WSJ* bestseller list and that ruined my chances, as you needed sales through a channel other than Amazon, and Apple Books is second-best for my genre. Now, I manually change my prices a week in advance. This makes my initial sales spike a little less extreme, since some readers buy the book when it's first discounted, but it also may help my book climb on Amazon's rankings, as they've adjusted their ranking system to account for sales over longer periods of time.

I have found it difficult to turn a profit within the duration of a BookBub Featured Deal, but the impact of a deal goes well beyond the deal itself. Awareness and sales of your book will lead to sales of any other books you have, so it makes sense to discount them to slightly-higher yet more-profitable price points. The big sales spike will make your book more visible for days or weeks, and you can slowly bring your price back up. If your book is discounted to $1.99, you only earn a 35% royalty on Amazon Kindle, meaning you only earn about 67¢ per book. But if once the deal is officially over you raise your price to $2.99, you qualify for the 70% royalty rate, and now you're earning a little more than $2 per book. On the bright side, you earn a 70% royalty throughout the deal on non-Amazon channels, such as B&N Nook, Kobo, Google Play, and Apple Books.

A common strategy for self- and traditionally-published authors alike is to run a BookBub Featured Deal about ninety days after a book has debuted. It gets those who became aware of the book, but weren't enticed enough, to finally buy. It's also your best chance besides the launch to make an attempt at a bestseller list.

BookBub Featured New Releases For Less

If you'd like to promote a book you're launching, BookBub has a promotion called "Featured New Releases for Less." I tried this when it was just "Featured New Releases," and I was launching *Mind Management* at $9.99 on Kindle. I found it to be worth it.

I paid $330 for my book to be sent to 600,000 subscribers, and I made $906 royalties across all books on all channels. I sold 68 ebooks and 8 paperbacks of *Mind Management*. My promotion took place one week after my book's launch day, so I was able to see the effects of the promotion pretty well.

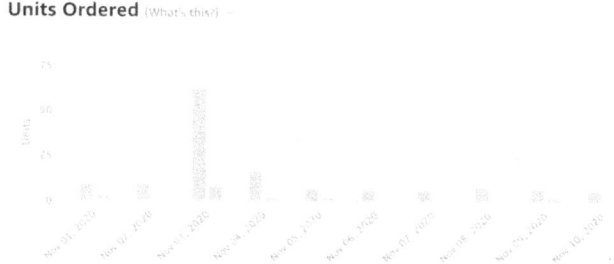

My BookBub Featured New Release led to a spike in sales.

However, when I ran my deal, Featured New Releases were not "For Less." BookBub now recommends your book be priced at $6 or less. I don't think I'll ever price a full-length book that low within the first few months it's out, unless I'm going for a bestseller list, yet I'm not likely to bother attempting to get on a newspaper's bestseller list in future launches.

Amazon Kindle Deals

In some ways, Amazon Kindle Deals are better than BookBub Featured Deals: Your book is promoted directly to Amazon shoppers, Amazon changes the price for you, and you don't even have to pay for the promotion! The catches are, you can't apply to Amazon Kindle Deals, and you can't control what type of deal your book is selected for.

You can't apply to Kindle Deals, but as of recently you can at least let Amazon know you're open to your book being selected for such deals. In the "Marketing" tab of KDP, you can currently nominate up to two titles for Kindle Deals. Each nomination lasts ninety days, and can renew automatically. This is also where you can

Run pricing promotions

nominate a book for a "Prime Reading" promotion, but only books in KDP Select are eligible.

Here is the process a book follows as it is selected, chosen, and promoted for a Kindle Deal.

- Nomination email: This email notifies you that your book has been nominated for a Kindle Deal. It indicates what market your book has been nominated for (such as .com, .co.uk, etc.), and within what dates the promotion would run.
- Accept the nomination: The Nomination email will have a link and a secret code you need to enter within a form on the page to which the link directs. You need to click on the link, copy/paste the code into the form, and submit the form.
- Selection: Sometime from as early as three weeks before the promotion period indicated in the nomination email to days *after* the promotion period has begun, you *might* get an email notifying you that your book has been selected for a deal.
- Discount/Promotion: Provided you don't manually change the price of your book, thus "breaking" the deal, your book's price will be automatically changed and promoted on Amazon.

How long your book is discounted and promoted depends upon the type of deal your book is selected for. Amazon can and will invent and retire various types of deals, but the main types are Kindle Daily Deals and Kindle Monthly Deals. One is of course a deal that lasts a day, and the other lasts a month.

You can't choose which deal your book is chosen for, and you can't gracefully opt-out of the deal once your book has been chosen. I say "gracefully," because, in my experience, if you change the price of your book manually, your book is no longer included in the deal. But I suspect doing this harms your chances of being included in future deals.

Before I get to why I think that, I'll say opinions differ on whether these deals are good, and which deal is better than the other. My first Kindle Deal was a Kindle Daily Deal for *The Heart to Start*.

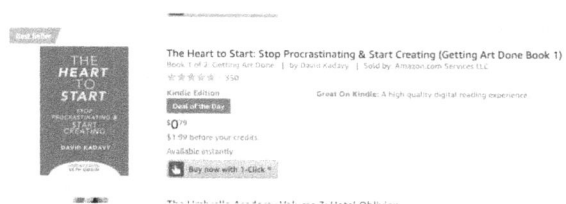

My book was discounted from $9.99 to $1.99. I sold 422 copies. (The previous day I had sold three.) Since being eligible for a Kindle Deal requires being in the 70% royalty plan, I still earned 70% royalties. I earned about $575 from my deal and it cost me nothing and required no work.

I've had Kindle Deals that performed even better. In March of 2022, *Mind Management* was marked down to $2.49 for a Kindle Monthly Deal. I sold 1,700 copies and made over $4,700 in revenue.

Some authors say the Kindle Daily Deals are great, but the Monthly Deals are no good. Some even say the reverse. I say, if your book gets chosen for a Kindle Deal, take it!

Kindle Deal restrictions and conflicts

Some of the restrictions when nominated for a Kindle Deal can be stifling and unrealistic. For example, I've received a Nomination email that gave me a six-month window in which my book might be chosen for a deal. This email also stipulated that to remain eligible

Run pricing promotions

for a deal, my price had to remain the same thirty days before and seven days after the deal. The upshot of this was that I couldn't change my price, in the hopes that *maybe* my book would be chosen for a deal. In my experience, I get notified my book is chosen for a deal no more than three weeks before the deal begins. Three weeks is less than thirty days, so any change in price would supposedly make me ineligible for a potential deal I don't even know about at the time.

The waiting period for hypothetical Kindle Deals caused a big conflict for me, causing me to miss out on a great opportunity. In February of 2023, my book, *Mind Management, Not Time Management* was nominated for a Kindle Deal, which would take place in April. This would have been great, because the first several months of the year is sort of "self-help season." People are motivated by their New Year's resolutions to buy books that help them with those resolutions.

But a few weeks before April, I still hadn't received confirmation my book had been chosen for anything. I had recently had a book included in a Kindle "Big Deal" that did almost nothing for sales, so I was less excited than usual about my book being chosen. I also really wanted to do some kind of pricing promotion within the first quarter, so I decided to apply for a BookBub Featured Deal. I knew from past experience applying didn't guarantee being chosen, anyway. BookBub did, in fact, accept my application! To prepare for the promotion, which would start March 31st, I marked my book down to $1.99.

Then, I received confirmation from Amazon that my book had finally been selected for a Kindle Monthly Deal, only four days before the April 1st–30th deal would start.

What had been a quandary became a pickle. I couldn't run the promotions in parallel, because the prices were different: My deal with BookBub was for $1.99, and my Kindle Monthly Deal was for $4.99. I could ask BookBub to reschedule the deal, but there were no guarantees, and after a month at $4.99, my book would probably have to be at $9.99 for some time before they would run the deal, so there would be a lot of delay for a promotion for which I had already paid $649.

Strangely, I received my confirmation for the Kindle Deal after I had already marked my price down to $1.99. So I had violated the eligibility requirement of not marking down the price within 30 days of the deal. Yet that seemed not to matter.

I tried calling Amazon to see if we could reschedule the Kindle Monthly Deal. I wasn't able to reach anyone who could help me, and was told someone would get back to me, but they never did.

I was disappointed to miss out on the Kindle Monthly Deal. I think having Amazon promoting my book at the $4.99 price point would have been very profitable. I also suspect that botching the deal may have put me on some kind of blacklist, because eighteen months have passed, and *Mind Management* hasn't been nominated for any more Kindle Deals in the U.S.

I did not take the best course of action, but hopefully my mistake will be useful to you. If you're nominated for a Kindle Deal in your main market, just be patient and wait until you're well into the period during which the deal should take place – maybe a week – before you mess with anything or schedule any other deals.

If you do find yourself in a situation where your book is supposed to be included in a Kindle Deal, but you've already changed your price, there is one trick I discovered in this experience that may or may not work for you. After my BookBub deal had passed and I had slowly stepped up my price to take profits on my higher sales rank, while browsing the Kindle Monthly Deals page and beating myself up for not being included, I changed my price back to $9.99 – the price from which my book was supposed to be discounted for the Kindle Deal. That seemed to trigger something within Amazon's system to include my book in the already-scheduled deal! My book suddenly showed up on the Kindle Monthly

Run pricing promotions

Deals page. Sadly, there were only a few days left in the month, so I didn't reap much benefit. I wish I had known sooner!

Part of why I was so hasty in applying for a BookBub Featured Deal was because I had had a reversal of this situation the year prior. A Kindle Deal had ruined my chances for a BookBub Featured Deal. After a March 2022 Kindle Monthly Deal, in which *Mind Management* was marked down to $2.49, and after my price had reverted to $9.99, I applied for a BookBub Featured Deal. They told me my book was accepted, but only internationally, because it had "historically been priced at $2.49."

According to BookBub's published requirements, a deal has to be at least a 50% discount to be eligible. Other than the Kindle Monthly Deal, the only time *Mind Management* had been priced below $3.99 – the point at which $1.99 would have been at least a 50% discount – had been nine months prior, in its previous BookBub Featured Deal. Apparently BookBub has unpublished requirements about the amount of time that needs to elapse within which a book is at least double its deal price.

I declined the international deal, because it would have required me to drop my U.S. royalty rate to 35%, just to meet the price in international markets. Instead, I applied again at least one month after my book had returned to $9.99. By that time, the editors' strategy must have changed, because again I was only selected for an international deal, which I again declined. I had to apply two additional times after that to finally be accepted for the deal. So the deal I had hoped to run in April didn't happen until late July.

As you can see, scheduling pricing promotions and reconciling requirements between Amazon and BookBub is not straightforward. You have to be patient and pay attention to potential conflicts, but it's worth it!

KDP Select pricing promotions

The only deals on Amazon you have complete control over are deals for books enrolled in KDP Select. As I'll talk about later regarding "wide" sales, when you enroll a book in KDP Select, you forfeit the right to distribute your ebook format on any other platform, including your online store, or as a free lead magnet. One feature you get in exchange for this exclusivity is the ability to schedule pricing promotions, in which your book is automatically discounted on the dates you choose. You can even give your book away for free during these promotions.

Because of the exclusivity requirements, I don't have any English-language books in KDP Select, so I don't participate in these promotions. There's not much to say about them other than that, like any pricing promotion, they're an opportunity to get more readers for your books.

* * *

Another great way to get more readers for your books is through influencer marketing.

Chapter 11
Influence influencers to sell your book

If an influencer recommends your book to their audience, some portion of their audience will buy it. So trying to persuade influencers to share your book is an effective way to sell books.

By "influencer," I don't necessarily mean the biggest names you can think of in your space. Nowadays, it seems just about everyone is an influencer to some degree, even if they merely have a few hundred actively engaged followers on social media.

Meet influencers

The more influencers you know personally, the easier it is to get their help when you want to sell a book. If you pitch your book to an influencer you hardly know, the chances they'll help you are very slim. So you should always be networking to some degree, building relationships with people you like and share similar interests with, who happen to also be influencers.

A great way to build relationships with influencers is by having a podcast, which I talked about earlier. Having a podcast is a tremendous amount of work, and only a small portion of your guests will become close enough friends to comfortably ask for help selling your book. But if you spend an hour having a deep conversation with someone, you'll certainly know them better than if you'd just emailed them.

The most important thing about networking with influencers is to network with people who you genuinely like the work of, and who you genuinely like. You can't tell if you're going to hit it off with someone before you meet them, but if you like and are at least interested in and curious about their work, that's a start. Don't try to build a relationship with someone just because they have a big platform. They're harder to reach because of the big platform, and your interactions with them will come off as phony, since they are.

The best way to network will differ based upon your life stage and resources. When I was in my twenties, I greatly reduced the comfort of my lifestyle to move to Silicon Valley. Networking happened naturally in the course of my social life, and those connections still help twenty years later. Over the years, I lived various "mini lives," spending a month at a time in various places, including two separate months in the NYC area. When I moved to South America, I started a podcast. Since I couldn't network much where I lived, I was forced to network worldwide. Now that I don't even run an active podcast and live in a rural area, I make it a point to take a couple trips a year where I can meet people in person. Sometimes I go to conferences, and I even took a special trip to Austin just to meet in person other writers I had interacted with on X.

While actively putting myself in situations where I will meet people is a component of networking, the most important thing about networking is the working. By that I mean putting your head down and doing work others will respect. Doors open when someone admires or has at least heard of your work. Even if they haven't heard of your work but they look at your online presence and see that you've created *something* – an app, an organization, a book, or even just an active blog – strangers who have also created things will be more interested in meeting you. The work is the work. The best way to "network" is put your work on the 'net.

Because I was born and raised in Nebraska with no creative professionals around me, nobody I met before the age of twenty-six, when I moved to Silicon Valley, has been instrumental in helping me sell books in the past decade-plus, and arguably, ever. But now I have a pretty great network that does help. I built that network from scratch by repeatedly putting myself in the right place, being genuinely interested in the work of others, and trying to do genuine and high-quality work myself. Those three things are the best you can do.

Give books to influencers

The first marketing dollars you should spend, even before running ads, should be put toward giving away copies of your book to people who might like it, and might recommend it to others. Whether it's worth giving your book to someone is a combination of the size of their audience and the likelihood of them telling others. If you have a friend with a book club of five people in your genre, give them a book! If you know an influencer with a million followers who isn't likely to recommend your book, might as well try!

Giving your book away is some of the most effective marketing dollars you can spend, because you can do it for cheap or even free. You can email a link to your ebook, or gift it with BookFunnel, and that costs you nothing. Or, you can buy "author copies" of hardcopy books at cost through Amazon KDP, and ship for cheap.

Whether you send ebook or hard copy will be a judgment call. If someone is willing to receive a hard copy and I can afford to send it, I will send a hard copy. A physical book has more presence and feels more like a gift. It's less likely to get lost in the shuffle.

When I do a big book, I make a spreadsheet in an app called

How to Sell a Book

Airtable (you could also use Excel or Google Sheets). I list everyone I know with an audience who might like a book, as well as some people I don't know. I divide them up by what phases of the project I'd want to send them a book, and apply tags for categories of things I'd hope to happen by sending them a book.

The project phases I used when sending *Mind Management* to influencers were: Preview Edition, First Edition Galley, First Edition, or just a Pitch Sheet (a one-page summary of what the book is about and its main points). By dividing by phases, I manage my workload, and make sure what I'm sending them is appropriate for the relationship. For example, if I barely know a big influencer who I know to be very busy, I'm more likely to send them a Pitch Sheet, offering to send a hard copy if they like.

The categories of things I hoped to get from influencers, which I recorded in my spreadsheet when sending *Mind Management*, were:

- Blurb: I want them to write a blurb for the book.
- Podcast: I want to be on their podcast.
- Media: I want more general media coverage, such as an article, or newsletter mention.
- Review: I want them to write a review of my book, for example, on Amazon.
- Wildcard: I don't know what would come of sending them a book, but have a gut feeling it could be good.
- Thanks: They helped me with the book enough that I just want to say thanks by sending them a copy.

Here's an actual email I sent to an influencer I know pretty well, who ended up writing me a blurb:

Hey [name]! Hope you're doing well – I assume you're still in [location]?

Influence influencers to sell your book

> My new book, *Mind Management, Not Time Management* [linked to Amazon page], comes out soon. You might dig it. It shows how to manage energy as a resource, to be more productive when creativity matters.
> Can I send you a copy? If you like it, it would be an honor to have a blurb from you gracing the pages.
> Let me know where to send (ebook available too)

And here's an email I sent to an influencer I hardly knew, which resulted in them writing an article about my book:

> Hey [name],
> Would you mind if I sent you a copy of Mind Management, Not Time Management? No obligation to do anything with it – it just seems up your alley.

Yes, that's it! Notice it's very low-pressure. I can't say this is the most-effective way to offer to send a book. Calls-to-action work in advertising, and they'd probably work one-on-one. But I personally hate being pressured to do things, so my strategy is simply to let people know about my book, and if they like it, that's great.

I also make a note in my spreadsheet about whether the influencer is mentioned in the book, and if so, where. This can be a marketing strategy to integrate into writing your book. I've known some authors who deliberately made sure to mention all their friends in their books, not only because friends are a good source of stories, but because then those friends felt even more motivated to share their books.

As I'm notifying influencers of my book, I keep track in the spreadsheet the status of the attempt:

- Pitched: I've pitched an offer to send them a book.

- Followed up: After not hearing back, I've sent a follow-up.
- Ready: They've accepted, and I've put their address information in the sheet. A book can be sent.
- Sent: The book has been sent.
- Received: They've received the book.
- Success: They've done something to promote my book.
- Failure: They haven't done anything to promote my book (admittedly, it's difficult to know how much time has to pass before marking this).

Be ready to send out a lot of books that don't result in anything. In promoting *Mind Management*, I had a list of 130 contacts. I marked 22 of my attempts as "Success," after sending out nearly 100 books, for a cost of $818 (retail value about $2,000). Unfortunately, I either didn't pitch or failed to follow up with about 30 contacts – I'm not perfect!

Give books to strangers (who might be influencers)

Paul Millerd, author of *The Pathless Path,* has a remarkable way of getting his book into the hands of readers, who might be influencers. He simply leaves his book in public places, where people can take them for free. For example, here are some books he left on the riverwalk in Austin.

Influence influencers to sell your book

Paul Millerd has left his book, free for the taking, in various public places. Photo copyright Paul Millerd. Used with permission.

He's also left books on tables in the communal areas of various conferences and in neighborhood book-exchange boxes. I wasn't sure where in this book to include this cool marketing strategy, but Paul lives in Austin, where there's a high likelihood his books will be found by some influencer. Still, he leaves books for people to take in various places such as public parks when he travels. He told me he's used this guerrilla gifting tactic to give away at least 1,000 books.

Paul explained, "When I launched the book, I didn't have grand ambitions. I was hoping to merely break even. As part of that plan, I decided that if I earned a profit I would buy books and gift them to people."

What's pure generosity on the part of Paul is also likely an effective marketing tactic. Gifting books has helped *The Pathless Path* sell more than 50,000 copies.

Make micro-influencers out of those who take action

In 2015, I was at a party at my friend Nick Gray's apartment, and he politely asked me to leave. I hadn't done anything wrong, it was just the party had abruptly ended.

In 2022, Nick launched his book, *The 2-Hour Cocktail Party*, wherein he introduced the party blueprint I had experienced in its infancy: A short gathering, with name tags and icebreakers, designed to maximize social connections, while minimizing burdens on the host.

To promote his book, Nick set a goal to get his readers to throw 500 parties. Each time a reader reported they had thrown a party, he numbered and documented it on social media and his website, along with a photo of the party. He essentially created micro-influencers who, by taking action, helped his book spread.

Nick explained to me, "It's one thing to get someone to buy a book, and another to read it and leave a review, but your goal as an author should be to get them to take action. Setting a goal to catalyze 500 parties gave me a larger purpose and a reason to talk about something bigger than myself."

Influence influencers to sell your book

Nick blew past his initial goal of 500 parties, and is now reaching for 1,000.

Pay influencers to promote your book

If you can't get your influencer friends to recommend your book, you can straight-up pay influencers to do so. I've found this to be a profitable way of selling books!

On Instagram, for example, there are many accounts on the "bookstagram" hashtag which share nothing but books. They share photos of covers and highlights, and video reels reviewing these books. Much of the time, they're sharing these because they've been paid.

I suspect that even more often, they're sharing these books for free. When they do so, they're usually sharing books that are already popular. Someone running a bookstagram account for the Business and Self-Help genres better have shared *Atomic Habits*, 7

How to Sell a Book

Habits of Highly Effective People, and *How to Win Friends and Influence People.*

Why? Because other bookstagram accounts have shared them. So by paying bookstagrammers to share your books, your book could potentially become one of the popular books other accounts feel obliged to share for free.

However, this process is not foolproof. First of all, a bookstagrammer sharing your book will only lead to sales if you have a compelling title, cover, and highlights for them to share, and if the book appeals to that bookstagrammer's particular audience. Additionally, any self-respecting bookstagrammer will only share quality books they feel confident will lead to engagement – people commenting on and sharing their posts or reels. After all, sharing books their followers actually engage with is their bread and butter. Finally, because being a bookstagrammer appears to be a low-effort way to build a social media page and make some money, there are tons of bookstagrammer accounts. Some are poorly-run, and others are committing outright fraud. All of the above likely applies to book influencers on platforms other than Instagram.

Like running ads, paying influencers to share your book is an investment in your education. You likely won't get it right the first time, but with some patience and money, you'll make profits on your campaigns.

To learn how to run effective paid influencer marketing campaigns, you need to keep records you can learn from. I keep an Airtable spreadsheet of bookstagrammers and my paid campaigns with them. On one sheet, I've recorded various accounts and their follower counts. I've direct-messaged them individually to find out what packages they offer, their rates, and to receive a screenshot of their accounts' reach over the previous thirty days. (This is one benefit of using Airtable: You can save images within your spreadsheets. Technically they call their sheets "bases.")

On another sheet, I record each campaign I run. I name the

Influence influencers to sell your book

campaign, indicate which influencer ran the campaign, and record the price and number of followers the influencer had when the campaign began. A couple weeks after the campaign, I ask the influencer to share a screenshot of the "post insights," so I can see how many accounts it reached and how many comments, shares, and bookmarks it received. I've tried not to overlap my campaigns with other marketing efforts, so I can watch my sales and attribute any spikes to the campaign. I record in the sheet my subjective opinion about how the campaign went: Great, Good, or Bad.

My budgets have ranged from $30 with a bookstagrammer with 123,000 followers, to $2,000 for a campaign across Instagram, Twitter, and TikTok for a total of 735,000 followers. I rated the former campaign as "Bad," and the latter as "Good." My best campaign was a $500 campaign for a bookstagrammer with 944,000 followers. The post went viral and reached nearly one-million accounts. Campaigns often involve multiple posts and post types. For example, I paid $150 to a bookstagrammer with 105,000 followers for an unboxing story, a post, two reels that included other books, and a photo post that also included other books.

In the month before my best campaign, *Mind Management* earned $2,848 on Amazon. In the month after that $500 campaign, it earned $3,983, with a big spike corresponding with the campaign.

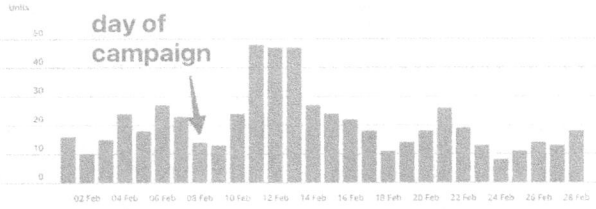

This influencer campaign doubled sales. Notice the spike happened a few days later. The post needed time to spread and paperback books had to be printed.

How to Sell a Book

For being my best campaign, that's not a huge direct profit. Influencer campaigns in my experience take time to reap benefits. Other accounts re-share the posts, or decide to share the book, too. People bookmark the posts and only get around to buying the book much later. I've also found that many of the accounts I've paid for promotion have started sharing my books in regular rotation, without further payment. Don't expect to make a big profit straight away with influencer campaigns. Also keep in mind that the audiences of bookstagrammers prefer hard-copy books. It takes a couple days for hard-copy sales to register in your KDP dashboard, as they're only counted once the book is printed and shipped.

I don't recommend revenue-sharing campaigns. I've done some campaigns based upon a share of revenue of book sales within some period, such as 50% of profits after ad spend for one week after the post (promising not to change anything about my ad spend). The revenue-sharing campaigns I tried didn't turn out to be worthwhile for the influencer, and tracking the revenue is difficult. It's downright impossible if your hard copy is fulfilled through IngramSpark (IS), as one sale on Amazon does not equal one sale in your IS dashboard. Amazon re-stocks books periodically, so you could sell a hundred books which end up fulfilled through Amazon's warehouse and aren't reflected on IS. Or you could sell five books, depleting Amazon's stock and causing them to re-stock with, say, a hundred books, which is then reflected on IS despite not being driven by the campaign.

If you choose to pay bookstagrammers to share your book, be prepared to get a lot of incoming messages from other bookstagrammers, eager to also share your book for payment. They apparently look to other accounts to see who to pitch and, who knows, maybe there's a secret underworld where they share client information. Almost all these pitches are not worth paying attention to. They're from either small and poorly-run accounts, or accounts with lots of fake followers and even fake engagement.

Influence influencers to sell your book

Whether you're responding to a pitch or evaluating a bookstagram account you've found on your own, don't evaluate based on follower count alone. Ask yourself if the influencer's content is genuine and unique. Look at the likes and comments on their posts. Do they look real, or fake? Are they by real people who you could see being interested in your book?

A ton of bookstagram accounts are based in India. I don't know why. Most of them are terrible accounts, but some of them are great. But keep in mind an India-based account will likely have lots of followers in India. Depending upon your book, that can be a good thing or a bad thing. *Mind Management* is being translated into many languages on the Indian subcontinent, and I think my influencer marketing has helped make that happen. On the other hand, some book ideas are compelling to an American audience but not an Indian one. This of course goes for wherever the account is based.

There is no standard cost-per-followers or -impression. I've paid $1.17 per thousand followers on a campaign that went horribly, and $17 per thousand on one that went at least okay. Whether doing a campaign with an account will sell your book profitably depends upon a lot of factors. The best way to learn is by doing.

Be a guest on podcasts

Being a guest on a podcast is a great way to sell books. The audience is highly-engaged and trusts the host to have worthwhile guests. But, getting onto podcasts that are worth getting on is not easy.

Some hosts are not as particular as I was about who they have as guests. I think the litmus test for lower selectivity is, Does the podcast have advertising? If an interview podcast has advertising and releases on a regular schedule, the host is obliged to find new people to interview, whether they are interested in and familiar with guests' work or not. They have ad slots to fill, and they'll make money by interviewing you. That doesn't mean getting on their show is a sure thing. If they've built a popular enough podcast to make money on advertising, they must've done something to ensure they've had quality guests.

I know from being a podcast host that hosts are bombarded with irrelevant pitches from authors, and PR agents who are focused on volume. Out of hundreds of pitches I've received, I've accepted and interviewed the guests in approximately two or three of those pitches. Usually that's been because the guest has been someone whose work I've already liked. I can only think of one time I've accepted a pitch for a guest I've previously known nothing about.

I have never hired anyone to pitch me as a podcast guest, and since I've rarely accepted these pitches, I can't recommend you do, either. Even as I write this, nearly a year after I stopped podcasting, and four years after I regularly had guests, I regularly receive pitches to have guests on my podcast. None of these pitches acknowledge that I no longer have guests nor publish new episodes, and few messages show any sign of being customized for me and what my show is about. It doesn't take much thought to see that businesses promising to get you on podcasts are probably usually scams. They blanket pitch clients as a guest to a bunch of podcasts, and tell the client they've been pitched to however many hundreds of podcasts. Clients of these podcast-booking businesses are paying to be pitched for my podcast, which isn't even active! They must get some interviews out of this spray-and-pray approach, but I doubt they're for good shows. Being on a podcast doesn't guarantee book sales, anyway. If a host isn't really into a guest's work, I believe it shows, and listeners won't be convinced to buy the guest's book.

This isn't to say you should never pitch yourself to be on podcasts, or even hire anyone to send messages on your behalf. But you'll have better chances of getting on better podcasts that

Influence influencers to sell your book

actually lead to sales if you put some care into your pitches. When you pitch yourself as a guest, you're essentially producing an episode for *that show*. So know what the show is about, what prior relevant topics the show has covered, and the general format of conversations on the show. Sell your proposed appearance to the host with a juicy topic and talking points that are right for their show.

Here's an actual email that landed me an interview with a big podcast:

> Subject: Aspiration procrastination
>
> Hey [hostname],
>
> Not sure if this resonates with you since starting a podcast and leaving a prestigious profession such as [profession] seemed to come naturally to you.
>
> But I bet a ton of your listeners dream of starting creative projects, and keep putting it off. Things like writing books, starting companies or podcasts – even traveling.
>
> I'd love to come on the show and help them finally get started. Here's how that might look:
>
> - **What is "aspiration procrastination?"** It makes sense we put off things like taking out the trash or going to the dentist, but all too often we put off our hopes and dreams.
> - **Why is "just get started" bad advice?** It's about as useful as "just put yourself out there" to be good at networking, or "just grow taller" to be better at basketball. [Examples taken directly from one of the host's prior episodes]
> - **What is the source of aspiration procrastination?** There's a fascinating psychology concept called "self-discrepancy theory" that breaks it

down into conflicts amongst the three domains of the self.
- **How can you stop putting off your aspirations?** You can strengthen or weaken facets of your self concept to overcome these conflicts, and finally take action.

The Heart To Start: Win the Inner War & Let Your Art Shine
› David Kadavy
☆☆☆☆☆ 158
#1 Best Seller in

My latest book, *The Heart to Start* [linked], was recently endorsed by Seth Godin (happy to send you a copy). But, this psychology-heavy pitch is the underwater part of the *Heart to Start* iceberg. I think your audience would dig it.

I could do this discussion over the Internet, or travel to you.

Does that sound like a good fit?

P.S. You can hear my guest-ing chops on Jeff Goins's The Portfolio Life [linked], and The Creative Penn [linked].

Notice that I start off immediately by relating to the host, and how this content may or may not be relevant to them. I really wasn't sure whether this content would be relevant to the host, and I expressed that, which turned out to be a subtle compliment. But I

Influence influencers to sell your book

thought their listeners would benefit, and I explained why. Then, like a book's sales blurb, I presented a bullet-point list of teaser/mechanism.

This pitch is heavy on psychology-related content, because many of the episodes of this podcast talked in-depth about psychology-related concepts. So I crafted this pitch especially for this podcast. I essentially produced an episode for them.

I'm reluctant to share this pitch with you, because, while I did land an interview, the podcast never ran the episode. It was a really disappointing career burn, because I put a ton of work into preparing for the interview, and traveled internationally on my own expense to do the interview in-person. But in the end the episode and/or my delivery of the concepts were not right for the show. The show didn't get as big as it was by running just any episode. I took the risk I did *because* it was a big show.

I think my mistake was trying to produce an episode about concepts that were only obliquely related to the book, rather than just talking about what's in the book. I think I had some impostor syndrome, perhaps because I and my book were ultimately not right for this show.

But I decided to share this pitch because it is still what I think is the best format for pitching to a podcast.

Here's another pitch, for a self-publishing focused podcast, and this episode did run:

> I'm a long-time listener to the show. It has really helped me as I've self-published my first book (after launching a traditionally-published book in the top 20 on all of Amazon).
>
> I just launched *The Heart to Start* [linked], and would be honored to chat on your show about overcoming self-doubt, perfectionism, and distractions to make one's work real.
>
> For example, I learned the art of "Motivational Judo" from the research of my former colleague, behavioral scientist Dan Ariely.

How to Sell a Book

Are you up for it?

Not to be presumptuous, but I've attached a PDF of the book. I know what it's like to get a ton of guest pitches, so no response expected if it's not a fit.

This is shorter than the above in part because of my intuitions about the amount of preparation the host did for their episodes. The prior pitch was for a podcast that was heavily-produced almost to the point of being scripted. This pitch was for a podcast I could tell had the more common casual preparation. So, instead of a bullet-point list, I kept what I envisioned talking about on the show to a couple short sentences

When I launched my second major self-published book, I already had relationships with several podcast hosts, so my pitches were more familiar and casual. For example:

Can I send you a galley of my upcoming book, *Mind Management, Not Time Management?*

Instead of trying to eke an extra bit of productivity out of our time, this book is about managing your creative energy to have better ideas, and turn those ideas into reality. In particular, it has a lot about how managing creative energy makes the writing process go more smoothly, even when the chaos of life gets in the way.

Mind Managment [sic], *Not Time Management* also chronicles my decade-long journey in optimizing my creative output. A journey that, as you know, led me all the way to South America.

If you like it, I'd love to chat with you about it on the podcast. My launch date is October 27th, which may be cutting it close in your production schedule, but I'd of course be willing anytime.

If you're interested in reading it, let me know where I can send the Preview Edition galley.

Congratulations on 500 episodes!

Influence influencers to sell your book

Embarrassingly, I misspelled my own book's title. I didn't even notice until editing this chapter. This drives home the point that the relationship is what matters.

Notice that I said my October 27th launch date might be cutting it close for this host. I sent my pitch on August 10th, about ten weeks before launch. I prefer launching fast over launching "right," but if you want to coordinate podcast episode debuts with your launch date, it's best to allow three to six months for hosts to respond to your pitch, read your book, conduct your interview, and work your episode into their publishing schedule. Many podcast hosts work faster than that, so if you aren't picky about the publish date of the episode, most of your episodes will go live faster.

Having a podcast yourself is a big advantage when trying to land podcast interviews. First, it helps you understand the motivations of other podcast hosts. You have some idea how many pitches they get, and you know what it's like to consider a guest. Second, it means you have experience producing episodes. You know the difference between a boring and interesting guest, and a boring and interesting topic. Third, it means you can return the favor.

The ability to do a "podcast swap," that is, have someone on your podcast in exchange for being on their podcast, is a double-edged sword. It gives you something to offer hosts of podcasts you want to be on. But it also means you'll get offers to swap from hosts whose work you're unfamiliar with or not interested in. If you're serious about running a good podcast and interviewing guests you're interested in, this can create some uncomfortable conversations.

The podcast swap is practically an industry standard. It really is a good way to grow your podcast, since podcast listeners listen to podcasts, but are hard to reach. But the whole thing makes me cringe. I think it really reduces the quality of a podcast if not done selectively.

While you may not want to interview every podcast host, I

personally don't think there's harm in being on any podcast whose host wants to interview you. If you're incredibly successful and in-demand you may have to be more selective about how you use your time, but 100,000 book sales in, I'm nowhere near that stature. My personal policy is, I'll be on any podcast with a genuine host who is interested in my work and doesn't expect anything in return (though I do promote every episode on various channels). I define "podcast" as a show that's available in Apple Podcasts. If it's only on SoundCloud or YouTube, it's not a podcast.

The reason I'll be on any podcast with a genuinely-interested host is not because I think it will sell books, but because I view it as part of my writing process. I'll take every opportunity to talk about my ideas in a free-form conversation, because it helps me talk about my ideas more crisply, and often helps me discover new ideas or things I can teach. In fact, I started writing this book because a podcast host asked how I had sold 100,000 self-published books. Anyway, what author isn't thrilled to talk with someone genuinely interested in their ideas?

If you have a podcast or are interviewed on podcasts, try listening to your episodes with a critical ear. Then compare to episodes of your favorite popular podcasts. Ask yourself honestly if the popular podcasts are more interesting to listen to than the episodes you're on. Through lots of repetition, you can be a more interesting and engaging guest. Part of it comes from being able to speak more fluidly and rhythmically. Part of it comes from knowing your material better.

You can even try writing out responses to questions you antici-pate being asked (some hosts will even ask you questions you provide). You can rehearse your responses and record your rehearsal to listen to over and over. This can make you a more engaging guest, so long as you don't overdo your rehearsal. You have to straddle a line between knowing exactly what you'll say and improvising in the moment. I find there's no substitute for having

Influence influencers to sell your book

written and thought about your subject matter from every possible angle.

In summary, I've never actively pitched a large amount of podcasts. Doing so can be a lot of work with little reward. Instead I choose to build relationships with podcast hosts over time, and talk to hosts interested in my ideas. Podcasts help sell books, but it's by no means necessary to be on a lot of podcasts to sell a respectable number of books.

Be on enough podcasts, and it will seem as if you're everywhere. But to make your books available everywhere, you have to go "wide."

Chapter 12
Go "wide" (or don't)

A dilemma top-of-mind in the world of self-publishing is, "Wide," or Kindle Unlimited? Your response to this dilemma will dictate trade-offs amongst how many books you'll sell, how much money you'll make, how much work you'll do, and how secure your business as an author will be.

To describe this dilemma in short for the unfamiliar, Kindle Unlimited is the consumer side of "KDP Select." As I talked about earlier regarding pricing promotions, when your book is enrolled in KDP Select, you can schedule pricing promotions, including giving your books away for free. The major feature of enrolling in KDP Select is it makes your book available in Kindle Unlimited (KU), so readers who pay Amazon a monthly fee can "borrow" your book and read it for no additional cost. Instead of being paid by the purchase, you're paid by the page read. This likely boosts your book in Amazon's search algorithms. When your book is in KDP Select, you can also earn a 70% royalty in markets in which other authors can only earn 35% (pricing restrictions still apply). Some current examples are Japan and Brazil.

While there are many benefits to being enrolled in KDP Select, there is one major catch: It requires you to make your ebook exclusive to Amazon. You cannot sell your ebook on any other stores,

Go "wide" (or don't)

such as Kobo, or Barnes & Noble's Nook. You cannot sell your ebook directly to readers on your website. You cannot make your ebook available for checkout at libraries. You can't even give your ebook away for free. Essentially, the rights to distribute your ebook are no longer yours while it's enrolled in KDP Select. They're Amazon's.

If you instead choose to be "wide," you will not enroll your ebook in KDP Select. Readers will have to buy your ebook to read it, any pricing promotions you run will require you to change your price manually, you won't be eligible for the 70% royalty in those other markets, and you won't get whatever boost there might be in Amazon's search algorithms. But, you'll still own the rights to distribute your ebook, and can sell it on any online store, including your own.

Part of what makes this dilemma agonizing is that Amazon is so dominant in the ebook market. I've been wide for almost the entire seven years I've been self-publishing, and 80% of *Mind Management, Not Time Management*'s ebook revenue has been from Amazon. For my first self-published book, the share is even larger: Kindle sales for *The Heart to Start* make up 98% of the ebook's revenue.

To get that 20% and 2% from other revenue sources, I've had to upload, keep updated, and market my books on dozens of other platforms. In recent years I've even built and started running my own online store. Meanwhile, I've had to forego what benefits I might've gotten by enrolling in KDP Select, which very well might have made up for the "wide" portion of my revenue. For *The Heart to Start*, that's almost certainly the case.

There are three main reasons I do all that extra work for arguably no extra money: legitimacy, morality, and security. Legitimacy: Having a "Kindle Unlimited" logo next to your book cover just screams self-published. There's nothing inherently wrong with that, but I enjoy the challenge of trying to make my self-published books traditionally-published quality in any way I can. One of those ways is by having it available in as many places as possible.

Morality: Letting Amazon have that much control over the ebook market is just wrong. I'm not an Amazon hater. I love Amazon, in fact, and they're responsible for making opportunities available to self-published authors that wouldn't exist otherwise. But if authors surrender power to Amazon, they'll have even more power. I want readers to have as many choices as possible for how they read my books. To enroll my books in KDP Select would be to give up on that goal.

Security: My business is more secure if I'm selling ebooks through many channels. The ebook market changes, and will continue to change. Part of the discrepancy between wide revenue of *Mind Management* and *The Heart to Start* is due to that change over the years. So far this year, *The Heart to Start*'s wide revenue is 7%, leaps and bounds above its lifetime share of 2%. Even Jeff Bezos has said, "Amazon will be disrupted one day." When that happens, KDP Select authors can certainly start offering their ebooks on other stores, but I'd rather have the wide reader-base and experience of marketing my ebooks on other platforms already in place. Even if Amazon remains dominant for the rest of my career, I don't want such a large share of my revenue coming from one place. My KDP account could become erroneously suspended for reasons beyond my control, and I would suddenly be in a desperate situation.

In sum, I'm wide because it feels like the right thing to do, as a full-time author I have the bandwidth to handle it, and while it doesn't make financial sense in the short term it probably makes financial sense in the long-term.

It's possible that being wide may actually make financial sense in the short-term, too: I can't prove but still believe the availability of my books in places other than Amazon helps me get BookBub Featured Deals. Even if that weren't so, a Featured Deal costs just

Go "wide" (or don't)

as much whether you're running it just for Amazon, or also including other retailers. Revenue from non-Amazon ebook retailers made up 27% of my revenue from my latest Featured Deal. Maybe a small number of those readers who buy on other platforms would buy on Amazon were it not available elsewhere. But I'd arguably be throwing away a quarter of my money every time I ran a BookBub Featured Deal, were I enrolled in KDP Select.

Whether publishing wide makes financial sense to you depends upon what genre you're writing in and how much time you have. There are some genres in which having your ebook available in Kindle Unlimited is practically necessary for success. I've heard this is true for romance, for example, as there are readers who read a few romance novels a week. They've already paid for KU, so if they can't borrow your book for free, they won't bother.

If you're building an author business on the side of your day job, or are otherwise very pressed for time, it can also make financial sense to enroll your ebooks in KDP Select. Publishing on Kindle and making these ebooks available in Kindle Unlimited is the best return-on-investment for your time in the publishing business. If you have no plans to go full-time, it's probably the way to go. If you do have plans to go full-time, the downside is that it takes years of publishing wide to build up significant revenue, as evinced by the bigger share of wide revenue for *Mind Management*, and the rising share of wide *The Heart to Start* revenue. So if and when you make the switch to wide, the high share of Amazon revenue will leave you still vulnerable should your account be suspended or otherwise perform poorly.

"Wide" or Kindle Unlimited? is not a decision you have to make all at once. When you enroll an ebook in KDP Select, you don't have to stay exclusive forever. In fact, the term is only ninety days. When I first launched *The Heart to Start*, it was enrolled in KDP Select for a ninety-day term. This enabled me to offer the ebook in a free promotion, to get early readers. Once the free promotion was over, many readers borrowed my ebook through Kindle Unlimited, and now, seven years later, I still occasionally get paid for page reads from those borrows. (Those who borrow during your ebook's term in KDP Select can read as long as they have a membership.)

Because KDP Select enrollment periods are only ninety days, KDP Select can be a part of your launch strategy. For example, you could enroll your ebook in KDP Select for its first ninety days, to get the benefits of scheduled pricing promotions, the algorithm boost, and the higher royalty-rate eligibility in select markets. Once your term expired, you could then publish your ebook wide, including on your own website. This is what I did with *The Heart to Start*. Also, it's worth noting a 7% portion of that 20% of revenue from wide sales for *Mind Management* I earned through a "Preview Edition," available before the Kindle edition was released (more on that in a bit). So in reality, only about 13% of my *Mind Management* ebook revenue came from wide sales that occurred while KDP Select was even an option.

While it may make sense to enroll books in KDP Select for their first ninety days, I don't think it's a good strategy to go back-and-forth between KDP Select and wide. Publishing wide is a long-term strategy. Especially don't "try" wide for ninety days then give up just because you aren't seeing sales. Give up if it's too much work for your available time, but keep in mind it takes years to build wide revenue.

It's also very important to keep in mind that *KDP Select's exclusivity only applies to your ebook edition*. I repeat: *KDP Select's exclusivity only applies to your ebook edition!* So some authors offer their ebooks on KDP Select, but have their hard-copy books available everywhere, including on their own online stores. 20% of my *Mind Management* units sold are hard-copy books, with about the same total revenue of the 56% of units sold in ebooks (audiobooks

Go "wide" (or don't)

make up 24% of my units sold). Certainly having your ebook available on other platforms drives hard-copy sales, but at least any customers who don't want to buy on Amazon can do so elsewhere, so long as they buy a hard-copy book.

Wide ebook marketing

As I've said, it takes years to build ebook revenue outside of Kindle. It will take fewer years if you put some effort into marketing your ebooks on other retailers. The top wide ebook retailers in the U.S. are Apple Books, Google Play, Kobo, and Barnes & Noble. For me, they're in approximately that order, with Apple Books a distant second to Kindle and the remaining three trading positions. Kobo is bigger in Canada than the U.S., and there is a smattering of many other ebook platforms throughout the world.

None of these other ebook retailers have an ebooks-native ad platform like Amazon does. Google obviously has an ad platform, but surprisingly they don't have a way to advertise your ebooks. So your options for advertising your wide ebooks mostly consist of advertising methods I've already mentioned: BookBub Ads, Meta Ads, and BookBub Featured Deals.

It intuitively seems a good way to market wide ebooks would be to discount your ebook on one platform at a time, and try to get people to buy on each, but Amazon will almost certainly price-match, and the others may, too. Technically, that doesn't stop you from announcing that, "My book is only $1.99 on Google Play!" But it will also be $1.99 on Kindle.

Most of my wide sales have been generated by BookBub Featured Deals and/or BookBub Ads. I say and/or because I often run BookBub Ads to wide platforms to supplement a Featured Deal, and sometimes run them even when I don't have a Featured Deal.

When you have a discount that puts you in the 35% royalty

bracket for Amazon, it's easier to run BookBub Ads profitably on the other platforms, because the other platforms still give you 70%. So while Amazon is only giving you about 70¢ for your $1.99 ebook, Apple is giving you close to $1.40. You'd think this would cause a huge discrepancy in the cost of generating a click on Apple over Amazon, but, based upon a quick glance of my past ads, that doesn't seem to be the case.

There's certainly lower volume, however, on wide platforms. So setting up an ad is the same amount of work with lower potential payoff. You also get less data to make a confident judgment on whether you're targeting the right authors. The lower volume can make advertising to wide platforms feel like a futile effort, but if you're committed to being wide in the long-term, sales will grow.

Don't fall into the trap of thinking wide ebook readers are the same as Kindle readers. They read on a different e-reader because they're different people with different motivations, and the entire ecosystem in which they shop for ebooks is different. For example, you may find that Kindle readers respond well to your ads when targeting readers of a particular author, but Apple Books readers do not. Maybe that author only offers their books in Kindle Unlimited, and that's why. Conversely, you'll find authors who apparently focus their efforts on Apple Books, and by targeting their readers on that platform, you can get much cheaper clicks than when targeting their readers on Kindle.

Like everything in this jungle that is self-publishing, you have to experiment to see what works. Fortunately you don't have to risk eating any potentially-poisonous plants. You just need money to experiment with.

Thinking about how to sell a book on four platforms other than Kindle can be overwhelming, so concentrate on one at a time, or just one. Browse the store, and see what it's like to be a reader on that platform. Buy an ebook or two. Think about how the experience is different from buying on Kindle, and you'll get some ideas.

Go "wide" (or don't)

You can also experiment with Meta Ads targeting readers of a particular store. You can target by interest, choosing the particular e-reader, but supposedly Meta's automatic targeting is so sophisticated it knows who to target based upon the link to your ebook. Adding a logo for the store to your image would probably help as well.

As with advertising Kindle ebooks on ad platforms outside of Amazon Ads, it's difficult to know whether your ads for wide ebooks are leading to sales. Part of the beauty of having almost no wide sales, though, is that if you have some wide sales, they probably came from your ads! So measuring the effectiveness of your ads can be as simple as looking at how much you spent in a given week, compared to how much you sold on that platform that week. Probably some extra sales will trickle in weeks after you've run your ads, so if you're breaking even, you're doing pretty well, especially if you're just building up your wide sales.

By far the easiest way to get wide ebook readers is to "simply" do BookBub Featured Deals. Having your book accepted for a deal is the hard part, but then BookBub does the rest. During a Featured Deal is also the best time to run ads on BookBub or Meta. Your ads will be far more effective if you're advertising a discount, and even more effective if you advertise that the discount is ending soon. (Amazon won't allow you to mention in your ads a discount or when it ends.)

Kobo promotes authors' ebooks through promotions. You have to contact their support team to get a "Promotions" tab in your Kobo Writing Life dashboard. Then, you can browse promotions and apply to them. If they select you, they promote your ebook. Sometimes there is a cost to the promotion, which may be a share of revenue generated.

Kobo's Promotions are only available if you publish your ebook directly through Kobo Writing Life, rather than through an aggregator. I pulled *The Heart to Start* from an aggregator to publish it directly to Kobo for over a year, and despite applying numerous times for promotions, was never accepted. I ended up switching back to an aggregator.

Aggregators make wide easy

To me, the biggest question in the "Wide" or Kindle Unlimited dilemma is not, Where will I make more money? It's, Do I have the time and energy to deal with this?

Aside from the three ebook retailers outside of Amazon that I mentioned above, there are dozens more where you could potentially make sales. That means there are dozens of places you could have to manage your ebooks and pay attention to your sales. So every time you correct errata and re-upload your book, or add a book to your "Also by [author name]" page and re-upload your book, you could potentially do that on dozens of ebook retailers. That's dozens of usernames and passwords to keep track of, and potentially dozens of CAPTCHAs to complete and two-factor authentication codes to retrieve, each so you can make a few extra bucks each month, if anything. And to find out whether you'd made anything, or nothing, you'd have to log in to each, individually.

This is why aggregators are a powerful if not totally necessary tool in the arsenal of the wide author. You upload your ebook once to an aggregator, and it publishes on dozens of retailers. You can log in once to an aggregator, and see your sales numbers for all those retailers.

The most popular aggregators are PublishDrive and Draft2Digital. They make money for their services by either charging you a monthly fee, or taking a share of your revenue. At the time of this writing, PublishDrive charges based upon the number of books you have – $25 billed monthly for up to six books,

Go "wide" (or don't)

for example. Draft2Digital charges 10% of your sales, based not upon your earnings but the *retail price* of your ebook.

If you're just starting to sell wide, being charged a percentage of your sale price probably sounds more enticing than a monthly fee, but it's worth thinking long-term about the implications of that. Ideally, you could start on Draft2Digital and switch over to PublishDrive once you started regularly making more than $250 a month. That's about what I did, though I'm grandfathered into a discontinued revenue-share plan with PublishDrive, and some of the books I switched from directly publishing to retailers.

The biggest drawback of changing aggregators, or switching between publishing directly to publishing through an aggregator, is you will lose all your reviews on some platforms and have to start over. Currently, PublishDrive says you can transfer reviews for Kobo, Barnes & Noble, and Amazon – though I wouldn't recommend publishing to Amazon through an aggregator. When I switched from publishing through Draft2Digital and directly to retailers to publishing through PublishDrive, I lost all my Apple Books and Google Play reviews, but was able to transfer my Kobo reviews (I didn't have any Barnes & Noble reviews at the time). For my one book I had twelve ratings on Apple Books and six on Google Play, and after much consideration, I gave those up to consolidate my wide ebook publishing through PublishDrive as I was publishing my second book, just to make uploading books and tracking sales less complicated. But, I recognized a few of the names of readers who had reviewed on Apple Books, so I documented their reviews and, after the book was republished, messaged them with a record of their reviews to ask them to re-post, which they all did.

At the time of this writing Draft2Digital lists on their website sixteen retailers they publish ebooks to, saying they distribute "to all the major retailers online, plus hundreds of storefronts worldwide." PublishDrive displays thirty-one retailer logos and claims to distribute to 400+ stores. One notable omission from Draft2Digital's list is Google Play. They don't distribute to Google Play, but PublishDrive does.

One very cool feature Draft2Digital has is automatic updating for your "Also by" page. If you have or plan to publish many books, instead of editing and re-uploading every ebook, you can change the books listed on all your "Also by [your author name]" pages in one place.

Both aggregators also offer print options, but unless you really want convenience and don't mind giving up more revenue, I wouldn't recommend using these aggregators for print. The same goes for IngramSpark, who I'll talk about shortly, vis-a-vis their ebook offering.

There are benefits to publishing directly to given retailers, so consider your strategy when deciding what mix of retailers you want to publish to directly, versus through an aggregator. The main benefits of publishing directly through a retailer's website are: you keep all your revenue, you're eligible for their exclusive promotions, and you have better access to sales analytics. For example, both major aggregators distribute to Amazon, but I wouldn't use them for that. It's better to publish directly to Amazon KDP because that's where you're likely to make the most money, so in the case of Draft2Digital you'd be giving up a portion of that revenue; and in both cases you'd miss out on opportunities to be picked for Kindle Deals. You might want to publish directly to Kobo Writing Life because you can be eligible for their promotions. Since reviews can be transferred after re-publishing through an aggregator it might be worth a shot.

I'm strongly considering publishing my next book directly to Apple Books, just to have better access to sales analytics. Sales analytics are real-time when publishing directly to Apple Books, but are delayed one to two days when publishing through PublishDrive. That doesn't sound like much, but it can make a big differ-

Go "wide" (or don't)

ence if you're trying to get on a bestseller list. That requires at least a couple hundred sales on at least one retailer other than Amazon. For me, Apple Books would be the best candidate by far. But without real-time sales data, I can't monitor how close I am to generating that many sales within a given week, and so can't adjust my advertising spend accordingly. Whether it makes sense for me to publish directly to Apple Books depends entirely upon whether I plan to attempt to make a bestseller list.

If convenience is king for you, publish through an aggregator for as many platforms as possible. If you're willing to put in some extra work for your efforts making wide sales, try publishing directly to some retailers other than Amazon. Kobo is a good one to try since they have promotions and you can always transfer your reviews if you switch to an aggregator.

Make your hard-copy books available everywhere, through IngramSpark

The industry standard way of making your hard-copy books available in as many places as possible is:

1. Publish your paperback or hardcover on Amazon KDP. Uncheck the "Expanded Distribution" option when doing so.
2. Publish that same paperback or hardcover on IngramSpark.

For whatever reason, Amazon KDP's expanded distribution isn't all that expanded. Some say it's because bookstores refuse to order from Amazon. In any case, Ingram is one of the largest book distributors in the world, and publishing on IngramSpark makes your book available to order from the same place bookstores around the world order much of their traditionally-published books.

How to Sell a Book

Don't panic if there are two versions of your hard-copy book available on Amazon for a short while when you do this. Wait a few days and see if they get consolidated into one, as this is a very common practice and Amazon handles it all the time. If there are still two versions of your hard-copy book, I'm sorry to say, you'll have to call Amazon and/or IngramSpark support, which can be annoying because they often blame each other. Because of this potential problem, expect it and give yourself plenty of lead time to sort it out ahead of any launch plans.

Some authors skip publishing their hard-copy on KDP and just publish on IngramSpark. For a time this was the most-profitable way to publish hard-copies. However, IngramSpark now forces authors to provide their books at a minimum 40% wholesale discount, which tends to make it less-profitable than KDP.

If you choose to publish your hard-copy only through Ingram-Spark, expect some "out of stock" issues on Amazon. When you publish your hard-copy on KDP, Amazon prints and ships your book quickly. If the only hard-copy version of your book is available through IngramSpark, Amazon either orders IS to print the book each time it's ordered, or orders several books so that it's in-stock, and they can ship quickly. If Amazon doesn't have your book in-stock in a warehouse, it may say on your book's page something to the effect of "Ships in 14–21 days," which as you can imagine harms your sales. If Amazon does have your book in-stock, it will show the "Prime" logo to Prime subscribers, and so ship very quickly, such as in two days.

However, it's possible that despite having your book uploaded to IngramSpark, Amazon still shows your book as "out of stock." If you call the customer service lines of both companies, they'll likely blame one another, and you'll learn that whether or not Amazon will order your book at all depends upon a variety of mysterious factors, such as traffic to your book's page, your wholesale discount, and whether or not you allow returns.

Go "wide" (or don't)

When I launched *100-Word Writing Habit*, Amazon mysteriously showed it as "out of stock" for weeks. Because of its non-standard size, I couldn't publish through KDP and fix this. It was available on other online stores, such as Barnes & Noble, but it really sucked to not have it available on Amazon and not have a straight answer for how to get them to show it as in-stock.

After some experimentation, the one thing that got Amazon to keep my book in-stock was allowing returns. Within days after I chose in my book's preferences on IngramSpark to allow returns, customers could finally at least order my book from Amazon. It also seemed to have triggered Amazon to order some books, because within a couple weeks my book was available with Prime shipping. Your results may vary, however, as Amazon takes into account a variety of factors signaling whether or not they can sell your book. But I can pretty confidently say that unless your book is already very popular, if you don't allow returns through IngramSpark, Amazon will not sell it to customers.

Don't *lose* money selling books: beware IngramSpark returns

It's very important you understand what you're signing up for when you allow returns on IngramSpark. If Amazon or some other store buys a bunch of copies of your book, then returns it, you could end up losing a lot of money. When allowing returns, you can choose for Ingram to either "Destroy" or "Deliver" the returned book. IngramSpark's policies are subject to change, but at the time of this writing, in either case, you are charged whatever the wholesale price is of your book at the time of returning. So if you have a $20 book you're offering at the current minimum 40% wholesale discount, you get charged $12. It's taken out of your future earnings, or if you end up with a negative balance, Ingram may send you an invoice.

How to Sell a Book

You earned that wholesale price when the retailer bought the book, so no harm, right? Don't forget that you've also paid to print the book. Let's say your book costs $7 to print. You're out $7 for each book that's returned. If some retailer orders 100 copies, you've earned $1,200. You'll be excited to see that on your earning's statement! But if they return them, it turns out not only did you not earn $1,200, you're out the $700 that was taken out of your earnings for printing all those books which will now be destroyed.

If you've chosen the "Destroy" option, that's the end of it. If you've chosen the "Deliver" option, at least the books won't be destroyed (so wasteful!), but now you will be charged $3 per book to send them to an address in the U.S. If you live in the U.S. and sell your books directly to readers, you can still make a profit off the book you've paid to have printed and sent to you. I don't live in the U.S. but currently rent warehouse space, and even after warehouse handling fees it's possible for me to make a profit.

The prospect of having a bunch of your books returned to you and actually losing money is scary. But I don't know how common it actually is. I've read horror stories on message boards, but I haven't yet had it happen to me. When there are returns of my books, it's usually one copy here and there. It's not fun to see a negative line-item on my statements, but so far those haven't been for big amounts.

Besides not allowing returns, the best way to sell books through IngramSpark without losing money on returns is to offer the wholesale discount least favorable to retailers: At the time of this writing, that's 40%. If some random bookstore owner finds your book and wants to take a chance on a few boxes of it, they're not likely to do so if your discount is 40%, because the industry standard is 55%. If a customer comes into their bookstore and specifically requests one copy of your book, however, they'll usually order one, even if your discount is only 40%. It's a guaranteed profit for them, after all.

Because I'm selling at a pretty good volume and am willing to

Go "wide" (or don't)

lose some money to learn a lesson that might help me sell more books, I've very recently started experimenting with a 55% wholesale discount on some of my books. I have noticed more copies sold on my statements in recent months, albeit at no increase in overall profits. I feel comfortable with this experiment because I've recently started selling books directly to customers, so can at least try to sell any returned copies.

Getting your IngramSpark book stocked in stores

Nothing makes your book feel "real" more than being able to walk into a physical bookstore and see your book in-stock on shelves. But while it's possible to get bookstores to keep your book in-stock, it isn't necessary and probably wouldn't affect your sales a great deal. Keep in mind I've sold more than 100,000 self-published books and have never seen one of my self-published books in-stock in a bookstore. That's not to say no bookstore has ever stocked my self-published books – they probably have, finding it through a *Publisher's Weekly* or *Kirkus* review. But I've never personally seen it, as I have with my traditionally-published book.

Probably the easiest way to get your book in-stock in a bookstore is to talk to a local independent bookstore owner. They likely have a section for local authors, and hold events in which local authors speak. If your book is published through IngramSpark, they can order it through Ingram's system, where they likely order their other books. I haven't personally talked to local bookstore owners, as my entire self-published career I've lived abroad in a non-English-speaking country.

If you have a large and loyal audience, you may be able to get a large nationwide bookstore, such as Barnes & Noble in the U.S., to stock your book. In 2016, blogger and podcaster Pat Flynn was able to accomplish this, and has written about it on his website. He ran a three-day campaign encouraging his readers to go to local Barnes &

Noble bookstores, and order his book with the help of staff. Once readers had picked up their books, they sent Pat photos of their receipts. He offered to reimburse the purchases of the first 500 receipts submitted, and drew a winner from all receipts for a 1-hour coaching call.

Pat has a large audience, so he was able to generate enough sales in Barnes & Noble bookstores to catch their attention, and they started stocking his book in physical bookstores. This promotion clearly could have been expensive, after reimbursing all those book purchases, but it was also a fun and mischievous experiment for his whole audience to participate in, which probably generated a profit over time. It was a fun "pseudo-event," which I'll talk about later.

* * *

Publishing wide through aggregators and IngramSpark is a good way to shift the balance of power from Amazon, toward indie authors, and make some extra money. But you can do both of those even more by selling direct.

Chapter 13
Sell directly to readers

You can make the biggest profit per-unit of your books by selling direct to readers. When selling hard-copy books, your only Costs of Goods Sold (COGS) are printing the books. When selling ebooks, you have none at all. What you pay for processing and delivering orders will vary, and is to some degree up to you.

Imagine, for example, you sell a book for $20, and it costs $7 to print. Through Amazon KDP, which offers a 60% royalty for printed books, you'd earn 60% of the $20 price, from which the $7 printing cost would be deduced. $12 minus $7 is $5. Selling directly to your readers, you'd get all $13 of gross margin. Your profits are more than double selling a hard-copy book direct, in this case.

Now, look at an ebook. With Amazon, the most you can reasonably charge is $9.99, so the most you can reasonably make in the 70% royalty plan is about $7 per Kindle ebook. Realistically, after digital delivery charges it will be more like $6.85. Selling that ebook direct, you can keep all $10. And since an ebook bought directly is actually *more valuable* than a kindle ebook "bought" (I'll explain in a bit), you can charge more – $12 or $15, for example. So again, you can make double the profit. Nothing's stopping you from selling an ebook with really valuable content for $20 or $40, or bundling it with a video course for $200. With Amazon's royalty structure, it feels silly to sell an ebook for $20, because you'd generally make about as much as if you sold it for $9.99.

Keep in mind, Amazon does a *lot* for the $8 they'd take in the above scenario per hard-copy book: They market your book to customers they've attracted to their website, they ship your book – often for free and within two days, and they handle all customer service inquiries and returns. They also collect any applicable sales tax. Your time and energy as an author are limited, and selling a book on Amazon saves you a lot of time and energy.

But why pay Amazon to sell a book to someone who's already a fan? What if they don't mind waiting a week or even three, for shipping they've paid for, to receive the book? What if they care about you, and much prefer giving you the extra $8 over giving it to Amazon? What if they'll be a low-maintenance customer, unlikely to complain over small details? You might as well sell them the book directly.

Start simple (or not at all)

Before you start selling direct, be aware that even more than selling wide, selling direct can greatly complicate your business operations, and take up time and energy you could use writing. I've gotten about as deep into selling direct as an author can go: I operate a Shopify store, run Meta ads, and even have books stocked in a warehouse. Setting up my store was a lot of work. Monitoring my ads, inventory, and order fulfillment, and handling the occasional customer-service inquiry doesn't take up a lot of time on a daily basis, but emergencies can pop up that I feel compelled to drop everything to address. Even with all this, I know I'm leaving

Sell directly to readers

money on the table, not optimizing my direct sales as much as I could. Like selling wide, selling direct to the degree I do is arguably not worth it. But I like the challenge of trying to figure it out, and I see it as another way to make my business more secure.

You don't have to set up a fancy store and contract a warehouse, and that's not how I started selling direct either. The easiest way to start selling direct is to collect payment through PayHip, and deliver ebooks through BookFunnel. PayHip makes it easy to set up a sales page for your ebook, and it integrates with BookFunnel so download instructions for your ebook are sent directly to your customer.

I currently pay $15 per month for BookFunnel, but it's worth it, because they are experts at making it easy for customers to download the format they prefer to any device they prefer. Depending upon how technically literate your customer base is, if you simply sell an ePub directly to customers, you'll likely get customer service inquiries from customers who need help loading the file onto their devices. When you deliver your ebooks with BookFunnel, the majority of those inquiries will go straight to BookFunnel. If any come to you, you can direct them to BookFunnel's customer service.

I also use BookFunnel to set up landing pages for free ebook giveaways, to build my email list. It integrates with many email marketing platforms, and if it doesn't integrate directly with yours, it integrates with Zapier, which likely can add new email addresses to your list.

When selling audiobooks direct, it's even more valuable to have the help of a service such as BookFunnel. Many customers wouldn't know what to do with a bunch of MP3 files. BookFunnel has its own app through which customers can listen to audiobooks on their favorite devices.

"You can just put books in the mail"

After selling ebooks directly to readers through PayHip and BookFunnel, the next level is selling hard-copy books. There are various ways to sell hard-copy books directly to readers, with various levels of complexity in set-up and work involved in each sale.

What I'm about to say will seem incredibly obvious to some, but will be a revelation to others. Coming from a tech background, where I always wanted to think of the most automated and hands-off way to do everything, it was a revelation for me: The simplest way to sell direct is to collect payment on your website with a payment service such as PayPal or Venmo, and manually send books to readers. You can keep a stock of books and padded envelopes in your home and mail one each time you receive a purchase. If you have a high order volume, you can make a trip to the post office once or twice a week.

Some authors even fulfill their orders by using the "Order author copies" option in the KDP dashboard to send the book directly to the customer (aka "drop shipping"). (Do not send "proof copies," as those will have a "Not for Resale" banner on the cover.) You can also order copies directly to a customer through IngramSpark. But be careful with these drop-shipping options. Your book will be delivered with a packing slip that shows how much you paid to print and ship the book. Ask yourself if your customers will be happy to see you spent, say, $12 to print and ship a book, when they paid you $20.

This is a good time for me to stress that selling directly to customers can be a very different kind of transaction than selling on Amazon. On Amazon, the customer may have never heard of you, and might even buy and read your entire book without remembering your name. On your own website, especially if you generate sales only from your email list, the customer knows your name, and even if you don't know them they might consider you a friend.

Sell directly to readers

So don't pass up the opportunity of selling directly to customers because you can't sell them a book as cheaply or ship it as quickly as Amazon. Just as some customers will appreciate honest, round-number pricing, such as $10 or $15, some won't mind paying a little extra, waiting a little longer, and paying their own shipping to buy a book directly from you. Some customers just refuse to buy from Amazon. Others like to know all the money is going to you. Think of it like buying an avocado directly from a farmer at a farmer's market for $4, instead of $2.69 from the supermarket. People do it all the time.

Yes, you *can* beat Amazon

But, most people still want to get the best deal they can, or at least not pay significantly more and wait significantly longer than other options. To attract these customers, you can beat Amazon in price, but not shipping speed.

For example, a paperback copy of my *Mind Management* would cost me $4.14 + $3.59 delivery, or $7.73 to drop ship to a reader from KDP. Charging my list price of $19.95, I could make $12.22. That's $4.39 more than the $7.83 in royalties I'd make if they'd bought straight from Amazon. But, it would take a week, maybe two, to reach the customer, and they could get it in two days from Amazon if they're a Prime member. In any case, Amazon has my paperback discounted to $17.96, so if I wanted to match Amazon's price, I could make $10.23 per book – still more than a sale through Amazon. I could sell my book for a much bigger discount, at $15.56, and still make the same $7.73 profit to match Amazon's royalty. But shipping would still be slow, and the book would still be shipped with a packing slip with my costs on it.

If I lived in the U.S., I could order author copies and store them in my closet. If I ordered ten books, shipping would be $8, or 80¢

each book. Add that to the $4.63 it costs to ship the book via USPS Media Mail, and the $4.14 it costs to print a book, and I could get a book to a customer for $9.57. On the list price, I could make $10.38, or if I wanted to sell for less than Amazon but earn the same profit, I could sell each book for $17.30, beating Amazon by 66¢. The books wouldn't ship with my costs on a packing slip, but they'd still take up to a week to arrive via Media Mail.

Think I could just pay more out of my profits and ship as fast as Amazon? Nope. As I write this, on a Wednesday morning, I could send it with UPS Next Day Air Saver, and it would arrive on Friday by 11 p.m. (so much for "next day"). Cost of shipping according to PirateShip.com, who claims to provide a 65% discount: $37.97.

While there's no way to match the speed of Amazon's shipping, when selling directly, you have many options for offering a more enticing deal than Amazon. Because shipping multiple books costs hardly any more and sometimes the same as shipping one book, your profits can really stack up.

Let's say someone bought all five books currently on my Shopify store. The total list price would be $87. It would cost me $39.08 to print and ship those books, so my gross margin would be $47.92. Because of Amazon's clever pricing and discounts, all these books together would cost nearly four dollars less: $83.32. Fortunately, I have a lot of wiggle room, as my royalties through Amazon would be only $28.59, and I'd make eighteen dollars more selling direct. I could provide a 20% discount for buying all my books and still make more than through Amazon. The customer would get for $69.60 what would've cost nearly fourteen dollars more, and I'd still make more profit.

But I don't have to give up profit to make the deal more enticing than Amazon's. Since none of these books are in KDP Select, I have total control over my ebook. Since my audiobook is not exclu-

Sell directly to readers

sive to ACX/Audible, I also have total control over my audiobook. I can offer my ebook and audiobook formats at a steep discount or *free* with each hard-copy purchase. Not all customers prefer to have all electronic formats instantly and wait two to three weeks for their hard-copy format, but for those who do, I can provide an insane amount of value over Amazon. I can certainly afford to offer free shipping for bigger orders like this.

I don't live in the U.S., so can't ship my own books personally. So books I don't already have in-stock in my warehouse I drop ship through BookVault (who does not print your costs on their packing slips). They're based in the UK, so the books take longer and cost more to ship. If you live in the same country as your customers and have a stash of books in your closet, you can make an even bigger profit, and ship your books faster.

I mentioned earlier that ebooks sold directly are more valuable than Kindle ebooks. The reason is that when you "buy" a Kindle ebook, you never own it. You merely license the right to read it. A friend of mine moved from the U.S. to the UK and, when he changed his Amazon U.S. account to an Amazon UK account, lost *all* his Kindle ebooks. I have 1,000 Kindle ebooks in my library, with 30,000 highlights, so that sounded horrible to me! Going forward, if I have a chance to buy an ePub over "buying" a Kindle ebook, I will choose the former. Not all customers will recognize that an ebook bought directly from you is more valuable than one "bought" on Kindle, or any retailer for that matter, but don't be afraid to charge more for your ebooks than the price on other retailers.

The customers you gain selling direct are also more valuable in some ways than the customers you gain on Amazon. Yes, one could argue that each sale on Amazon increases your sales rank and perhaps leads to more organic sales, but the problem with customers on Amazon and other retailers is you have no way of contacting those customers. When a customer buys directly from you, you get their email address and even their mailing address. If they give you permission, you can send them follow-up deals, such as coupon codes, or sell them higher-margin online courses and consulting. If you're a prolific author, the customer lifetime value (CLV) can be so high, it can arguably be worth it to make even less on a direct sale than you might have made selling the same books through Amazon. Running ads at break-even or even a loss is a good way to build your email list with leads of the highest quality: people who buy!

As you can see, when you sell directly to customers, you have lots of options for how to make it a good deal and experience. You can provide discounts and freebies, and even sign your books. But I'll stress again that selling directly is an advanced tactic that can get endlessly complicated and take up unlimited time and energy. Just because my Shopify store exists, I'm often thinking about all the things I could be doing to maximize profits.

If you choose to ship your own books personally out of your closet or garage, ask yourself what your time is worth. The math may work out so that you make three dollars more per sale than selling through Amazon, but if you're making one sale a week, are spending an hour processing that order, are burning gas on a trip to the post office, and are buying a padded envelope, is it worth it? That time may be spent more profitably writing your next book.

The above examples, for simplicity, don't include payment processing fees. Unless you find a way to collect money with no transaction fees, such as through Venmo, the fees for a $20 transaction are about $1: On Shopify Payments, they're about 88¢, and on PayPal, they're about $1.19. So what might have looked like a three-dollar increase in earnings over Amazon may actually be two. When you figure in gas and materials like padded envelopes the advantage may be eliminated completely.

Sell directly to readers

But like anything, if you are committed long-term, you can't decide so easily whether it's worth it, and a deficit in time or even money in the short-term can be an investment in the future. You can start simple, and build up. I started selling directly using PayHip and BookFunnel, started selling one hard-copy book through a PayHip integration with BookVault, built up to a five-dollar-per-month Shopify "Starter" plan, and now have a fully-fledged Shopify store, and books in a warehouse. It's not a huge profit center and takes up a lot of time and attention, but it gets easier as I learn, and I love having control over the experience. Plus, I just feel closer to my readers and more appreciated for my work when readers buy from me directly.

Why direct sales are the future

Even if my online store is a lot of work and not a huge profit center, I could see it being a big source of profits in the future. As someone who has been a customer of Amazon for more than twenty-five years, it seemed unlikely to me that people would go to my online store just to buy my books. When I lived in the U.S., I loved Amazon's "one-click buy" button. Every time I thought of something I needed, I'd just click. I had so many boxes showing up at my house, every day was like Christmas morning, because I had forgotten what I had ordered.

Once I started building my store with Shopify, I started to understand why it and other online store builders will continue to erode Amazon's market share. Shopify is essentially building "one-click buy" for the entire internet. You can connect various apps to your store, which publish the catalog you've built in Shopify on other stores, including social media platforms. With the Meta app, you can generate stores on Instagram and Facebook. With the TikTok app, you can generate a store on TikTok. With the "Google

& YouTube" app, you can build a store on your YouTube channel, and display your products through Google Merchant Center, which enables customers to shop for your products through search results.

Now, instead of going to Amazon's website to make purchases, customers are shopping right in the apps they use every day. Once they've made a purchase in any of these places, their payment and address information is stored for easy checkout. Shopify is just the hub that distributes information about products to these storefronts while making payment easy and providing retailers like us one central place to handle orders.

My Instagram store, created through the Meta app for Shopify

Premium editions and crowdfunding

So far, I've been talking about selling the same ol' books on your website as you sell on Amazon. But since selling directly skews towards more intimate transactions with your most-loyal readers, it makes sense to create special editions for them. I only sell the hardback editions, if they exist, on my online store, which are a little more special than paperback editions. BookVault has a "bespoke" service, which allows you to add premium details to your books, including foil or holographic stamping and placeholder ribbons. I recently developed a special hardback edition of a journal-prompts workbook, which features a silver-foil stamp and placeholder ribbon.

Sell directly to readers

The premiere edition of my *100 Journal Prompts Workbook*, printed through BookVault's Bespoke service, featured a silver foil and a placeholder ribbon.

Extra touches like this can take some extra work to develop, and are expensive unless produced at higher volume, so it makes sense to run crowdfunding campaigns, such as on Kickstarter. By offering special editions only for a short period of time, you can focus all the demand of your most loyal readers to increase the number of sales and your margins.

With Kickstarter, you can announce your book project, and set a funding goal. Your readers only get charged for your book at the end of your campaign, if your funding goal has been reached. So, instead of printing each book as orders come in, you and your readers can save on volume for premium flourishes.

For example, I've just completed a successful Kickstarter campaign for the above workbook. Printing one of those workbooks costs $12.14 through BookVault. If I include shipping for one book to the U.S., the costs alone rise to $21.37. But my costs drop 15% even at modest volume. If I print 100 copies, the printing cost per book drops to $11.78. If I could ship those books myself, it would end up costing $13.96 to get each book to the U.S. If I add $4.63 for Media Mail, my costs drop to $18.59 to get each book to a customer, not including envelope costs.

As quantity increases, costs decrease. BookVault is print-on-demand (POD), but if I order a large quantity of books with the same specs from an offset printer such as PrintNinja, I can save big: At 500 units, each copy would only be $8.63 (the next lowest quantity available would be 250, at which it would cost $15.20 to print each book – more than POD through BookVault). If I printed 750, they'd cost $6.48 each. 1,000, $5.64. But shipping the books would cost more than through BookVault, since they're printed in China. At 750 units it would cost $1.89 each to get them to the U.S. Printing would be cheaper and higher-quality, but would also take 9–10 weeks for production and delivery. If I did a rush job it would take 4–5 weeks, but shipping costs would triple.

Whether you print a bunch of books offset or only use POD, it's more expensive to fulfill orders as they come in than all at once through a crowdfunding campaign. You either have to spend a bunch up-front and store the books, or pay more to produce each book as it's ordered. But through a crowdfunding campaign, you can determine how many books you need to print, and therefore know the most economical way to print them. You don't have to print the books until you actually have the money, and you don't have to store the books for longer than it takes to pack and ship them. You can produce a higher-quality book at the most cost-effective price. So you can decide to make more profit, pass on the savings to your readers, or a bit of both.

A crowdfunding campaign also adds natural scarcity and urgency to your special editions. It's a way of saying, "Buy it now. This is your one chance." Scarcity and urgency are time-tested qualities of effective marketing campaigns, and in my experience they multiply your rate of conversion. But making fake scarcity and urgency feels weird. In this case it's real.

So with a crowdfunding campaign for special editions of your books you make the most effective use of your resources to sell the most books and make the most money possible in a short amount of time. This isn't just a great way to do business, it's an avenue for self-respect and focus. Don't "wait by the phone" for your readers to call. Set the time and date for your loyal readers to show up, and they will. The rest of the time, you've got plans: You're busy writing.

Preview editions

The last 10% of getting a book into the world is the most exhausting, and seems to take 90% of the whole project's energy. During the last 10% you're in an awkward position because you're eager to launch the book, since you've been working on it a long time without pay, yet also afraid to launch, since that's just normal. Dancing back and forth between your eagerness and your fear can lead to feeling desperate and eventually defeated. This puts you in danger of running out of steam entirely.

My favorite way to deal with this conundrum is through a Preview Edition. A Preview Edition is a well-polished draft of your book, released serially to paying customers. A Preview Edition gives you money and motivation to help you finish your book. It also gives your most loyal readers the earliest access possible. You can also get feedback from your Preview Edition customers, which can greatly improve your First Edition.

I first used the Preview Edition model when I was writing *Mind Management, Not Time Management*. I had spent many years working on the concepts within the book, and a few years actively writing the book, so naturally I was running out of money and motivation. I released a Preview Edition, and earned $4,000 to keep me going as I completed my final draft.

The basic technology behind my Preview Edition worked like this:

- I created an individual ebook out of each chapter, using a Mac program called Vellum
- I collected payment through PayHip, which triggered delivery of the ebooks for the completed chapters through BookFunnel
- As I completed chapters, I used BookFunnel's "Certified Mail" to deliver them to existing customers, and added them to the "Delivery Action" that delivered chapters to new customers

Now that I have a Shopify store, I sold the Preview Edition of the book you're reading through a hidden product on my store. Directing email subscribers to my Preview Edition on my Shopify store also led to sales of my other books, as potential buyers, directed to the store through my emails, browsed the rest of the store.

I'm most comfortable doing a Preview Edition when I already have well-polished chapters completed, and can "see" the rest of the book in my mind's eye. I want to feel like writing the rest of the book is mostly a minor detail that needs to be completed, and like offering a Preview Edition will give me an extra push to get it done. So I'm not certain a Preview Edition would have been a good idea for my first time writing a book. I'm comfortable offering it because I have experience writing books. Whether offering a Preview Edition is a good idea for you depends upon your experience and what motivates you.

You can get motivation when offering a Preview Edition by publishing a schedule on which you promise to release new chapters. I like to already have parts of the book ready to deliver when I launch my Preview Edition, have additional parts almost ready to deliver, and feel really good about my ability to write the rest of the parts. On the sales page for the Preview Edition, I list the parts that

Sell directly to readers

customers will get immediately, and a schedule of approximate dates on which I'll deliver the additional parts. Once I've collected payment on a page that outlines a schedule I feel highly motivated to stick to that schedule.

What I see as an added bonus but which is also an integral benefit of a Preview Edition is the feedback you get from early readers. For *Mind Management*, I offered a temporary Facebook Group where readers could discuss with me and amongst themselves the techniques described in the book. I also set up a Google Doc for each chapter, in which I accepted comments and corrections. My Preview Edition readers essentially edited my book!

I recommend setting a higher price for your Preview Edition than you plan to charge for your First Edition. I like to charge $20. In writing your sales email and page emphasize that buying the Preview Edition is a chance to get the material earlier than anyone else, and to be a part of bringing the book into the world. In addition to the chapter ebooks, you can offer a discussion group or promise to list those who gave you useful feedback in the acknowledgements of the book.

Close sales to your Preview Edition well before you release your First Edition, even before you deliver the final chapters of your Preview Edition. You don't need the distraction of trying to generate Preview Edition sales when you're finishing your book. Also, you want to get feedback from your Preview Edition readers before you finalize your First Edition, and to provide feedback they need to have had enough time since buying it to read the book. Announcing that you're closing sales will also motivate people to finally get around to buying your Preview Edition.

A few weeks after you've delivered all of your Preview Edition, solicit feedback from your readers. Announce that you're closing down comments on the Google Doc(s), and send out a survey to get their overall impressions of the book. I like to ask for a star rating,

1–5, what their biggest takeaway was, what they would cut if they had to, and any additional comments. I give them a chance to do this anonymously, to encourage honest feedback.

Phased releases

You can have the best of all worlds – KDP Select, wide ebook sales, direct sales, and preview editions – if you plan a phased release strategy. That might look like this:

- Phase 1: Preview Edition: Give your biggest fans a chance to read it first, and shape the future of the book.
- Phase 2: Direct Ebook Sales: Make a higher margin selling an ebook directly to the rest of your audience.
- Phase 3: KDP Select Exclusive: Close your direct ebook sales temporarily and sell your ebook only on Kindle throughout one ninety-day term of KDP Select.
- Phase 4: Wide Ebook Sales: Once your KDP Select term ends, publish your ebook everywhere you can, including direct ebook sales.

With a phased release, you get as much value as possible from various avenues. You get early and motivating revenue and feedback to improve the book from Preview Edition customers, higher margins from customers who buy direct, and wide ebook sales, while still giving your book an early boost by giving Kindle Unlimited members a chance to read your book on their subscriptions.

To get maximum value from all channels, you could also add a crowdfunded premium hard-copy edition. Since your initial direct ebook offering would be temporary anyway, you could add it to the crowdfunding campaign, to further leverage scarcity before publishing your ebook exclusively for a KDP Select term.

Sell directly to readers

The one good reason I could think of to not do a phased release like this would be if you were going for a bestseller list. In that case, you'd want to concentrate all your initial demand through retail channels. I'll talk more about that in a bit.

But first, a little on audiobooks.

Chapter 14
Interlude on audiobooks

I'll keep my thoughts about audiobooks brief, as much of the same tactics for selling ebooks apply to audiobooks. Audiobooks account for nearly one-quarter of my sales of *Mind Management*, so I'd be remiss to not mention them.

You can produce your own audiobook if you have a good audio-production set-up, i.e. a high-quality mic and a quiet place to record. You want as much padding as possible on any hard surfaces around you when recording, such as the walls, ceiling, and floor. I recorded the audiobooks for both *The Heart to Start* and *Mind Management, Not Time Management* in walk-in closets, with clothes hanging all around me.

Don't underestimate how hard the vocal performance is of reading your audiobook. If you're thinking, "It's just talking! Talking is easy," you are grossly underestimating it. Voiceover is an art form that many professionals dedicate their lives to perfecting. To do an at least passable vocal performance, you need to enunciate well without sounding too stiff, apply inflection to your voice appropriate for the content, and control your breath so your voice resonates and you aren't inhaling every couple words or having to take giant gulps of air while out of breath and exhausted.

If you're committed to reading your own audiobooks, make a

Interlude on audiobooks

habit of reading your work aloud. Having your own podcast, where you read articles you've written, is a great way to practice voice over, and also builds your skills in basic audio production. This was one of my main motivations for having my own podcast. I still hired professionals to do post-production on my audio, preparing the files according to the specifications of audiobook publishing platforms.

Voice lessons are also very helpful, even if they're singing lessons. So long as you learn to appreciate what a deeply technical art form it is to use your voice effectively. I took singing lessons at a music school in Chicago. It improved my voiceover and as a nice side-benefit leveled up my karaoke performances. At the very least look up some vocal warm-up routines on YouTube. I've warmed up before nearly every podcast and audiobook recording.

You can hire a studio to supervise your audiobook production, though I imagine that to be grueling, and have heard such from authors who have done it. When you produce your own audiobook, you can do a half hour here and there, and record your files over a couple weeks. If you're paying a studio, you'll have to do it all in one day or a couple long days. Your mouth feels like mush after too long reading aloud.

Definitely if you hire a studio but even if you record your audiobook yourself, rehearse. By reading aloud your whole book at least once, preferably several times, you program the words into your mind and muscles. I can't tell you how many times I've simply not been able to say a word or sentence, but just by having a night's sleep between rehearsing and recording suddenly it became easy. Rehearsal is especially powerful if you enunciate to an exaggerated degree and ridiculously slowly. When you record, you'll pronounce the words more crisply, without getting tongue-tied.

You can hire a narrator to read your audiobook for you. It's expensive to pay them outright for it, so you can do a revenue-share deal. I've never done either of these but there's a marketplace on ACX, through which you can publish to Audible and Apple.

How to Sell a Book

Like for ebooks, there is a "Wide, or ACX" dilemma. Findaway Voices is an aggregator, now owned by Spotify, that distributes to a bunch of platforms. But if your audiobook is exclusive to ACX, you earn a higher royalty rate: 40% if you're exclusive, and only 25% if you're not. The volume of sales on Audible is so high for audiobooks that once again it's hard to justify financially not publishing exclusively to ACX. More than 75% of my audiobook revenue for *Mind Management* has been through ACX. If I had earned that revenue with the higher royalty rate for exclusive sales, I would have made about 60% more, rather than the remaining 25% I've made from Findaway and direct sales.

You can distribute to Audible through Findaway, but like with wide ebooks, most wide audiobook authors distribute directly to Amazon's Audible through ACX, and to the rest of channels through Findaway.

If you agree to an exclusive contract with ACX, the term is for seven years, though I was able to simply email them and cancel that contract. You can only do this if you've produced your own audiobook. If you have a revenue-share deal with a narrator, you're committed to that contract.

AI voiceover is getting pretty good, and is now available on all major ebook retailers. It's a viable option if you simply don't have the funds, skills, or desire to produce an audiobook.

For promotion of your audiobooks, there are special links for giving away audiobooks in the ACX and Findaway dashboards. If your audiobook is on Findaway Voices, you can also apply for Chirp audiobook deals through the BookBub Partners dashboard. These promotions discount your audiobook, and you pay for the promotion through a share of your revenue. In my first Chirp deal, of *The Heart to Start* in March 2021, I sold 577 copies and made $211.

I've only recently discovered that through Findaway, you can schedule pricing promotions on other retailers, such as Spotify,

Interlude on audiobooks

Apple, and Barnes & Noble, as well as on Chirp, to run your own promotions or complement your Chirp deals. I'll be experimenting with that as I attempt to increase my wide audiobook sales.

Don't feel like you have to launch with an audiobook. They take a long time to produce, and ACX can be very slow in approving them for publication, so it makes timing your audiobook release with your other formats hard.

* * *

I'll talk about launches next.

Chapter 15
Don't launch the "right" way

How you launch your book can make or break your author career, but not for the reasons you'd think. You probably think I mean you have to launch the "right" way: Create a "wall of sound" by expertly timing the release of all formats of your book, along with a bunch of influencer promotions, editorial reviews, and podcast and traditional media appearances. Make sure everyone is talking about your book.

But what I really mean is that launching the "right" way is a tremendous amount of work. It's enough work, it could burn you out so bad you never want to write a book again, thus ending your author career after your first book.

The "right" way to launch exists not because it's the only way for a book to succeed. It's not. The "right" way to launch exists mostly because of the parameters of traditional publishing. When launching a traditionally-published book, here's the reality: The first run of books has been printed and paid for. Thousands of books are stored on a palette in a warehouse. The marketing and PR staff of the publisher are assigned to this book. They're also assigned to a bunch of other books. Your book is one of many the publisher is releasing this week, and this year. The publisher has now spent tens if not hundreds of thousands of dollars on your book, and they need to know if it's a hit or a flop before they invest more.

The "right" way to launch makes the best use of a publisher's resources. The publisher's resources are numerous and scalable, and there are many books competing for those resources. Publishers take the portfolio approach I talked about early in this book. They make lots of bets on books, not knowing which are going to be hits. If they see signals that a book is going to be a hit, it makes sense for them to focus money and people on that book. So they'll focus resources on your book for a few weeks, and see what happens. At the very least they want to recoup their expenses for printing and storing that palette of books sitting in a warehouse, and they don't want to pay to store that palette any longer than necessary.

The slow-motion launch

Your resources as a self-published author are likely neither numerous, nor scaleable. If you do everything yourself, like I do, you have a certain amount of time and energy each day and week, and the money available to you depends upon the performance of the very books you're trying to promote. Yes, you can and maybe should do some advanced planning to coordinate and time some promotions to coincide with your launch. But some elements of promoting a book require the book to be finished. The longer you wait to launch your book while lining up promotions, the longer you delay getting paid for the book you've worked so hard on. Working on the promotions you can line up before finishing the book uses time and energy you could be using to finish the book.

Because your resources as a self-published author are different from those of a traditional publisher, I recommend a "slow-motion" launch. The optimal way for a traditional publisher to launch a book is by focusing their resources to do as many things in as little time as possible. The optimal way for a solo indie author to launch a book is by getting the book out as fast as possible, and applying their limited resources consistently over an extended period of time thereafter.

The upshot of this is that a book can succeed even if there is no real coordinated "launch." Books can and have flopped even when the richest publishers launched the "right" way.

When I've launched my short read books, I've done little more than publish them then send an email to my list. When I've launched my major books, I've done slow-motion launches. I've done what I could to coordinate promotions, but have been far from launching the "right" way.

Launching books is a skill, and you can learn and get better each time you do it. When I "launched" *The Heart to Start*, I released only the Kindle edition. Then I worked on and released the paperback edition. Then I worked on the audiobook, which I released several weeks after the Kindle edition. I launched with a couple blurbs, and sent out evaluation copies here and there in the months after the book launched. I didn't add the blurb on the cover, from Seth Godin, until about nine months after launch, after Seth had read the book and written a blog post mentioning it.

When I launched *Mind Management*, my launch was slightly more coordinated. I launched the Kindle edition, the wide ebook edition, and the paperback edition all at once. By the time I launched, I had already sent out ARCs to influencers, gotten a few blurbs, and lined up some podcast interviews. I still didn't launch the audiobook for several more weeks.

The degree to which I'm able to coordinate a launch depends upon my skills and level of experience. When I released *The Heart to Start*, I had never self-published a Kindle ebook, a paperback, nor an audiobook. I had never sent out ARCs. I was doing all those things for the first time, so naturally each took more time and energy. When I released *Mind Management*, I had done many of those things and others several times, thanks to my short reads, and

Don't launch the "right" way

had even written documentation of what steps to follow. So those things took less time and energy than before, which freed up time and energy to coordinate other elements of my launch.

The Heart to Start has sold over 30,000 copies, and *Mind Management* over 40,000. So I think they were both successful despite not being launched the "right" way.

It's not that launching the "right" way isn't in any way better than launching in slow motion. Having your book talked about in as many places as possible at the same time, aka the "wall of sound," is probably a force multiplier. If you have a very specific target audience, you don't need for your book to be in many places at once before it seems as if it's "everywhere." It's definitely a way of cutting through the noise.

But launching the "right" way is only marginally better in a hypothetical situation where you have unlimited resources. If you don't have unlimited resources, you can launch in slow motion. The most costly element of launching the "right" way is the sanity of the author. A traditional publisher may have more resources than an indie author, but in either case everything involved in the launch hinges on the author. So many traditionally-published authors come out of launching their books exhausted, swearing they'll never write another book.

Have faith that if you've written a good book, it will spread. Look at the sales graph, over time, of *Mind Management*.

How to Sell a Book

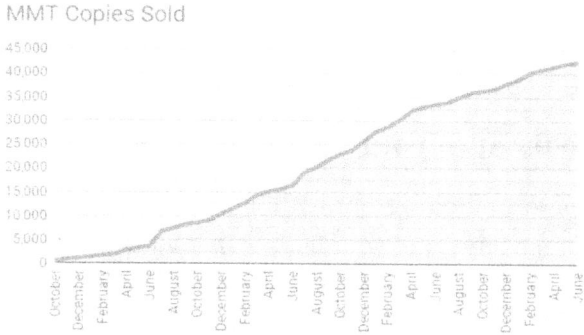

It took about five months to sell the first 2,500 copies. Five months after that, I had sold at about double that rate: 5,000 more, with the help of the book's first BookBub Featured Deal. Sales then accelerated a bit over the course of a couple more years, then started to level off after about three years. Time will tell if the book gets a second wind.

Notice also how my profit margin has grown over the years.

Early on, I was spending a good portion of my profits on *Mind Management*, but over time, the growth of my revenue has outpaced my spending.

The best thing you can do to "launch" a book is write a book that people enjoy reading enough to recommend it to friends.

Then, whatever you can do to get books into people's hands will lead to more sales. You don't have to do it all at once.

Make the most of your launch moment

Still, if you are an indie author with limited resources, one of those resources at the launch of your book is that you have a new book. You can more easily persuade people to take an action when there is a reason. I've already talked about how the scarcity built into, say, a crowdfunding campaign provides a good reason for people to take action. Because your book is new when you launch it, that alone is a reason that will persuade some people to buy your book, so long as they hear about it.

A very common marketing tactic for book launches is to give away things for buying multiple copies of your book, within a short period of time after your book launches. Giveaways are really commonly used with traditionally published authors, such as Tim Ferriss and Ryan Holiday, and you can probably find on the web the pages describing their old giveaways. Rewards might be a PDF of a deleted chapter for buying three copies of the book, some audio interviews for buying five copies, coming to speak at somebody's company for buying five-hundred copies, and various levels in between.

When I launched my very first book, *Design for Hackers*, I ran a giveaway, mostly of free subscriptions to various software-as-a-service platforms that were hot in the startup world at the time. Coincidentally, that was a traditionally published book. It was easy for me to line up those giveaways because there was already a lot of buzz about the book, as I had gotten my first book deal through writing articles that performed well on a Reddit-like news aggregator called Hacker News.

Running a giveaway during a pre-order period, and/or for the first week your book is out, is an effective way to motivate sales upon launch. Aside from the fact that your book is new, it creates a sense of scarcity of the extra value you're offering for acting right now. But be careful what you give away. You don't want to have to do a hundred one-hour video calls, for example, with each person who simply bought a copy of your book. That's a hundred hours of your time for what, several dollars an hour? It's much better to give away something of value that was integral to writing the book, such as a chapter you cut or an audio and/or text interview with a subject-matter expert. Reserve anything that requires your personal one-on-one time for larger quantities. You could, however, invite all those folks who bought three books to a single one-hour webcast where they can ask you anything.

All this said, I personally haven't run a giveaway for a book launch in more than a decade. I'd much rather spend my time and energy writing my next book.

Since getting your book into the hands of readers is the best marketing for a good book, your launch can also be an opportunity to do whatever you can to do that, even if it means giving your book away. If your Kindle edition is free for the first week, for example, that is a motivating reason for people to download your book. The flood of downloads will increase your book's Amazon rank, and likely help others discover it organically.

It's easiest to give your book away for free if it's enrolled in KDP Select and you run a Kindle Countdown Deal. Pricing your book free when not in KDP Select, aka "permafree," requires pricing it as free on at least one other platform, emailing Amazon KDP customer service, and hoping they'll honor your request to price match.

When I first launched *The Heart to Start*, I gave away the Kindle edition free for the first week. More than 3,000 people downloaded it (not counted in my "copies sold" numbers). When

Don't launch the "right" way

Nir Eyal debuted *Hooked: How to Build Habit-Forming Products*, he gave it away for free. That started a snowball that led to so many sales, he sold the book to Penguin, and it's now traditionally published.

A huge factor in how you decide to launch your book is whether or not you're trying to make a bestseller list.

Chapter 16
Make a bestseller list (or don't)

One case where you'd want to put a lot of effort into a coordinated launch is if you're attempting to make a bestseller list. Whatever bestseller list you're trying to hit, you need a high volume of sales in a short amount of time. Coordinating as many promotions as possible at once is the surest way to produce a high volume of sales in a short amount of time.

The most well-known bestseller list is the *New York Times* bestseller list. If your book is self-published, you might as well forget about it being a *New York Times* bestseller. The NYT list is based upon sales in a wide selection of brick-and-mortar stores. You can't get your book stocked in those stores unless you're working with a distributor. The stores in which the NYT list counts sales is a closely-held secret, though there are agencies that you can pay hundreds of thousands of dollars to generate sales in the stores that matter.

Even if you somehow generated that many hard-copy sales of your book at retailers, your self-published book might not be included on the list. The *New York Times* editorializes their list. It's not based solely upon the number of copies a book has sold. If they don't think your book is the right fit for their list, they will straight up not include it.

Make a bestseller list (or don't)

A couple other prestigious lists within reach of self-published authors are the *USA Today* and *Wall Street Journal* lists. The *Wall Street Journal* bestseller list was discontinued in November of 2023. It was a great option to get a traditional-media bestseller designation, because as long as your ebook cost at least 99¢, your sales on major ebook retailers would count toward the list. The *USA Today* list is somewhat editorialized, and is an uncategorized list of the top 150 bestselling books in the U.S. for a given week.

Even though the WSJ list is discontinued, I'll still write about it as if it exists. It ended pretty recently, and I've heard rumors it may be coming back.

To make the NYT list, you need roughly 5,000 to 10,000 hard-copy book sales, bought individually in bookstores around the country (bulk sales don't count). To make the WSJ ebook list, you needed to sell 3,000 to 5,000 ebooks. To make the *USA Today* list, you need to sell 5,000 to 9,000. I've also heard from multiple author friends who have made the WSJ or *USA Today* lists, at least 500 of those sales need to come from a retailer other than Amazon. But, author Nicholas Erik wrote in 2018 that retailers such as B&N and Apple Books report as few as 150–200 sales. Since you need to make some sales outside of Amazon, if you're exclusive to Amazon through KDP Select, you're not eligible to make these lists.

An Amazon bestseller is a "real" bestseller

Another bestseller designation is the Amazon bestseller, or having your book ranked in the top of a category on Amazon, thus getting a "Best Seller" tag next to your book. But this is controversial.

Many authors, myself included, take this to mean they're a best-selling author, and then include that on their covers and in their bio. Some people think being on top of a category on Amazon does not make a book a "real" bestseller. Scribe Media, most likely founder Tucker Max at the time of writing, calls the Amazon bestseller designation "ridiculous" and a "nonsense status symbol." Their, or Tucker's, reasoning being his friend Brent Underwood pulled a clever stunt by releasing a one-page Kindle ebook featuring only a picture of his foot, got a few friends to buy it, and rose to the top of the "Transpersonal Psychology" category, thus causing a "#1 Best Seller" tag to appear next to his book.

Brent's stunt was really funny and brilliant. But I don't think it says about bestseller lists what he thinks it says. When he outlined his stunt on *Observer*, he called the "Amazon Bestseller" designation "complete and utter nonsense," then went on to promote the marketing consultancy he runs with author Ryan Holiday, saying they've helped launch thirty "legitimate New York Times best sellers."

The whole thing was a really smart marketing stunt (or "pseudo-event," which I'll talk about in a bit). But the logic of Brent's argument doesn't hold together. The first bestseller list more than a hundred years ago had *four* books on it. Now bestseller lists, even for "legitimate" newspapers, rank over a hundred books, divided by categories. Whether Amazon bestsellers are legitimate depends upon your definition of a bestseller. If a bestseller is a book on a list somewhat-arbitrarily deemed important by a powerful institution, then yes, a NYT bestseller is a "legitimate" bestseller, and an Amazon bestseller is not. If a bestseller is an objective measure of sales rank within a period of time, then the NYT bestseller is illegitimate, and the Amazon bestseller is legitimate. Amazon has objective data about what books are selling well in the largest book marketplace in the world, and their "Best Seller" tags reflect that data.

It makes sense Brent would have the perspective he does. Brent and Ryan help mainstream traditionally-published authors get on the NYT list, amongst other things. Tucker is Brent's friend and is an effusive guy, so that might explain why he thinks the Amazon bestseller is nonsense. A funny fact is that Brent and Ryan's consultancy is called Brass Check, which is named after a book by Upton Sinclair, in which he talks about corruption in the media and explains he named the book after a brass "check" patrons would be issued to redeem for services in brothels. The inside joke at Brass Check seems to be that they're handing out figurative brass checks to their clients to redeem for NYT bestseller status.

So people who help authors get on the NYT bestseller list think Amazon bestsellers aren't legitimate. I'm a self-published author and I think they're clearly legitimate, as they are based on actual sales data. But more importantly, I don't think people should rely on some authority, whether editorialized or accurately quantified, to tell them what to like.

Amazon's ranking algorithm, then and now

Achieving Amazon bestseller status isn't as easy as it was when Brent pulled off his stunt, in 2016. Amazon's ranking algorithm has gotten more sophisticated. It used to be based purely off sales velocity in a given hour. Now nobody other than Amazon knows exactly how it works, but it clearly takes into account sales data over the course of several days, if not weeks.

A short anecdote from my career will serve both as a lesson on how to boost sales velocity, and on how touchy Amazon's sales-rank algorithm used to be. When I launched *Design for Hackers* in 2011, I aimed to generate as many sales on launch day in as short a time as possible, to try to achieve the best possible sales rank. I had run a Kickstarter campaign to raise money for a book tour, and one of the rewards was my book. But since the book was traditionally published, the most cost-effective and easiest way to send books to

How to Sell a Book

my supporters was to buy them with my Amazon Prime account and ship to each supporter individually.

Since I was going to buy all those books anyway, and I figured purchasing them would help my sales rank, I made sure everything was set up for these books to be bought in as short a time as possible. I hired an assistant to enter all the addresses into my Amazon account in advance of launch day, so he could later buy the books as quickly as possible at a designated moment in time. When launch day or rather launch *hour* came around, my assistant bought the books so quickly Amazon support called me, sounding concerned, to confirm I was actually ordering that many books that fast. In all he ordered about seventy books.

My book reached the #18 spot on all of Amazon that morning. I don't know for sure that ordering all those books within an hour directly contributed to that sales rank (maybe orders from the same account didn't count?), but I posit it did. One thing that definitely contributed was that the front page of the news aggregator Hacker News featured not one but two links about my book. One was my blog post announcing the book, and another was simply the Amazon link.

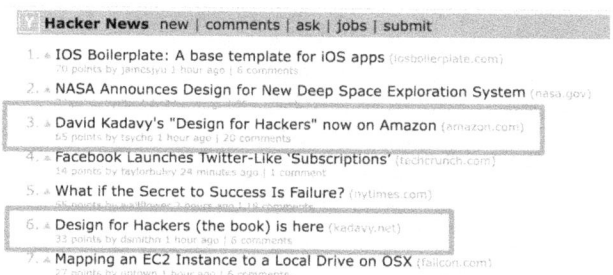

In any case, I had high sales velocity for a short amount of time, and for a shining moment my book was outselling all but seventeen books that ever existed. Those whose books mine closely outranked included Tim Ferriss and former Vice President, Dick Cheney. No

Make a bestseller list (or don't)

doubt that high rank led to some organic sales to readers who had never before heard of my book.

With the same sales velocity and volume, my book wouldn't rank as highly today. But what rises fast falls fast, so whatever rank a book that climbed more slowly achieved today, it would hold near that rank for a longer period of time. If achieving a high Amazon rank is a goal of yours, the currently accepted wisdom is to have some sales in the days before you expect to generate a spike. For example, if you have a BookBub Featured Deal scheduled, you could schedule the same pricing promotion to be sent beforehand to other smaller discount ebook email lists, such as BookGorilla (aka "promo stacking") and/or promote it to your email list.

As you check the rank of your book, take lots of screenshots! You never know which will be the highest rank you ever achieve. I'm glad I still have evidence, well over a decade old, of my moment at #18.

If you're trying to hit a newspaper's bestseller list, you can greatly contribute to your sales velocity in a given week by scheduling the release of your ebook and generating pre-orders. All your pre-orders will count towards your sales that qualify you for the bestseller list. Pre-orders also appear to help your Amazon rank on launch day. Make sure your book is released at or towards the beginning of the weekly period that your target bestseller list counts. For example, one list might count sales from Monday through Sunday, and another might count Sunday through Saturday. Check the criteria of your target bestseller list before you design your campaign.

One Amazon list I don't think anyone debates the veracity of, which didn't exist when Brent Underwood did his stunt, is the Amazon Charts list. This list features the top 20 books in Nonfiction and Fiction, respectively, with a list for both most read and most sold, respectively. It's updated once a week. You'd have to be crazy to say these books aren't bestsellers. Surprisingly, you rarely hear an author brag about being an "Amazon Charts bestseller." Maybe because so few books achieve it. Maybe because the books that do likely have other honors that currently carry more clout.

When and how to go for bestseller status

There are two times in the lifetime of your book when you have the best chance of making a bestseller list on purpose. One is when you launch your book, and another is a few months after you launch your book. Both require sacrifices.

If you're going to attempt to hit a bestseller list when your book launches, you might as well launch your ebook at a 99¢ price. When it was active that was the minimum price at which an ebook qualified for the *Wall Street Journal* bestseller list, and they didn't care how much profit you made or whether anyone actually read your book – only the number of copies sold counted. So you should charge the minimum viable price for your ebook and generate lots of pre-orders (confirm pricing requirements of your target list before you design your campaign). You could even watch your pre-order sales and keep pushing back your launch date until you felt

Make a bestseller list (or don't)

comfortable with your numbers (KDP will punish you for delaying your launch date more than once by taking away your right to take pre-orders on future releases for one year).

The downside of charging the lowest possible price to attempt to make a bestseller list at launch is you miss out on profits from the readers most willing to pay a reasonable price for the book you worked so hard on. You might sell 3,000 ebooks at 99¢, and make about $1,000, but if you had been charging $9.99, you would have only had to sell about 150 ebooks to make the same amount. If you're optimizing for sales on ebook retailers, you're also missing out on direct sales, from which you could make even a higher profit.

From one perspective, launching at a low price to make a bestseller list is missing out on profits. From another perspective, it's giving a gift to your loyal readers for being the first to buy. Also, if you launch at a low price and generate a lot of sales, you could make more profit in the long run, as your book spreads. If you make a bestseller list, that will possibly generate more sales. If your book is meant to build your business and/or increase your speaking fees rather than make profits itself, it can be worth it to take whatever measures possible to make a bestseller list.

Besides launch, the other time in which you have a good chance to make a bestseller list on purpose is three to six months after the book has launched. If you do a pricing promotion and get a BookBub Featured Deal, it's possible to generate enough sales to rank on a list. If your ebook has been offered at a higher price for its short lifetime, that can create a slingshot effect that drives high sales velocity once the ebook is discounted. Some people want to buy the book but are expecting it to be discounted, and Amazon's algorithms will probably boost the book, especially if it's been selling well anyway in its first few months.

Waiting a few months after launch before attempting to reach a bestseller list allows you to maximize profit upon launch, but it greatly reduces the amount of control you have over whether you make enough sales to be included on a list. If you make your attempt upon launch, you can keep stacking up pre-orders, charge the minimum viable ebook price, and even delay your launch if you need to stack up more pre-orders.

If you wait a few months before trying for a list, you're leaving many things up to chance. There are no guarantees you can get a BookBub Featured Deal. Even if you get a Featured Deal, you don't know if the timing of the deal will be good: You want a deal that occurs early- to mid-week, such as Tuesday or Wednesday, which gives a chance for the sales spike to drive organic sales (you can always ask BookBub for particular days, but again there are no guarantees they'll honor your request). Even if you get a Featured Deal which occurs on a good day, you might not be able to get a deal at the minimum viable ebook price. Featured Deals currently tend to be $1.99 at a minimum, while the minimum price WSJ accepted was 99¢. Even if you get everything lined up perfectly, will you be able to drop your price in time for the Featured Deal, but not so early the initial spike from dropping the price gets counted for the prior week? I've learned the hard way that aggregators don't always change your price on time, if at all. There will likely be no moment in the lifetime of your book in which the "slingshot effect" of dropping your price will be as strong as when you first discount your ebook, so don't blow it.

If it's really important to you to make a bestseller list, make your attempt at launch with a healthy and warm email list, and be prepared to not only miss out on profits, but spend thousands of dollars on supplemental ads and promotions to drive sales velocity. I've written on my blog about how I spent $6,000 on a BookBub Featured Deal and supplemental ads attempting to get *The Heart to Start* on the WSJ list, and failed, selling 2,500 copies and making less than $2,000 in revenue. By the time I did my first Featured Deal for *Mind Management*, I was trigger-shy from that experience. I spent only $3,900, made more than $2,000 revenue, and

Make a bestseller list (or don't)

sold 2,700 copies. Had I spent more, and had my aggregator not failed to change the price in time, I definitely could have breached the 3,000-copy lower limit at which it was supposedly possible to make the WSJ list.

Ask yourself seriously how badly and for what reasons you want to make a bestseller list. After two attempts, I'm not sure that I'll try again, and may simply try to maximize profits for my next book release, even if the WSJ list is reintroduced. Having "*Wall Street Journal* bestseller" in my bio would no doubt impress some people and sell some books I might not have otherwise, but my business isn't set up such that selling more copies of books rather than making a profit is my goal. Nor do I want to use such bragging rights for higher consulting or speaking fees. Additionally, I know that making an attempt at a bestseller list is exhausting, both financially and emotionally. It's even more draining emotionally when you reflect on all that preparation and effort, asking why you did it, and can't come up with a better answer than To feel important. I don't even read the *Wall Street Journal*. Why else would I care?

Aside from making a bestseller list on purpose, it's also possible to make one by accident. At some point during the lifetime of your book, an influencer with a big audience may recommend your book. Srinivas Rao is not a self-published author, but out of nowhere Rush Limbaugh recommended his book, which put Srinivas's book onto the WSJ list. So maybe that's the best way: Do your thing, make money selling your book to people who care, and if it makes a list at some point, that's great.

* * *

Another time you might make a bestseller list is if you plan a really effective "pseudo-event," which I'll talk about next.

Chapter 17
Do media stunts (aka create "pseudo-events")

Bestseller lists are a kind of "pseudo-event." Pseudo-events, as defined by Daniel J. Boorstin, are events planned so they will be covered in the media. By covering the event in the media, the event reinforces qualities about the subject of the story.

So when Brent Underwood created his one-page Kindle ebook, he created a pseudo-event. He intended for the book to get a "Best Seller" tag, then he intended to write an article about that. The ostensible purpose of the article was to attack the legitimacy of the Amazon bestseller, but Brent was likely confident the article would be shared on social media and covered by traditional media. In creating this pseudo-event, Brent brought attention to his PR firm, while reinforcing the message that PR firms like his are a means to the only "legitimate" bestseller status.

When Pat Flynn was trying to get his books on the shelves of Barnes & Noble, the campaign had many qualities of a pseudo-event. Yes, he genuinely wanted to get his books on the shelves of Barnes & Noble, but because of the highly interconnected and participatory nature of social media, he couldn't separate that goal from the coverage of the event itself in media. He wrote the blog post and mobilized his audience. His audience then went to various

Do media stunts (aka create "pseudo-events")

Barnes & Nobles, sharing the stories of their purchases on social media, which further spread the word that Pat was trying to do this cool thing. People naturally wanted to be a part of getting a self-published book onto the shelves of Barnes & Noble. Even today, eight years later, I'm talking about Pat's pseudo-event in this book. Since Pat Flynn writes about small-business entrepreneurship, this event reinforced his expertise in that field, which naturally appealed to his readers.

The "pseudo" in pseudo-event is not about the consequences of the event, other than its coverage in media. When Kim Kardashian wore one of Marilyn Monroe's dresses at the Met Gala, that was a pseudo-event, despite that she allegedly damaged the dress. She knew the press would be there, taking photos, and that people would talk about it on social media. In designing this pseudo-event, she was attempting to connect her image to that of an icon. The Unabomber's bombings were very much pseudo-events, despite that they killed and injured people. Ted Kaczynski knew they would be covered by the media, striking terror in the public. He used the threat of further bombings to coerce the *New York Times* and *Washington Post* into publishing his 30,000-word manifesto. Millions have read it, and nobody would have had he not used his deadly pseudo-events.

As you can see, pseudo-events can be anything from fun to horrifying. To design a pseudo-event, plan an event that's worth being covered in the media, and ensure that when the event is covered, the story will reinforce some quality of your brand.

So getting your book on a bestseller list is a pseudo-event. You run a campaign and spend lots of money to get the designation, and for the rest of your life you can put *"Wall Street Journal* bestselling author" in any media about you, such as in your bio and on your book's cover. And you can bet when you're a guest on a podcast, the host will mention it.

How to Sell a Book

I created a pseudo-event when I advertised my book on a billboard in Times Square.

My friend Robbie Abed had done this for one of his clients, and told me a site called Blip Billboards allows you to buy ads on billboards across the U.S. One of these billboards is in Times Square.

I didn't care who passing through Times Square would see my ad, but I did care about how having my book advertised in Times Square could be a pseudo-event. After running an experiment with a cheaper billboard in Chicago, I scheduled an ad to run in Times Square. I hired a photographer to take the above photo and record video. Then I created media about the media the photographer had created (a photo) of my media (a billboard). I shared it on social media, wrote a blog post, talked about it on my podcast, posted on Reddit, and sent a story about it to my email list.

It was remarkable as a self-published author to have my book advertised in Times Square, so my readers were excited about it. But part of what was remarkable about the story was how cheaply I was able to run the ad. I paid as little as $20 for each time one of my ads showed up on the billboard in Times Square. (Amongst the photographer, my test ads, and running two ads several times, I spent a total of about $450.)

Do media stunts (aka create "pseudo-events")

Once I had created and talked about my pseudo-event, I was excited to see what would happen next. Tim Ferriss retweeted a video of my billboard to his 1.8 million followers, a self-publishing podcast had me as a guest where we talked about my pseudo-event, and the New York Public Library started stocking my books and invited me to speak in their CEO Series, via videoconferencing. My talk is now listed on NYPL's website, alongside those of Marie Forleo, Seth Godin, and A.J. Jacobs. The page links back to my website, giving me a powerful .org link that boosts my SEO.

If I'm to critique my own pseudo-event, I'll say that what it reinforced about the book wasn't exactly clear. I liked the idea that my book had "time" in the title, and that it was in Times Square, in a city obsessed with time. I also thought it was fun to use deliberately vague language in my ad to suggest something that wasn't true: My ad said it's a "#1 bestseller," which was true (Amazon) and it said "New York is reading," which was technically true (people in New York were reading it). But somehow those facts got scrambled up in the brain to suggest that my book is a *New York Times* bestseller. The ad said "bestseller," was in New York, and was in Times Square. In retelling the story, I even caught myself several times starting to say, "*New York Times* Square." So my pseudo-event was a fun and mischievous satire of traditional media, by a self-published author with no traditional-media presence. It didn't reinforce much about my book, in particular. But part of my story as an author is that I'm self-published, and thus have to be resourceful, and advertising in Times Square for $20 is a good example of that.

✷ ✷ ✷

Pseudo-events are one of many ways to sell a book, but there may be no better way than simply writing more books.

Chapter 18
Write more books

It's far easier to make a profit selling books if you have multiple books. If you're an indie author playing a portfolio strategy, publishing multiple books gives you more chances to get lucky and have a hit. Each book you publish also teaches you more about choosing the right book idea and marketing your book. Each book is a chance to improve as a writer, even if only by starting from scratch to avoid mistakes you've made in earlier books.

It's very common for writers who have never published a book to have one book they've been working on for years, that they expect to be wildly successful. They've hired multiple editors and cover designers. They've taken multiple writing workshops and each time re-written the book from scratch using the new tricks they've learned.

If one of these writers encounters me somewhere along their journey, naturally they'll want my advice, too. Without fail, they've done nothing to publicly test the content of their book and so have no audience to sell it to. They're wandering through the mountain range, looking to anyone with experience as if they might be a wizard that will bestow on them a magical amulet that will unlock the secrets to publishing success. Being asked for advice by them is frustrating, because I know there's nothing I can say that can get them to accept the truth. I try to avoid conversations with these writers altogether, but if I knew they'd listen, I'd say: "Publish that book, then start writing the next."

I know from personal experience how they feel, and what they're thinking. I was in a similar position when I had written multiple book proposals and tried to get a book deal for my second book. I was fortunate to get past that for two reasons. One was that I interviewed Seth Godin on my podcast, and he told me I should be publishing a book a week on Kindle. Two was that I had already published one book, motivated by a traditional publishing contract, so I knew that publishing is scary and fear can make you come up with any reason in the world why you're not ready. Still, it took several months for Seth's advice to sink in and motivate me to act. I didn't publish a book a week, but once I did begin self-publishing, I published three books in six months. One was the full-length *The Heart to Start*, and the other two were my first "short reads."

Two is two, three is six

Publishing lots of books diversifies your portfolio and teaches you lessons, but it also provides multiple entry points into your catalog. If a reader enjoys your writing, from each of those entry points they may next jump to any other book you've written. There's more likely to find something enticing if you've written two other books rather than one, or three other books rather than two. If you've written no other books, the next book they'll read will be by a different author.

You can see the power laws of writing multiple books by visualizing and quantifying two-book paths a reader can take through your catalog. In other words, how many different ways can a reader go from the first time reading a book by you to the second time?

If you've written two books, A and B, there are two paths they can take: A→B or B→A. One more book is just one more book, but it's four more paths a reader can take. If you've written three books, there are now six two-book paths. By writing a fourth book, you can increase the number of potential two-book paths to twelve.

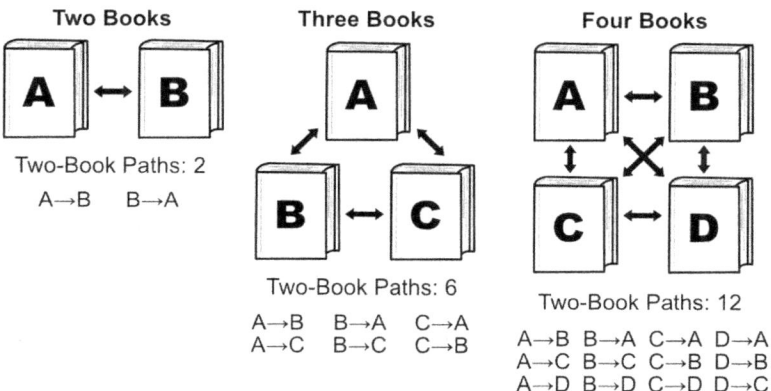

If a reader reads two books by you, they'll naturally be interested in a third. Each additional book doesn't just increase potential entry-points into your catalog, it multiplies the number of ways a one-time reader of your books can become a habitual reader.

As I've described in the section about direct sales, it's also much easier to turn a profit and beat Amazon's prices selling directly if a customer buys multiple books at once. It's impossible for them to buy multiple books at once if you've only written one!

Write in series

The surest way to get a reader to keep buying your books is to publish a series of books that belong together. Writing in series is standard practice amongst indie fiction authors. Fiction authors have the advantage that their series' continue stories, and reading each subsequent book is essentially the same "product" as the previous book. Enjoyment of reading the story is the product. If

Write more books

they enjoyed the last book, they'll likely enjoy the next. And if the author has finished the previous book with a "cliffhanger," the reader will be motivated to keep reading the story.

With nonfiction, it's not as easy to provide a series of books that must be read together. Nonfiction is typically meant to solve a problem or provide knowledge, and once you've read a book it takes time to absorb and apply the content. Certainly people also read nonfiction just for the enjoyment of reading a particular author's writing style, or to reinforce concepts they already know but either want validated or need constant reminders to apply. I like to read Nassim Taleb's *Incerto* series because it's fun to try on his perspective. But I've let years pass between reading one of Taleb's books and another. They're related, but don't compel you to read them in order, the way a fiction series does.

Breaking a nonfiction book into a series that must be read together would feel unfair to the reader, unless the book is so long it makes sense. I broke *Getting Art Done* into a series not only because one book would have been too long, but because the struggles I wanted to address in the series tend to take place in different parts of someone's creative journey. Getting the courage to start creating projects is its own challenge, optimizing the use of your creative energy is another, and finishing and shipping projects is another. It would be weird to have seven short books on each of those three topics.

Now that I've published two books in that series, I've seen some of the benefits of having multiple entry points into a series. Notice the revenue and ad spend of *The Heart to Start* and *Mind Management*, in the graph below. For the first couple years in the life of *The Heart to Start*, I could barely make more revenue than I spent on ads. Once *Mind Management* came out, suddenly I was making more profit on *The Heart to Start*.

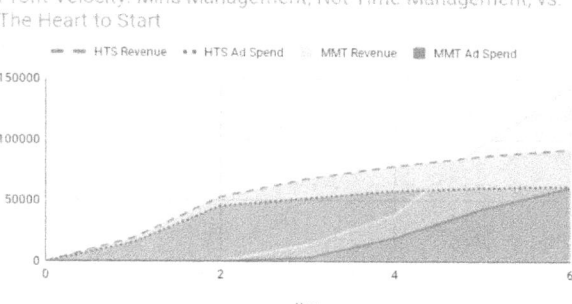

I posit that once I finish the final book in the series, the profit margins of both these books will rise. Retailers such as Amazon promote with one another books in series, and the human mind naturally feels more compelled to read another book by an author if it's in the same series as the previous book they've read. I could also bundle the books into a single ebook "box set," or run a Kickstarter for a premium collector's edition physical box set, with a sleeve that holds all three books, and printing flourishes such as foil stamping.

Write diversely

You'll probably see a bigger lift in profit per additional book if each new book you write clearly belongs in a series with your previous books, but that doesn't mean you should restrict yourself to writing in series if your interests tempt you to do otherwise. I've written several books outside of the *Getting Art Done* series. *Design for Hackers* is about design, and *Digital Zettelkasten* is about an obscure note-taking method. You can draw connections amongst all my books simply because they all come from my mind. Even if you have diverse interests, the topics you're interested in will tend to be related somehow. Design is a creative field, which connects *Design for Hackers* to the *Getting Art Done* series on creative productivity. People interested in creative productivity tend to be interested in

Write more books

How to Write a Book, and if you're a writer, it's no surprise if you're interested in building a Zettelkasten. Even design and Zettelkästen apparently attract people with similar interests: When I announced *Digital Zettelkasten* on the r/zettelkasten subreddit, one of the first comments was, "*the* David Kadavy wrote a Zettelkasten book? Fastest sell ever." Turns out this reader had loved *Design for Hackers*.

Don't be afraid to write books about a lot of different topics. Mark Manson's first book, *Models*, was about dating, and his follow-up hit, *The Subtle Art of Not Giving a F*ck*, was a broader self-help book. *Subtle Art* was such a massive hit it got Mark a gig writing a biography of Will Smith. Ryan Holiday's first book, *Trust Me, I'm Lying*, was about media, and now he's writing books about Stoicism. I hope to release a book about golf in coming years, which seems wildly unrelated to anything I've written before, but you can bet it will be written in the deconstructive and analytical style of my previous books.

If a book is highly unrelated to your previous books, you can release it under a pen name. This arguably helps with marketing, as it trains algorithms to associate your name and pen name with their respective topics. But a pen name is probably more useful for your creative mindset as an author than anything else. I've written and released some fiction under a secret pen name, mostly because I enjoy embodying a different persona when I write fiction. I also appreciate the anonymity as I learn in an area where I'm not confident in my abilities. But Steven Pressfield has had no problem in his career writing creative productivity books such as *The War of Art* alongside historical fiction novels such as *Gates of Fire*. It seems all roads from authors who write on a variety of topics lead to Will Smith. Smith starred in the movie based upon Pressfield's novel about golf, *The Legend of Bagger Vance*.

When you have multiple books, it's much easier to make a profit off pricing promotions, such as BookBub Featured Deals.

Many readers discover you for the first time during these deals, and if your other books are also discounted, some will buy those books, too. This is a good tactic to make up for the lower royalty rate on Amazon during pricing promotions. You'll only make 35% on a book discounted to $1.99, but if you discount your other books to $2.99 or $3.99, you'll still motivate sales, but will earn a 70% royalty. Pricing promotions are even more effective for authors of fiction series. They can promote the first book in a series for cheap or free, and charge more for the rest of the books in the series, which readers will want to read if they get hooked on the story and characters in the first book.

In sum, don't think you only have one book in you, and that it has to be perfect. The more books you write, the more of all your books you'll sell.

You'll also have more books for which you can sell foreign rights.

Chapter 19
Sell foreign rights

Selling foreign rights to your books is free money for work you've already done. It helps you sell more books and make more profit. Other than one report I've received that 500 books of the first print run of one of my foreign-rights deals sold out, I don't count my books from foreign publishers in my 100,000 self-published books sold, though the first print runs of the fifteen deals I've made amount to about 30,000 additional books. But I definitely count the money I've made off these deals. These foreign-rights deals have made nearly $18,000, and helped me reach readers I couldn't have otherwise.

Translate yourself? (Nope.)

You might wonder, since I've been focused in this book on how to sell a book as a self-published author, why I'm talking about making deals with foreign publishers. Why don't I hire translators and release my books in various languages? I've actually tried that. I paid a translator to translate my short read, *How to Write a Book* into Spanish, and I released it on Kindle and paperback through Amazon KDP, enrolled in KDP Select. After several years, that version has barely made back the few hundred dollars I spent on translation. I've confirmed through this experiment what I've heard from other self-publishing experts, such as Joanna Penn: You shouldn't bother trying to create and market your own foreign translations.

The first reason not to bother creating and marketing your own foreign translations is that foreign book markets are not like your local book market. Amazon is not as dominant in many countries as it is in the U.S., for example. Nor are ebooks as popular around the world as they are in the U.S. What works to sell a book in the U.S. doesn't necessarily work to sell a book in Spain. A foreign publisher knows its market. It knows how to sell a book in its territory, and it's more complicated than simply uploading a foreign translation to Amazon KDP.

The second reason not to bother with your own foreign translations is managing a foreign translation is more complicated than you expect. When I experimented with a Spanish version of one of my books, there were lots of tiny things that needed to be translated beyond the obvious. For example, sales copy for Lockscreen Ads. Fortunately for me, I speak Spanish well enough to be married to someone who only speaks Spanish, which also means I live with someone who natively speaks Spanish. I did a lot of little translations myself, with her assistance. And I still have barely made back my investment.

Which brings me to the third reason not to bother with your own foreign translations, which is that it's a lot of extra work for very little money. If you have the privilege of writing in English for English-speaking markets, your time and energy is better spent marketing your books in that language.

Making a deal with a publisher for foreign translations and sometimes even foreign versions of your original book is better than doing it on your own. The only work you have to do is negotiate the deal, review and sign the contract, and watch your bank account for a wire to arrive. Free money!

If you still want to try making your own translation, give it a shot. Just know you're risking failure and wasting time and energy that could be better spent elsewhere. But some authors claim to have no problems doing their own translations. And if you're writing natively in, say, German, and want to do your own translation into English, that's probably very much worth trying, as it opens opportunities in a huge market.

Finding foreign-rights deals

I've learned through experience you don't get foreign-rights deals the way you might expect, which for me was to search for foreign publishers and send them pitch emails. The best way to get your first foreign-rights deals is simply to sell a lot of books in your native language. Especially if you publish in English in the U.S. or UK, publishers in other markets are sifting through Amazon, looking for books they already know sell well and that they think will also sell well in their markets. Just make sure that if someone searches for your author name, they can find a way to contact you, such as a website that lists an email address. Then, sell as many books as you can in your language. If you sell a lot, someone will contact you.

When someone contacts you, it's not unusual for them to ask for a PDF of your entire book. Lots of authors worry this is a scam to pirate your book, but it's normal. Since I do my own page layout, I can quickly and easily make a watermark featuring the publisher's name on every page of the PDF I send, by exporting from my page layout software. There are other tools to watermark PDFs, such as Adobe Acrobat.

I at least look up the publisher, to confirm they have a website and that I'm receiving an email from an address on the same domain as their website. I also check the LinkedIn profile of the person emailing me. All of this could be faked, but I make a judgment call. So far I've never been victim of a scam due to sending a

PDF of my book. If your book is good, someone's going to pirate it anyway, but many more will buy it, so it's not worth missing out on real opportunities just because you won't send a publisher a PDF.

If you don't hear back from a foreign publisher, follow up. Follow up until you feel uncomfortable about bothering them. Follow up like a fly at a Sunday barbecue. Follow up until they either offer you a deal or tell you to get lost. I use a Gmail plugin called Boomerang to send any email thread back into my inbox if there hasn't been activity in, say, four weeks, to remind me to follow up. Four weeks is a good amount of time within which to follow up, because publishers work slowly. But follow up, follow up, follow up. I have made many foreign rights deals that wouldn't have happened had I not followed up. Following up with foreign publishers is the easiest money I've made as an author.

Is it a good deal?

After you send a PDF of your book, and follow up several times, you may get an offer. Most foreign-rights deals consist of the following parameters:

- Language: What language do they want to translate to and sell in? (if applicable)
- Territory: In what country or countries do they want to sell?
- Duration: How many years? (five is standard)
- Advance: How much money will they pay you up-front?
- First Print Run: How many copies do they want to print?
- Royalty Rate: What percentage will you earn of each sale?

Sell foreign rights

- Retail Price: The price at which they plan to sell your book.

The parameters that affect how much money you make are the First Print Run, the Royalty Rate, and the Retail Price. But in my experience, there's no point negotiating the First Print Run or the Retail Price. The publisher knows their market way better than you could ever hope to, so they know the right price for your book in their market, and they know how many books they're willing to print.

The one parameter that affects how much you make that you can and should negotiate is the Royalty Rate. Out of all my deals, the lowest Royalty Rate I've had was 6% for Korean, and the highest I've had was 10% for Russian and 10% for English in Malaysia. (Yes, I've even sold English rights. More on that later.) Some authors claim to get a Royalty Rate as high as 12%, but I haven't. Most my deals are at 9%. Most deals don't cover ebook and audiobook rights, but the only Royalty Rate I've seen for those is 25%.

So the Royalty Rate, times the Retail Price, times the First Print Run tells you *approximately* what you'll make on the deal. In my opinion, this group of parameters is secondary to the most important number in your foreign-rights deal: the Advance.

Personally, I'd rather have a big Advance than a high Royalty Rate. I keep a spreadsheet where I evaluate and record my foreign-rights deals, and I have a column called "Copies to Pay Out." The formula for this column calculates:

Advance ÷ (Retail Price in USD × Royalty Rate)

So if I have a $1,000 Advance on a $10 Retail Price book on which I'm earning a 10% Royalty Rate, I'm earning $1 per book, so they have to sell 1,000 copies before I earn out that Advance.

How to Sell a Book

The quantity calculated in the Copies to Pay Out column is right next to the quantity of the First Print Run. In my opinion, if the Copies to Pay Out number isn't larger than the First Print Run, the deal *stinks!* I don't care if the Royalty Rate is 1% or 100%, if the Copies to Pay Out Column number isn't larger than the First Print Run number, I need to negotiate a better deal.

Why? Because I don't trust foreign publishers beyond the money they wire to my bank account when they pay me the Advance. They're in another country, often operating in a different language. I have no idea how many copies they're selling, and don't have the resources to travel to their offices to conduct audits, nor hire lawyers to take them to court. If a publisher has paid me $1,000, they'll probably have a hard time stiffing me for $1,000 more even if they try. $1,000 is still significant money to me, but it's hardly enough to justify going to small claims court at a county courthouse in central Nebraska, never mind an international trial.

Your foreign-rights contracts will likely stipulate compensation beyond the First Print Run and/or Advance. For example, my contract for Arabic rights, with a Saudi Arabian publisher, paid me $1,200 for a First Print Run of 2,000 copies. The contract stipulates they'll pay me $750 per 1,000 additional copies they print. That's my only contract where additional copies are compensated in that way. Most simply promise that I'll be paid additional royalties beyond the Advance, calculated by multiplying the Retail Price times the Royalty Rate. For example, a Vietnamese publisher also paid me $1,200 for a First Print Run of 2,000 copies. After earning a 7% Royalty Rate on books with a Retail Price at about $6.72, they need to sell 2,549 copies before I've earned out my Advance. For each copy sold thereafter, they have to pay me 7%, lumped together on an annual basis.

Since the number of copies the Vietnamese publisher needs to sell before I earn out my Advance is higher than the First Print Run, that suggests to me I've gotten a big Advance. They'll need to

Sell foreign rights

print again before I earn out my Advance. On paper it might sound like you'd rather have a quantity of Copies to Pay Out smaller than the First Print Run, because you'd be owed more money before the First Print Run is sold, but that would only matter if you trusted the publisher to pay you beyond the Advance. I've heard some authors in forums claim they've never had a foreign-rights deal that *didn't* pay beyond the Advance, but more commonly you hear they've never had a deal that did. I've personally never been paid beyond an Advance for a foreign-rights deal. I've even had trouble getting some publishers to send me my contractually-stipulated author copies. Granted, I made my first self-published foreign-rights deal three years ago, and despite paying me, that publisher never released the book. The next-newest deals are only two years old, so there's still time for my lack of trust to be proven incorrect.

One of the major terms stipulated in foreign-rights deals for which unrealistic advice gets thrown around is Territory, or where in the world the foreign publisher has the rights to distribute their version of your book. The advice I heard before I made my own foreign-rights deals was that you want to restrict the Territory in your contract to the smallest area possible. For example, supposedly if you make a deal for Spanish with a publisher in Spain, you should restrict the Territory to just Spain. That way, you can make separate deals with publishers in other Spanish-speaking countries that know how to market to readers in their respective countries.

After fifteen deals, I have yet to restrict Territory on deals in foreign languages. The first reason is I have yet to make a deal in a language that is spoken many places other than its country of origin. Languages spoken in multiple countries, such as Spanish and French, tend to already have many great books written natively in those languages. When you make a deal in Spanish or French, you know your book has "made it," because you've written something that isn't fully covered by authors writing in those languages. More likely, your first foreign-rights deals will be in Vietnamese,

Polish, or Korean. I've sold, or had sold through my traditional publisher, rights to each of those three languages multiple times.

The second reason why I have yet to restrict Territory on deals in foreign languages is that even if you sold rights to, say, Vietnamese, and those rights were restricted only to Vietnam, just imagine the conversation of trying to sell Vietnamese rights outside of Vietnam:

"We'd like to buy Vietnamese rights to your book."

"Great, you can have them everywhere except…Vietnam."

So all my translation deals so far grant worldwide rights.

English rights abroad

The one type of foreign-rights deals I make extra sure *not* to grant worldwide rights is my foreign-rights deals in English. Why would I make foreign-rights deals in English? Amazon has online stores around the world, and IngramSpark has "global" distribution, so surely everyone in the world can order my books? That's not technically true, and even if it's possible to order my books, it's not economically feasible in some parts of the world.

For example, if someone in India wanted to buy a copy of my KDP Print paperback edition of *Mind Management*, it would cost 1,717 Rupees, which right now is about $20.50. That doesn't sound too bad to an American since the cover price is $19.95. But consider that the average annual income in India is $1,314. Yes, that's *annual* and I didn't misplace the comma. That's about two-dozen times less than the average annual income in the U.S. This isn't due to a lack of ambition or hard work, their economy just hasn't developed as much as that of the U.S., so there are few opportunities to make more.

Certainly there are wealthy Indians who can afford a $20 book, but for the rest, if there's a way I can get my book into their hands for cheaper, I'm interested. That's where Territory-restricted

English rights come in. I made a deal with an Indian publisher who can sell my book in English for $4.24. I haven't held one of these books in my hands yet, and I'm sure the print and paper quality is far below what I use for the books I sell in the U.S., but that's impressively cheap. That deal is restricted to the Indian subcontinent, including Pakistan, Sri Lanka, Nepal, Bhutan, Bangladesh, and the Maldives. You can bet the contract does not say "worldwide rights." Those belong to me, except where I've made Territory-restricted English deals.

Before I made any of my Territory-restricted English deals, I was sure to make clear to the publishers to what extent I could prevent distribution of my own versions within their territories. For the Kindle and KDP Print versions, I can restrict distribution to a country by un-checking a box. I don't have that granularity of control for the paperback and hardcover editions distributed through IngramSpark. So, we've stipulated in the contract that my versions being available in their country isn't a violation of their rights. Their versions are much cheaper anyway, and they know more about how to make books available in their country in the stores where people buy books.

Hire a lawyer?

I've now used the "C" word a number of times in talking about foreign-rights deals, so I need to address it because I know it makes lots of new entrepreneurs nervous. Yes, all these foreign-rights deals have *contracts*. Yes, the first versions of these contracts sometimes have sneaky things written into them. Yes, there are some contracts that are downright predatory. So yes, absolutely, you *should* hire a lawyer to review all these contracts. But I've never hired a lawyer to review my foreign-rights contracts.

I've never hired a lawyer to review these contracts because that would cost as much or more than I'm making on some of these contracts. I'm a writer. I know how to read. I understand words. I know that if a contract says, "worldwide exclusive English rights, in perpetuity, including any future formats heretofore unknown," I'd be signing my work away were I to sign that contract. There could be some crazy loophole of international law I don't know about that would screw me despite a contract making sense and seeming fair. So far that hasn't happened. But that's a risk I take not hiring a lawyer. We're all entitled to take our own risks and potentially suffer the consequences.

So read and understand your foreign-rights contracts carefully, review them with the help of an LLM such as ChatGPT or Claude, then hire a lawyer to review them. Or use your best judgment and take your own risks, at your own risk. You might be able to find a lawyer working pro-bono. The Alliance of Independent Authors claims to provide contract reviews, but when I was looking for help with my first contract, the response I got was that they had a queue a few weeks long, and I would hear back from them once they got around to reviewing my contract. But I never heard from them again, and didn't follow up. I still join their organization for some of the discounts, but I don't bother asking for help with contracts.

Foreign-rights agents

You can lower your risk of signing an unfavorable contract and earn more money on your deals with the help of a foreign-rights agent. Foreign-rights agents find and negotiate deals on your behalf, in exchange for a commission as a percentage of your deal. Some take 10%, and others as much as 20%. That sounds like a lot, but in my experience, good foreign-rights agents more than make up for what they take in commission by negotiating a better deal.

When I was negotiating my deal for the Indian subcontinent, I had two publishers interested in my books. The deal also poten-

Sell foreign rights

tially involved two books across six languages, including my first territory-restricted English deal, so it was more complex than I was comfortable managing on my own. So, I handed off the negotiation to an agent I had worked with previously (we agreed upon a reduced fee, since the deals had come to me, first). In a single email, she was able to nearly double the advance I had negotiated over a few weeks' time. There didn't appear to be anything unique about what she said in the email. My best guess is that publishers know an agent knows what good terms are, and agents work with publishers repeatedly, so long-term relationships are at stake. The whole thing feels like a racket, but again, as long as I'm not giving up my worldwide English rights, I'm willing to work with an agent to make more money and get ostensibly more fair terms. I still read my contract carefully, and if you can get a lawyer's advice on the contract, all the better.

When you work with an agent, the publisher pays them, not you. So you have to trust that the agent is going to pass on your share of payments. This is easy to monitor for the Advance, as it's written right into the contract, but thereafter, you're trusting that agent to pay you if you earn out your Advance and earn further payment. From one perspective, your agent has experience and relationships with foreign publishers, so can fight for you to make sure you get paid. From another perspective, when working with an agent you often don't even have a contact at the publisher, so have no idea whether the publisher has sent additional payments. Since long-term relationships between agents and publishers are at stake, perhaps an agent would rather *not* fight a publisher they want to make future deals with. All the more reason to write more books. Your agent is more likely to pay you for a past deal if a potential future deal is at stake.

I heard one author claim, while giving a talk on foreign rights, "Every agent I've ever had has stolen from me." The alternative is to make your own foreign-rights deals, negotiating your own contracts and collecting payments on your own. After making fifteen foreign-rights deals over the past couple years, I still don't know the best way. So far, I prefer working with agents because it's less work for me, for more money up-front. I'm not working on big deals yet. They've ranged from Advances of $200 each for five different languages in the Indian subcontinent, to $4,000 for the Korean version of *Digital Zettelkasten*. So whatever mistakes I'm making likely don't amount to a lot of money. But I'm learning through doing so I can be prepared when I make bigger deals.

Like finding foreign-rights deals, I don't have much better advice for finding a foreign-rights agent other than to sell as many books as you can in your language and wait for them to come to you. Sometimes when I get an email asking about foreign rights, it's from an agent who is already working to arrange a deal with a publisher, and so I work with that agent. I also work with an agent I got introduced to by reaching out to a successful author in my genre. When I've otherwise gone searching for a foreign-rights agent, all I could find was a high-profile agency, 2 Seas, who wasn't accepting inquiries, and another agent who had represented a bunch of books I had never heard of, and who had what I considered predatory terms in her contract (she wanted 20% of any foreign-rights deal I made with or without her help, worldwide, for two years).

Many self-published authors have the attitude about foreign-rights deals that they're free money for selling rights they aren't yet using anyway. That's about the attitude I take, but unlike many with this attitude, I at least try to negotiate.

* * *

You can sell a book in another language on the other side of the planet, or you can sell a book to someone standing right in front of you.

Chapter 20
Try in-person sales

You can sell your books in-person by setting up a booth or table at a trade show, craft fair, farmers' market, or conference. Whether this is an effective way to sell your book will depend upon whether it makes sense for that book to be sold in that context. If you're a fantasy author and want to sell books at Comic-Con, that would make sense. If you have a keto cookbook, you could probably sell several copies at your local farmers' market.

The main challenges in selling your books at in-person events are setting up and paying for a booth that will generate sales, and knowing how much inventory to bring with you. Since decorating your booth has up-front costs, and setting up to make in-person sales has a learning curve, I wouldn't recommend trying it unless you can think of several events in your area where you can try as you learn, and you're willing to lose some money in "tuition" to learn in-person sales.

Since I live in a Spanish-speaking country, there are no viable events in my area for selling books in-person, but I've sold books at one event, just to see what it was like. I paid $50 for a booth at the RAVE event in Las Vegas, as part of the 20BooksTo50k conference (now Author Nation), and sold $100 worth of books. Here's what my "booth" looked like.

How to Sell a Book

I had bought the smallest possible half-table at the conference, which was to be two feet wide. When I showed up, it turned out I had a four-foot half-table. That was good for letting my books spread out, but it made my tablecloth not fit so well: I had purchased one exactly two feet wide at a fabric store, which in Colombia only cost me a few dollars.

I couldn't justify the cost to print a standing banner, like the one you can see on the right side of the picture, belonging to my neighbor. A 24" x 62" vinyl banner would have cost at least $90, and I had no plans to do future shows.

But, I wanted to attract the attention of passers-by somehow, so I lugged my antique typewriter on the plane to display on my table. I printed special cards, 100 for $32, which would hold about 100 words from my typewriter, and invited people to start their 100-word writing habits on the typewriter. Next to the typewriter, I also kept my iPad, opened to the sign-up page for my free *100-Word Writing Habit* email course. I bought plastic risers and book stands on Amazon, which together cost about $45. I also printed bookmarks, 150 for $57, which featured a coupon for my online store.

Not many people actually typed on the typewriter, but it definitely got people to stop and talk to me. It was useful to talk to

Try in-person sales

people in-person and see how they reacted to my books, but I wouldn't say that was so valuable as to justify the whole project.

Planning my table at the show turned out to be much more work than I had expected. I measured the space on furniture I already had, to set things up, see how they'd look, and even mock-up the printed material I had planned onto the photo.

I lost money doing this and spent a lot of time. I don't plan to do it again.

I used furniture in my house to simulate and plan my in-person event display.

Authors who succeed at in-person sales tend to have lots of books, and live within driving distance of several viable events. Driving to events helps a lot because not only does it make it easier to bring your inventory to the event, it doesn't leave you in the position where you're desperate to sell your remaining inventory for cheap as the event is shutting down (so you don't have to bring it on a plane). Some event-goers know authors are in this position at the end of a show, and descend like vultures as the show is shutting down.

A self-published author who has had a lot of success selling in-person, and who has talked and written a lot about it online is science-fiction author Ben Wolf.

How to Sell a Book

Author Ben Wolf's in-person event display. Copyright Ben Wolf. Used with permission.

In most states, if you're selling at an in-person event, you're liable for sales tax in that state. When I sold at RAVE, we simply paid the event organizers, who had arranged to file sales taxes with the state of Nevada.

* * *

Another way to sell books in-person is by going on a book tour.

Chapter 21
Go on a book tour (maybe)

One of the first things people think about when they think about selling books is book tours. But I've put them last indeed because they are least. Most likely the lowest ROI you can have for your marketing dollars and hours is by organizing and going on a book tour.

As I mentioned when talking about launches, I organized a book tour for my first, traditionally-published, book. I raised money on Kickstarter for a ten-city tour in the U.S. I broke that tour up into a few different trips, and while I was on the tour, people from a couple more cities reached out. So I ended up going to twelve cities.

My book tour did work, but it probably wasn't the best use of my time and money, and the reasons it did work were unique to my book. *Design for Hackers* came to be through grassroots support of the budding startup community, circa 2010. I got my book deal because the Hacker News community loved my content. At that time, there was a lot of excitement about startups, as incubators were popping up around the country, outside of Silicon Valley. So there was a lot of excitement about my book in the startup community in general, and in various cities around the country there were local communities with incubators and meetup groups that were eager to have me come speak. Finally, it was the right time in my life for a book tour. I had been holed up in my apartment in Chicago the previous winter, writing, didn't have any reason to want to be in Chicago all the time, and was eager to travel.

Raising money for my tour on Kickstarter was integral to making my book tour successful, and to launching my book. People came out to see me speak, or invited me to speak to their local startup communities, because they had seen the campaign. As I mentioned when talking about launches, fulfilling the backers gave me a good way to generate a lot of sales for my book in a short amount of time, to boost my Amazon rank within a particular hour on launch day.

I didn't raise enough money to actually cover the expenses of my book tour. I raised about $5,800 for the ten cities I had planned, and local startup communities paid to help get me to a couple other cities. Aside from having to buy several dozen books for backers with that funding, I had to pay for plane tickets, transportation, meals, and hotels, though a couple readers reached out and offered me places to stay, and fortunately that worked out.

Overall, my book tour worked fine and was a life-changing experience for me. In fact, it led me to speak in Chile at a conference organized by someone I met on the tour, which in a roundabout way led to me living in South America.

But I wouldn't recommend a book tour as a marketing tactic for most authors, unless it's a tactic that's integrated with an appropriate strategy. If there is a vibrant nation- or world-wide community behind the topic of your book, if that community is just your huge following, or if there is simply a physical-space, participatory element to your book's topic that you could best bring to life by being in various places, a book tour *could* work. There may be local meetup groups who would love to have you come talk about your book. If traveling around the country for weeks or months doesn't

Go on a book tour (maybe)

feel exciting to you, I'd recommend you focus on other more cost-effective ways to market your book, other than a book tour.

In fact, here come a bunch more.

Chapter 22
43 tactics to sell a book

From this book and your own brainstorming, you likely have an overwhelming number of ideas for how you can sell a book. But you probably don't have the time and money to do all of them at once. Even if you did them all at once, it would be impossible to know what worked – any increase in sales could be due to one or two tactics, but not the others.

Over the years of selling my books, I've been inspired by what Benjamin Franklin did for his "Thirteen Virtues." For one week at a time, he would focus primarily on one of his thirteen virtues, such as frugality, cleanliness, or humility. By focusing on one at a time, he made more progress in learning to uphold each virtue than if he had tried to uphold all at once.

So, I've kept a master list of book-marketing tactics. Each time I've had a new idea of how to sell a book, instead of springing into action, I've added the idea to the list. I've tried to focus on one at a time, which has helped give myself a decent chance to succeed with each tactic, but has also helped me better estimate whether the tactic has increased my sales.

Admittedly, I haven't been perfect at trying all these tactics, and I haven't kept great records of whether each of them worked.

43 tactics to sell a book

That's probably for the best, because what has worked for me won't necessarily work for you, and vice-versa.

Here are forty-three tactics to sell a book. Try each one for a time, and add your own ideas to the list.

1. Ask a local bookstore to host an event featuring your book.
2. Enter your book into contests. A few reputable contests are BookLife Prize, Self Publishing Review's SPR Book Awards, and the Independent Author Network's Book of the Year Awards.
3. Have fellow authors recommend your book on their BookBub profiles.
4. When your ebook is free, post it on Reddit's FreeEBOOKS subreddit.
5. Black Swan social engineering: Figure out ways to get your book in front of influencers who could create a positive "Black Swan" event for the book. Brainstorm who those people are, what they might do, and how you could influence them to do that thing.
6. Book website: Build a website just for your book, to generate email subscribers and direct people to the various buying options.
7. Post a presentation on SlideShare describing in a compelling way the main idea behind your book.
8. Journalist outreach: Identify journalists who might like to cover your book. Analyze their work, develop and send pitches, and follow up. (You can also try to figure out what smaller outlets they get story ideas from, and get covered by those outlets – what Ryan Holiday calls "Trading Up the Chain.")
9. Email course: Develop an email course based upon

your book. Send out a short lesson in each email, referencing further information in your book.
10. Podcast course: Produce a podcast-based course on topics in your book.
11. Facebook Group: Set up a Facebook, Discord, or other group for readers of the book. If you don't want the long-term commitment of managing a community, it can be a "flash" group that ends after a certain amount of time.
12. Workbook: Develop a workbook for learning to implement the concepts covered in your book.
13. Submit to BookBub as a Featured New Release for Less.
14. Submit to BookBub as a Featured Deal pricing promotion.
15. Submit a request to Blinkist to summarize your book.
16. Buy a list of addresses of libraries or bookstores and send them promotional material via mail.
17. Answer questions related to your book's topic on Quora.
18. Advertise using Quora Ads.
19. Test out new cover designs by running BookBub Ads and seeing which covers have the highest click-through rate.
20. Test out description copy by running test ads on Meta.
21. Run a giveaway using KingSumo Giveaways. Give away related books, to boost your book's ranking in the "Also Boughts" recommended on Amazon.
22. Identify a popular blog in your industry, then brainstorm and pitch a guest post idea.
23. Run a giveaway of your book using Goodreads Giveaways.

24. Run Google Ads targeting searches for books related to yours.
25. List on your website ways readers can help spread the word about your book, including "swipe copy" they can copy and paste into their email newsletters or social media posts.
26. Write on your blog reviews for books related to yours, so you can rank highly when people search for those books.
27. List on your website a page featuring "Top 10 Books About [Topic]," for the topic of your book.
28. Amazon Reviewer Outreach: Find the contact information for top Amazon reviewers who have reviewed books related to yours, and offer to send them copies of your book.
29. Keyword Optimization: Monitor your book's ranking for various keyword searches on Amazon. Run test ads to gauge volume of searches for those keywords. Change your back-end keywords in KDP and optimize your description to help rank highly on the most-relevant keywords.
30. Podcast Appearances: Identify and analyze podcasts you'd like to be on. Work hard brainstorming ideas for each podcast, and pitch proposals to the hosts and producers.
31. Educator Outreach: Identify professors at universities who might teach classes that could use your book. Write proposals and pitch those professors.
32. Blogger Outreach: Identify bloggers who have reviewed related books. Contact them and offer to send them books.
33. YouTuber Outreach: Same as above, but with YouTubers.

34. Goodreads Ads: Use Goodreads' "Advertise With Us" contact form to explore direct advertising on Goodreads.
35. Also-Bought Hacking: Keep a spreadsheet that tracks your book's position as an "Also-Bought" on related books on Amazon. Use various tactics trying to get readers of those books to also buy your book. You can over-bid on ads on those books' pages, run a giveaway of those books, and/or have the authors of those books on your podcast.
36. Book Trailer: Create a flashy video to get people excited about your book.
37. Online Conference: Organize an online conference which you livestream on YouTube, and on which you invite other authors in your field to speak or be interviewed.
38. YouTube Videos: Do keyword research to identify topics related to your book on which you could create videos.
39. Multi-Day Livestream Course: Promote a schedule of lessons you will livestream on TikTok, YouTube Live, Instagram, etc. Show up on that schedule and give a lesson every day for a week or two.
40. Electronic ARCs: Set up your ebook as an ARC on NetGalley and/or Edelweiss, so journalists and book professionals can read your book in advance.
41. Advertise with *Publisher's Weekly*, through BookLife's "PW Select Module," to reach booksellers and librarians.
42. Try to get listed on libraryreads.org, such as by networking with people on the Steering Committee.
43. Editorial Reviews: Submit for or pay for reviews from BookLife, Readers' Favorite, American Library

43 tactics to sell a book

Association, Best Seller's World, Kirkus, Blue Ink Review, and/or Indie Reader.

As I review this list, I'm reminded of many promising tactics I have yet to try!

Appendix

As mentioned in the Introduction, the following screenshots are included to "show the receipts" of the 100,000 copies I've sold of my self-published books.

My Amazon dashboard shows more than 75,000 copies sold.

My ACX dashboard shows nearly 15,000 audiobooks sold.

Appendix

My PublishDrive analytics show more than 5,000 sales.

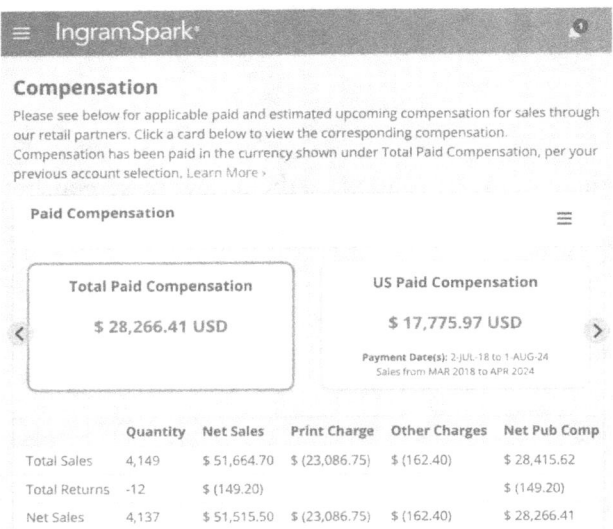

My IngramSpark compensation report shows more than 4,000 sales.

Appendix

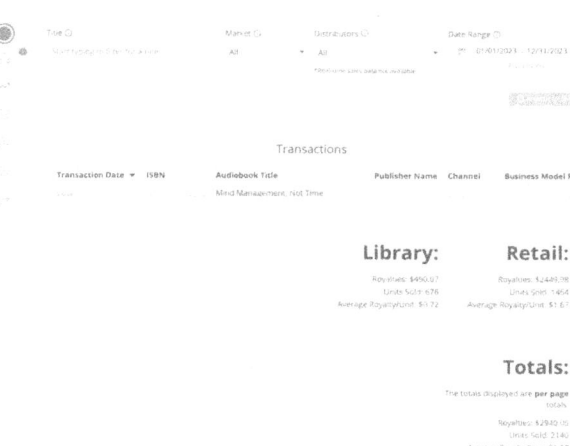

My Findaway Voices analytics shows 2,140 sales, just in 2023.

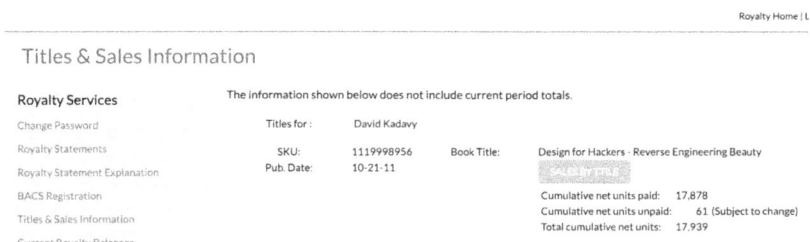

My 100,000 self-published sales don't include sales of my traditionally-published book, which are near 18,000 copies.

Acknowledgments

While I've had to figure out a lot of self-publishing on my own, I couldn't have done it without help from others who have generously shared their knowledge with the public, with me personally, or both. My best resources have been *The Creative Penn* podcast by Joanna Penn, *The Sell More Books Show*, by Bryan Cohen and Jim Kukral, and the 20BooksTo50k Facebook group, started by Craig Martelle and Michael Anderle. Thanks to all of you, and everyone in the 20BooksTo50k Facebook group. Thanks also to Seth Godin for pushing me to try self-publishing, to Garrett Kincaid for providing valuable feedback on this book, everyone mentioned in the book for their contribution, and all the Preview Edition readers who helped fund the book and provide motivation. Thanks also to others who have provided me with publishing advice and inspiration over the years include Ramit Sethi, Robbie Abed, Tynan, Clay Hebert, Ryan Holiday, Lisa DiMona, Nir Eyal, Stephen Hanselman, Chris Webb, David Fugate, and Jeff Siarto. Writing books is the best job in the world, so thank you, finally, to everyone who has bought my books!

Index

100-Word Writing Habit (Kadavy) book, 130–31, 188; email course, 42, 255
2-Hour Cocktail Party, The (Gray), 161–62
2 Seas, agency for foreign rights, *see:* foreign rights
20BooksTo50k; conference, *see:* Author Nation
3-2-1 Thursdays, 47
3:2:2 dynamic creative system, *see:* Meta Ads
4-Hour Body, The (Ferriss), 25–26
4-Hour Work Week, The (Ferriss), 24–25
7 Habits of Highly Effective People (Covey), 162–63

Abed, Robbie, 41, 57, 233, 271
ACX, *see:* audiobooks
ActiveCampaign, *see:* email marketing
Advantage+, *see:* Meta Ads
advertising; Amazon Ads, *see:* Amazon Ads; billboards 233–34; BookBub Ads, *see:* BookBub Ads; Goodreads Ads, 265; Google AdWords, *see:* Google; in *Publisher's Weekly*, 265; Meta Ads, *see:* Meta Ads; Quora Ads, *see:* Quora; X Ads, *see:* X
Advanced Reader Copies (ARCs); electronic, 265; Edelweiss, 265; lead time for sending, 101, 215; NetGalley, 265
Affinity Publisher, *see:* page layout software
agents, for foreign rights, 251–53; 2 Seas, 253; how to get, 253
aggregators, 10, 138, 145, 183–86, 230; Draft2Digital, 145, 183–86; Findaway Voices, 10, 211, 269; PublishDrive, 10
AI, *see:* Artificial Intelligence
Alliance of Independent Authors, 103, 251
Allen, David, 56
"Also by" pages, 183, 185
Amazon; "Also Boughts", 72, 263; algorithm, 30, 175–76, 179, 224, 240; Amazon Ads, *see:* Amazon Ads; Amazon Associates, 126; Amazon Charts, 227; ASIN, *see:* ASIN; bestseller status, 222–24; categories in Kindle Store, 26–28, 30, 222–23; drop-shipping KDP author copies, *see:* drop-shipping; expanded distribution, 186; gift cards as survey incentive, 96–97; Kindle Countdown Deals, *see:* pricing promotions; Kindle Deals, *see:* pricing promotions; Kindle Direct Publishing (KDP), 28, 30, 67, 117–18, 120, 126, 138–40, 147–48, 165, 185–88, 192, 195–96, 219, 228, 242–43, 249, 250, 264; KDP Select, 138, 148, 153, 175–79, 197, 207, 219, 222, 242; Kindle Unlimited, 138, 175–79, 181, 183; out-of-stock status, 177–78; Prime Reading promotion, *see:* pricing promotions; pricing restrictions 135–39, 149–52, 175, 192–93, 241; Product details on book's page, 27; proof copies, 195; reviews, *see:* reviews on Amazon; royalty plans, 135–39, 146, 149, 152, 175–76, 179–80, 193; sales rank, 126–30, 137, 146, 151, 198, 219, 222–28, 259; search rankings, 28–30, 63–64, 67–68, 175–76; shipping time, 187–88, 196–97
Amazon Ads, 107–21; bidding on, 107, 112–13, 116–17, 265; evaluating performance of, 119–20; Lockscreen Ads, 109, 115–18; Sponsored Brands ads, 119; Sponsored Products, 109–15; three-campaign structure, 110–15
American Library Association, *see:* editorial reviews
Anderle, Michael, 217
anecdotes as marketing devices, 25
AOV, *see:* Average Order Value
Apple Books, 145–46, 180, 184, 185–86, 222
ARCs, *see:* Advanced Reader Copies
Ariely, Dan, 32, 171
Artificial Intelligence (AI), 54; ChatGPT, 30, 54, 251; Claude, 251; for ad targeting, 115, 128, 182; for contract review, 251; for creative brainstorming, 30
ASIN, targeting of in Amazon Ads, 114
assonance, 24
Atomic Habits (Clear), 162
Audible, *see:* audiobooks
audiobooks, 61, 179–80, 194, 209–12; ACX, 198, 210–12; Audible, 198, 210–11; Chirp deals, 211–12; Findaway Voices, 211–12; pricing promotions for, 211–12; selling direct, 194; Spotify, 211
Author Alliance, 68
Author Nation, 254
authority in search for idea/author fit, 31–34; doing as source of, 26, 33
Average Cost of Sale (ACoS), 118
Average Order Value (AOV), 131

Barnes & Noble (B&N), 146, 176, 180, 184, 188, 190–91, 212, 222, 231–32
Bauer, Elise, 56
Bennett, Paul, 57
bestseller lists, 137, 144–47, 186, 208, 221–30, 232; Amazon bestsellers, 222–27; definition

) of a bestseller, 222–24; *New York Times*, 101, 221–24, 234; pre-orders and, 218–19, 226–29; strategy for achieving, 130, 144, 146, 186, 208, 221–22, 227–30; timing of attempts, 227–30; *USA Today*, 222; *Wall Street Journal*, 144–45, 222, 227, 229–30, 232

Best Sellers Rank on Amazon, *see:* Amazon, sales rank

Best Seller's World, *see:* editorial reviews

Bezos, Jeff, 177

bidding on Amazon Ads, *see:* Amazon Ads

bids on keywords, *see:* keywords

billboards, *see:* advertising; Blip Billboards, *see:* Blip Billboards

BISAC subject codes, *see:* categories

Black swans, 14, 262; kind of book, 14–15, 19, 33; relative to white- and gray-swan books, 14–15, 17–20

Black Swan, The (Taleb), 14

Blip Billboards, 233

blogger outreach, *see:* Public Relations

Blue Ink Review, *see:* editorial reviews

BookBub 74–77, 262; Featured Deals, 123–24, 142–52, 177–178, 180, 182, 217, 226, 228–29, 240–41, 263; Featured New Releases, 124, 146–47, 263

BookBub Ads, 122–26, 180, 181; for testing titles, subtitles, and book covers, 74–76, 116, 145; marketing through recommendations on profiles, 262

BookFunnel, 156, 184, 200, 205; for audiobooks, 194

BookLife, *see:* editorial reviews

BookLife Prize, *see:* contests

book tours, 38, 224, 258–60

BookVault; for drop-shipping, *see:* drop-shipping

Boomerang, Gmail plugin, 245

Boorstin, Daniel J., 33, 99, 231

bookstagram, *see:* Instagram

bookstores, making your books available in, 186, 190–91, 263; as a sales-data source for the *New York Times* bestseller list, 222

box sets, 239

Brass Check, 224

broad keywords, *see:* keywords

Brown, Brené, 65–66

build the audience as you build the book, 35–62

calculator; of hard-copy book royalties on Amazon KDP, 140; of sales based upon sales rank, *see:* Kindlepreneur

Case, Steve, 56

categories, 26–28; BISAC subject codes, 26; on Kindle Store, *see:* Amazon

chapter names as a sales tool, 46, 93

ChatGPT, LLM, *see:* Artificial Intelligence

Checklist Manifesto, The, 64

Cheney, Dick, 225

"chicken little" books, 22

chiasmus, 24

Chirp, *see:* audiobooks

Cialdini, Robert, 43

Claude, LLM, *see:* Artificial Intelligence

Clear, James, 11, 47

CLV, *see:* Customer Lifetime Value

COGS, *see:* Cost of Goods Sold

Cohen, Bryan, 107, 119, 271; *Sell More Books Show, The*, *see:* Sell More Books Show, The

commitment, *see:* persuasion

community-first, 37–39

conferences, 155, 160, 265; running online; selling at, *see:* in-person sales

content marketing, *see:* Search Engine Optimization, *see:* podcasts; reviews of related books, 264

contests; BookLife Prize, 102, 262; Independent Author Network's Book of the Year Awards, 262; Self Publishing Review's SPR Book Awards, 262

contracts, for foreign rights, *see:* foreign rights

ConvertKit, now Kit, *see:* email marketing

copywriting, *see:* sales blurbs

Cost of Goods Sold (COGS), 192

covers; design style strategy, 69–72; designing yourself, 68–69; hiring a designer, 68–69; testing, 72–76

CreateSpace, 138

Creative Penn, The, podcast, *see:* Penn, Joanna

crowdfunding, Kickstarter, 201–204, 207, 224, 239, 259

Customer Lifetime Value (CLV), 199

Daring Greatly (Brown), 65

Data Guy, The, 137

Deep Work (Newport), 22–23, 63, 66

deliverability, *see:* email marketing

Design for Hackers (Kadavy), 19, 31, 37, 42, 49, 216, 224, 239, 240, 258, 273, 274

DiMona, Lisa, 271

direct sales; of audiobooks, 194, 198; of ebooks, 194, 197–198; drop-shipping, *see:* drop-shipping; of IngramSpark copies, *see:* drop-shipping; of KDP author copies, *see:* drop-shipping; payment processing fee comparison, 199; preview editions, 204–207; pricing on, *see:* pricing; shipping, 196–198; through BookFunnel, *see:* BookFunnel; through BookVault, *see:* print-on-demand; through PayHip, *see:* PayHip; through Shopify, *see:* Shopify, 127, 130, 140, 197, 199–201, 205

Discord, 37, 263

discounts, *see:* pricing promotions

Digital Zettelkasten (Kadavy), 18, 29, 33–34, 38, 77–78, 98, 239–40, 253, 273

Draft2Digital, *see:* aggregators

drop-shipping, 195; of IngramSpark copies, 195; of KDP author copies, 195; with BookVault, 198, 200, 202–03

Dynamic Creative ads, *see:* Meta Ads

East of Eden (Steinbeck), 24

Eat, Pray, Love (Gilbert), 25, 26, 33

ebooks; aggregators, *see:* aggregators; direct sales of, *see:* direct sales; pricing, *see:* pricing; top retailers, 180; value to customer when sold directly versus through Kindle, 198

Edelweiss, *see:* Advanced Reader Copies

editorial reviews, 102–03; American Library Association, 265–266; Best Seller's World, 266; Blue Ink Review, 266; *BookLife*, 265; Indie Reader, 266; *Kirkus*, 102, 190, 266; *Publisher's Weekly*, 102–03, 190, 265

Ego is the Enemy, The (Holiday), 25

Elements of Eloquence, The (Forsyth), 24

elevator pitch, *see:* sales blurbs

Eilish, Billie, 108

email marketing, 39–49, 51, 54; ActiveCampaign, 39; building your list with Meta Ads, *see:* Meta Ads; deliverability, 39, 46, 132; Email Service Providers (ESPs), 39; email courses, 40–45, 51, 131, 255, 262; email newsletters 46–50, 59, 62, 132, 157, 264; GDPR compliance, 48; Kit (formerly ConvertKit), 39; lead magnets, 45–46, 54, 131–32, 153; legality, 39–40, 48; MailChimp, 39; quarantining new email addresses, 131–32; sender reputation, 39, 46, 132; why not use Gmail?, 39

Email Service Providers, *see:* email marketing

Erik, Nicholas, 222

ESPs, *see:* email marketing

event sales, *see:* in-person sales

exact match keywords, *see:* keywords

exact targeting of ASIN in Amazon Ads, *see:* ASIN

expanded distribution, on Amazon KDP, *see:* Amazon

expanded targeting of ASIN in Amazon Ads, *see:* ASIN

explosive email courses, *see:* email marketing, email courses

Eyal, Nir, 22, 220, 271

Facebook, 52, 200; Facebook groups, 37, 118, 206, 263, 271

fan-fiction, 38

farmers' market sales, *see:* in-person sales

Fat Chance (Lustig), 25

Ferriss, Tim, 26, 47, 218, 225, 234

Fifty Shades of Grey (James), 38

Findaway Voices, *see:* audiobooks

Fire Me, I Beg You (Abed), 41

first pages of book as sales tool, 89–93

Five-Bullet Friday (Ferriss), 47

Flynn, Pat, 190–91, 231–32

foreign rights, 242–53; agents for 251–53; contracts, 250–51; finding deals for, 244–45; in English, 249–250; translation, 242–44

forewords, 104

Forleo, Marie, 234

Forsyth, Mark, 23

Franklin, Benjamin, Thirteen Virtues, 261

Freakonomics (Dubner, Leavitt), 25

free, marketing by offering books and ebooks for, 135, 143, 159–60, 175–76, 178–179, 198, 219–20, 241

FreeEBOOKS Reddit subreddit, 262

Fried, Jason, 56

Fugate, David, 271

Gates of Fire (Pressfield), 240

GDPR compliance, *see:* email marketing

Getting Art Done (Kadavy) book series, 32, 38, 42, 71, 119, 238, 239; email course, 42, 45

Getting Things Done (Allen), 27, 56

gifting books as a marketing tactic, 159–60

Gilbert, Liz, 26, 33

gift cards as survey incentive, *see:* Amazon

giveaways, 218, 219, 263; as a launch tactic, 218, 219; for influencing recommendation algorithms, 263, 265; Goodreads Giveaways, 263; KingSumo Giveaways, 263

Gladwell, Malcolm, 22

Gmail, why not use for email marketing?, *see:* email marketing

Godin, Seth, 56, 101, 106, 169, 215, 234, 236, 271

Google; Google AdWords, 132; Google Calendar, 32, 83; Google Docs, 206; Google Forms, 96; Google-ability of a title, 25; Google & YouTube Shopify app, 200–01; Google Merchant Center, 201; Google Play, 146, 180, 184–85; Google Search Console, 53

Google-ability of a title, *see:* Google

Goodreads; Goodreads Ads, *see:* advertising; Goodreads Giveaways, *see:* giveaways

Gray, Nick, 56, 161

Great Gatsby, The (Fitzgerald), 24

Hacking of the American Mind, The (Lustig), 25

Hacker News, 37, 218, 225, 258

Hanselman, Stephen, 271

hard-copy books; pricing of, *see:* pricing; printing costs, 139–40, 189, 192, 196–97, 202–03

hardcover books, *see:* hard-copy books

Heart to Start, The (Kadavy), 19, 23, 29, 31–32, 70, 72–73, 81, 87, 94–95, 98, 101–02, 116, 144, 149, 169, 170, 176–79, 182, 209, 211, 215–16, 219, 229, 238

Hebert, Clay, 271

Helium 10, 114

Hillman, Saya, 56

Holiday, Ryan, 25, 48, 218, 223, 240, 262, 271

hook, 80–81, 83–85, *see:* sales blurbs

Hooked: How to Build Habit-Forming Products (Eyal), 23, 220

How to Do Nothing (Odell), 66

How to Live with a Huge Penis (Jacob), 66

How to Win Friends and Influence People (Carnegie), 63

How to Write a Book (Kadavy), 18, 57, 131, 240, 242

Howey, Hugh, 137

HTML influence upon SEO, *see:* Search Engine Optimization

HTS, *see: Heart to Start, The*

Hunter, Rob, 57

"I don't have an audience" Catch-22, 35–36

idea/author fit, 31–34; idea/author statement, 32–33

idea/author statement, *see:* idea/author fit

ideas for books, The four M's of a good book idea, 22–25; assessing sales potential, 26–30

idiom jacking, 25

income, *see:* revenue

Independent Author Network's Book of the Year Awards, *see:* contests

In Defense of Papyrus (Kadavy), 19

Indie Reader, *see:* editorial reviews

Indistractable (Eyal), 22–23

influencer marketing, 154–74; being a podcast guest as a marketing tool, *see:* podcasts; meeting influencers, *see:* networking with influencers

Influence (Cialdini), 43

INeedABookCover.com, 69

IngramSpark, 186–91, 250; for drop-shipping, *see:* drop-shipping; returns, 188–90; sales reporting, 165

in-person sales, 254–57; displays for, 255

Instagram, 52, 162–64, 201, 265; ads, *see:* Meta Ads; bookstagram, 162–65; Instagram Live, 265

interior design, 77–78, 18

Jacobs, A.J., 234

journalists, pitching story ideas to, *see:* Public Relations

Jorgenson, Eric, 18

Kaczynski, Ted, 232

Kahneman, Daniel, 32

Kagan, Noah, 41, 55

Kardashian, Kim, 232

KDP, *see:* Amazon

keyphrases, *see:* keywords

keywords; as advertising targets, 110–14; as search terms customers use, 28–30; bids on keywords, 113; broad, 112–14; exact, 112–14; in Amazon KDP back-end metadata, 30, 264; in auto-suggest, for market research, 29; in book titles and subtitles, 67, 106; influence over category inclusion, 30; negative exact, 112–13; negative phrase, 112

Kickstarter, *see:* crowdfunding

Kindle Direct Publishing, *see:* Amazon

Kindle sample, *see:* first pages…

Kindlepreneur; Publisher Rocket, 30; sales rank calculator, 27

KingSumo Giveaways, *see:* giveaways

Kirkus, *see:* editorial reviews

Kit, formerly ConvertKit, *see:* email marketing

Kobo, 146, 176, 180, 182–86; Kobo Promotions, 182–83; Kobo Writing Life, 182–85

Kounios, John, 56

Kukral, Jim, *Sell More Books Show, The, see: Sell More Books Show, The*

launching books, 101, 172, 179, 187, 204, 212–20; attempting bestseller lists, 226–28;

changing launch date, 228
Lauffenburger, Katie, 42
law; lawyers for contract reviews, 250–51; legality of email marketing, *see:* email marketing, legality; legality of obtaining reader reviews, 95–97
lead magnets, *see:* email marketing
Legend of Bagger Vance, The (Pressfield), 240
length of books, *see:* short reads
library marketing, 102, 234, 265; libraryreads.org, 265
libraryreads.org, *see:* library marketing
Libsyn, 62
Limbaugh, Rush, 230
livestreams; Instagram Live, *see:* Instagram; TikTok Live, *see:* TikTok; YouTube Live, *see:* YouTube
Love Mondays (Kadavy), 47–48, 132
Love Your Work (Kadavy), 62
luck, 16–18
Lustig, Dr. Robert, 25

mailboxes for CAN-SPAM compliance, 39–40
MailChimp, *see:* email marketing
Martelle, Craig, 271
Mastering Amazon Ads (Meeks), 118
Manson, Mark, 11, 57, 240
Max, Tucker, 223–24
McLuhan, Marshall, 79
Medium, 36, 38
Meeks, Brian D., 118
Met Gala, 232
Meta; Facebook, *see:* Facebook; Instagram, *see:* Instagram; Meta Ads, *see:* Meta Ads; Meta app for Shopify, *see:* Shopify
Meta Ads, 74, 77, 127–32; 3:2:2 dynamic creative system, 128–30; Advantage+, 128; Dynamic Creative ads; for building your email list, 131–132; for testing titles, subtitles, and book covers, 74, 77; Forms, 131; Lead Ads, 131–32; retargeting, 130
Mind Management, Not Time Management (Kadavy), 19, 23–24, 30, 32–33, 50–51, 54, 70, 78, 80, 82, 84–86, 98, 102, 116, 146, 149, 150–152, 157–159, 164, 166, 177–179, 196, 204, 206, 209, 211, 215–217, 229, 238, 249
MMT, *see: Mind Management, Not Time Management*
Monroe, Marilyn, 232
"must be nice" trap, 36
mysterious mechanism, *see:* sales blurbs

negative exact keywords, *see:* keywords
negative phrase keywords, *see:* keywords
NetGalley, *see:* Advanced Reader Copies
Never Give Up (Trump), 65
Never Split the Difference (Voss), 25
networking with influencers, 101, 154–156, 265; by having as guests on your podcast, 55–58, 62, 172–73; by reciprocating for having you as a podcast guest, 59, 172–73; by sharing their work in your newsletter, 48
New York Public Library, 234
New York Times, 108, 232; bestseller list, 101, 221, 223, 234
Nook, *see:* Barnes & Noble
number of sales; assessing for other books, 26–28; of other author's books, 16, 27–28, 32, 108, 160; of the author's books, 9–10, 18–21, 32, 34, 68, 78, 130, 216, 219, 267–269

Obstacle is the Way, The (Holiday), 24, 64
Omar, Ilhan, 108
One Thing, The (Keller), 64
out-of-stock status on Amazon, *see:* Amazon

paperback books, *see:* hard-copy books
page layout, *see:* interior design
page layout software; Adobe InDesign, 78; Affinity Publisher, 78; Sigil, 78; Vellum, 78, 205
payment processing, *see:* direct sales; with PayPal, 195, 199; with Shopify, 199; with Venmo, 195, 199
PayHip, 194, 195, 200, 205
PayPal, *see:* payment processing
pen names, 240
Penn, Joanna, 138, 243, 271; *Creative Penn, The,* podcast, 271
persuasion; commitment, 43–44, 47; reciprocity, 43–44; scarcity, 44, 203, 207, 218, 219; urgency, 41, 203
phased release, 207–08
phrase keywords, *see:* keywords
PirateShip.com, *see:* shipping
Play it Away (Hoehn), 68
podcasts, hosting as marketing tool, 55–62; as part of writing process, 61, 173; attracting guests, 57–60; being a guest on as marketing tool, 166–74; course in format, 263; swapping with other hosts, 172–73
POD, *see:* print-on-demand
point of difference, *see:* sales blurbs
polyptoton, 24

portfolio approach, 16–18, 214, 235–36
PR, *see:* Public Relations
pre-orders, 218–19, 226–29
Pressfield, Steven, 240
Prestozon, 111, 114
preview editions, *see:* direct sales
pricing, price points, 18, 38, 134–37, 143; by currency, 137–39; effects on royalty rates, 135–39, 146, 149, 152, 175–76, 179–80, 193; in direct sales, 140–141, 146, 192–93, 195–97; of ebooks, 197–98, 227–29; of hard-copy books, 139–40, 195–97
Professor Charley T, 129
promotional, *see:* pricing promotions
pricing promotions; BookBub Featured Deals, *see:* BookBub; BookBub Featured New Release for Less, *see:* BookBub; BookGorilla, 226; Chirp deals, *see:* audiobooks; for audiobooks, *see:* audiobooks; Kindle Countdown Deals, 153, 219; Kindle Deals, 147–52; Kobo Promotions, *see:* Kobo; Prime Reading promotion, 148; promo stacking, 226
Prime Reading promotion, *see:* pricing promotions
print-on-demand (POD), 202–03
printing, 202–03; foil or holographic stamping, 201–02, 239; offset, 203; placeholder ribbons, 201–02; print-on-demand, *see:* print-on-demand
printing costs, *see:* hard-copy books
Product details on book's page, *see:* Amazon
promo stacking, *see:* pricing promotions
proof copies, Amazon, *see:* Amazon
pseudo-events, 99, 191, 223, 230, 231–34
pseudonym, *see:* pen names
psychology, 130–31; of pricing, 134–36; of titles and subtitles, 23, 65–67
Public Relations (PR), 213; blogger outreach, 264; journalist outreach, 262, 265; Trading Up the Chain, 262; YouTuber outreach, 264
PublishDrive, *see:* aggregators
Publisher Rocket, *see:* Kindlepreneur
publishers, 16, 21, 71, 79, 101, 108, 213–16; foreign, 242–53
Publisher's Weekly, see: editorial reviews; ads, *see:* advertising
Publisher's Marketplace, 99
Pyatesky, Alex, 57

Quora, 263; Quora Ads, 263

randomness, 13–18

Rao, Srinivas, 230
RAVE book fair, 254, 257
reader blurbs, 99–101
reciprocity, *see:* persuasion
Reddit and subreddits, 37–38, 52, 233, 240, 262; FreeEBOOKS subreddit, 262
returns, IngramSpark, 187–89
retargeting, *see:* Meta Ads
revenue, by market, 139
reviews, 94–97; dealing with negative reviews, 97–99; getting first reviews, 94–97; obtaining reviews legally, 95–97; of related books as marketing tool, 264; on Amazon, 94–97, 264; transferring reviews after switching to/from an aggregator, 184–86
Roeder, Laura, 56

sales, *see:* revenue
sales blurbs, 79–86; as writing tool, 87; call-to-action, 86–87; elevator pitch, 82–83; hook, 80–81; mysterious mechanism, 84–85, 170; point of difference, 85–86
sales rank, *see:* Amazon; calculator
scams, 103, 167, 244–45
scarcity, *see:* persuasion
schools, marketing to, 264
Scribe Media, 18, 223
Search Engine Optimization (SEO), 52–55, 67, 234, 264; relevance to titles and subtitles, 67
self-actualization, in process of finding idea/author fit, 32–33
Self-Publishing with Amazon Ads (Cohen), 107
Sell More Books Show, The, 271
sender reputation, *see:* email marketing
SEO, *see:* Search Engine Optimization
series, writing in, 10, 107, 119, 237–39, 240
Sethi, Ramit, 271
shipping; competing with Amazon in direct sales, 196–98; PirateShip.com, 197; time displayed on Amazon, *see:* Amazon; UPS, 197; USPS Media Mail, 197, 202
short reads, 17–18, 19, 69–70, 130–31, 215, 236
Siarto, Jeff, 271
Sigil, *see:* page layout software
Sinclair, Upton, 224
SlideShare, 262
Smith, Will, 240
social media marketing, 43–44, 49–52; as part of writing process, 50–51, 82, 116
So Good They Can't Ignore You (Newport), 66
Spotify, *see:* audiobooks

statistical significance of ad tests, 76–77
stories as marketing devices, 25, 158
storytelling technique as sales tool, 89–93
Start With Why (Sinek), 64
*Subtle Art of not Giving a F*ck, The* (Manson), 33, 57, 240
subheads as a sales tool, 46, 93
Substack, 36
Summer of Design (Kadavy), 40, 41–42, 45
Summer of Marketing (Kagan), 41
Summer of Quitting (Abed), 41
summits, online, as underhanded method of audience building, 58–59
surveying readers, 96–97, 206–07
swipe copy, 264

table of contents (TOC) as a sales tool, 93
Taleb, Nassim, 14, 22, 71, 238
Ten Passive Income Ideas (Kadavy), 36
Telegram, 52
testing ideas through lead magnets, 45–46
Thanks for the Feedback (Stone, Heen), 66
Thinking, Fast and Slow (Kahneman), 31–33
three-campaign structure for Amazon Ads, *see:* Amazon Ads
Thompson, Phil, 42
TikTok, 50–51, 62, 164, 200, 265; TikTok Live, 265
Times Square billboard, advertising on, 233–34
Timberlake, Justin, 108
Tipping Point, The (Gladwell), 25
titles, 23–25, 63–67, 74; psychology of, 23–25, 63–67, 74; subtitles, 29–30, 67–68, 74; testing, 74–77; turnkey titles, 64; whether they pass the cocktail party test, 23, 65–66, 106
TOC as a sales tool, *see:* table of contents...
trade shows, *see:* in-person sales
Trading Up the Chain, PR tactic, *see:* Public Relations
traditional publishing, 16, 18, 21, 71, 79, 86, 99, 101, 108, 213–14; economics relative to self-publishing, 213–14; launch strategy relative to self-publishing, 213–16; pricing relative to self-publishing, 136–37
trailer, video for promoting book, 265
translation, *see:* foreign rights
Trump, Donald, 65
turnkey titles, *see:* titles
Twilight (Meyer), 38
Twitter, *see:* X

typography, *see:* interior design
Tynan, 56, 271

Unabomber, The, 232
Underwood, Brent, 223, 227, 231
UPS, *see:* shipping
UPS Store, *see:* mailboxes...
urgency, *see:* persuasion
USPS Media Mail, *see:* shipping

Vellum, see: page layout software
Venmo, *see:* payment processing
viral loop as part of explosive email course, 43
VirtualPostMail, *see:* mailboxes...

Wall Street Journal, 144–45, 222, 227, 229, 230, 232
War of Art, The (Pressfield), 19, 240
Washington Post, 232
Webb, Chris, 271
website, for book, 262
wide publishing, 153, 175–91, 193–94, 207, 211–12
wholesale discount, on IngramSpark, 187–89
Wolf, Ben, science-fiction author's in-person sales display, 256–57
Wonder City Studios, 42
workbook, 42, 131, 201–02, 263

X (formerly Twitter), 24, 49–51, 62, 132–33; advertising on, 132–33

Yeh, Chris, 117
YouTube, 200–201, 264–65; app for Shopify, *see:* Shopify; store; videos for marketing, 265; YouTube Live, 265; YouTuber outreach, *see:* Public Relations

Zapier, 194

Also by David Kadavy

Mind Management, Not Time Management: Productivity When Creativity Matters

The Heart to Start: Start Procrastinating & Start Creating

Design for Hackers: Reverse-Engineering Beauty

Short Reads

How to Write a Book

Digital Zettelkasten: Principles, Methods, & Examples

About the Author

David Kadavy is the bestselling author of *Mind Management, Not Time Management, The Heart to Start,* and *Design for Hackers.* His self-published books have sold more than 100,000 copies, and are being translated into a dozen languages. His weekly newsletter, *Love Mondays,* has over 10,000 subscribers. David lives in a cabin in the mountains outside Medellín, Colombia.

 x.com/kadavy

 instagram.com/kadavy

www.ingramcontent.com/pod-product-compliance
Lightning Source LLC
LaVergne TN
LVHW010312070526
838199LV00065B/5535